NEW
ENGLISH DRAMATISTS

7

INTRODUCED BY J. W. LAMBERT

CHIPS WITH EVERYTHING
Arnold Wesker

AFORE NIGHT COME
David Rudkin

EVERYTHING IN THE GARDEN
Giles Cooper

PENGUIN BOOKS

Penguin Books Ltd, Harmondsworth, Middlesex
AUSTRALIA : Penguin Books Pty Ltd, 762 Whitehorse Road,
Mitcham, Victoria

—

Chips With Everything
First published by Jonathan Cape 1962
Published in Penguin Books 1963
Copyright © Arnold Wesker, 1963

—

Afore Night Come
First published in Penguin Books 1963
Copyright © David Rudkin, 1963

—

Everything in the Garden
First published in Penguin Books 1963
Copyright © Giles Cooper, 1963

—

Made and printed in Great Britain
by Cox and Wyman Ltd,
London, Reading, and Fakenham
Set in Monotype Bembo

CONTENTS

INTRODUCTION *by J. W. Lambert*   7

CHIPS WITH EVERYTHING   15
  Arnold Wesker

AFORE NIGHT COME   73
  David Rudkin

EVERYTHING IN THE GARDEN   141
  Giles Cooper

INTRODUCTION

THE three plays printed in this volume were not the only outstanding new pieces to be seen in London in 1962. But it is perhaps a sign of the times, and no mere coincidence, that they should all share the same basic theme: the undermining of order by chaos – to put it one way – or the revolt, articulate or inarticulate, intelligent or instinctive, of the individual against any social framework. And all three, curiously enough, also demonstrate that however much people may wish to break the mould which shapes their lives, they will unite in distrusting – even in attacking – any individual who successfully exists outside that mould.

Arnold Wesker's fifth play, CHIPS WITH EVERYTHING, has more in common, structurally and emotionally, with his first, *The Kitchen*, than with the intervening trilogy, *Chicken Soup with Barley*, *Roots*, and *I'm Talking about Jerusalem*. In the trilogy he explored, or illustrated, the organization of society in terms of the aspirations and disillusion of one family, struggling against political imbalance, unthinking ignorance, and personal weakness to establish a valid image of a good life. A strongly autobiographical element greatly weakened two of the plays in particular: a shrill *raisonneur*, Ronnie Kahn proved ever more irritating in himself and overbalanced the first and last plays with a too soft-centred emotional gloss, leaving *Roots*, in which he appeared only by reflection, by far the most effective of the three in terms of both argument and theatrical effect.

In *The Kitchen* Wesker had avoided these cramping pastures and turned to his experiences as a pastrycook to provide, in a much tighter form, the framework of men in society. Here the owner of a restaurant stood for the world of established order. He was presented without rancour as a man who genuinely could not understand how those who worked for him could be discontented with their lot. The head chef and assistant chefs stood for those who, invested with a little brief authority, lived in a non-committal limbo. Below them the assorted cooks worked and grumbled and in a small way dreamed, but lacked any sort of impetus to do anything about themselves. The

7

rogue in this herd was a young German in whom an overplus of animal energy turned easily to rage.

In *Chips with Everything* the R.A.F. provides a similar framework, but – in, of course, a much longer play – Wesker's working out of his theme has become immensely more complex and more dramatically forceful. It is a much less sympathetic play than *The Kitchen*. Wesker's own rage against all levels of society seems to have gained ground – and his feeling for individuals to have diminished. This is due in part perhaps to the intervening influence of Brecht – wholly for the good in so far as it has encouraged Wesker to some stunning theatrical *tours de force*, wholly harmful in that it has greatly weakened his ability to see human beings as such, and encouraged him to use them as counters in a game whose concealed basis is contempt.

I don't lightly accuse a writer whose concern for the betterment of the human condition is so plain, in his life as well as his works, of treating his own creations with contempt, even of set aesthetic purpose. But his characterization of the senior officer in this play compares ill with that of the restaurant-owner in *The Kitchen*. The Wing Commander is again the representative of order. Order is the point of his whole being. The raw recruits who, in peacetime, are thrust upon him are by their ignorance and stupidity a threat to that order. So far, so good. But then Wesker weakens his case, and coarsens his drama, by making the Wing Commander not merely distressed, baffled, or even angry, but downright vindictive. Such men exist, but special cases make bad drama, or at least bad didactic drama. Again, it is true that Authority often does display impatient spite against its subjects; but this is not the point Wesker is trying to make. His thesis is quite simply that all power corrupts, and that we must work towards a world in which the exercise of authority by one human being over another is no longer necessary or possible; and he would have illustrated it better by a more balanced tyrant – unless indeed he had gone the whole Brechtian hog and made the figure entirely a caricature.

At the other end of the scale, too, his treatment of the recruits is questionable. Wesker wishes to say that the structure of society has made these boys the stupid, malleable creatures they are; but it is impossible not to feel, and to regret, the strong undertow of scorn with which he has drawn them – in their opening exchanges, for instance, or in the joke made about the inability of one of them to pronounce the word economics, or in their pathetic readiness to hero-worship. Only one of them, Smiler Washington, is given serious attention; and he, after a theatrically splendid monologue of despair, is turned into a half-hinted Christ-figure in a manner which suggests that Wesker was carried by his own rhetoric far beyond the point of significance.

Against this uncertainty of touch stands the force, power, and absolute sureness with which he has handled Hill, the hut corporal. This man is a mere highly trained instrument, of what he does not care; he turns clumsy recruits into processed airmen, and that is enough for him. He is intended to be only one of the distorting pressures of society; yet something – almost it seems a certain latent admirableness – has made him very nearly the dominating figure of the play. But not quite: in the end the central figure, Pip, the upper-class recruit, retains his puzzling authority. Pip is in revolt against the world that made him; he is also angry with the underlings for their willingness to be so; and he maintains against both sides his own particular cross-fire of contempt. It is impossible not to see in Pip Mr Wesker's mouthpiece, impossible not to recoil from the note of hectoring priggishness (the part desperately needs an actor who can mitigate this quality); impossible, though, not to follow with total absorption his successive clashes with one aspect after another of the system he hates. Some of them are obscure, some of them are more than obscure, they are downright silly – notably his encounters with the awkwardly drawn young Pilot Officer whose identity he finally more or less assumes; but all of them make their mark in the theatre.

The dramatic viability and unflagging impact of *Chips with Everything*, in fact, sweep all before them. In the dovetailing of his twenty-three scenes Wesker can beat Brecht at his own game. In the expression of group emotions through action *Chips with Everything* is hardly to be equalled. The scene in which the recruits are introduced to one level of the Station hierarchy after another is brilliantly and economically comic. The square-bashing assumes a deadly accurate insane hilarity. The Christmas Eve jollifications in the Naafi canteen, with their interpolated ballads, triumphantly override the threat of folk-art absurdity. The coke-stealing scene, on either side of a strip of wire netting, 'has to be', says Wesker's unabashed stage direction, 'silent, precise, breathtaking, and finally very funny'. And so it is. The dreadful make-believe of bayonet practice jabs hatefully at the audience's guts. And though, theatrically speaking, the play loses its thread a little half-way through the last act, it recovers magnificently to end in the startling ambiguity of the moment when all the recruits, shaped at last like so many sausages, stand rigidly presenting arms while the National Anthem rings out in a blazing ironic comment on ends and means.

David Rudkin's AFORE NIGHT COME won for itself widespread though not universal critical acclaim when it was presented at the Arts Theatre as part of the Royal Shakespeare Company's experimental season, untimely nipped; and Rudkin was subsequently the winner of the *Evening Standard* Drama Award for 'the most promising playwright of 1962'. Rudkin, twenty-six years old, is a schoolmaster in the Midlands and comes, he has told us, of a Revivalist family in which he grew up with a considerable sense of guilt in ever going to a theatre or a cinema at all. No wonder then, perhaps, that his first play, or the first of his plays to be seen, should be heavy with the sense of doom. To English ears the title must immediately conjure up precisely the picture of powerful rustic menace which in fact pervades the play – so much so that many initially supposed that it must be some sort of parody on the lines of *Cold Comfort Farm*. And it very nearly is; only a hair's breadth preserves it, time and again, from toppling into absurdity: the balance being saved usually by its theatrical grip.

Here the group is made up of seasonal workers picking pears in an orchard not far from the great Midland industrial conurbations. At the play's very beginning the gathering riff-raff establish a sense of the corruption of cities over the hill, to set against the isolation and routine brutalities of country life. Rudkin's attitude towards this bunch is at all times perfectly neutral; he has an excellent ear for one sort of demotic speech and never allows his dialogue to be coloured by any hint of intellectual comment (though once or twice he allows improbable allusions and turns of phrase to slip through). Into their midst comes first a student – nervous, quiet, and in his well-meaning way nearly as priggish as Wesker's Pip. But his place as the Outsider is soon taken by a wandering Irishman, Roche, a filthy old fantasist, wearing dark glasses and with his head wrapped in a tea-cloth, who soon becomes the focus of the group's discontent and bewilderment. The pity, disgust, and fear felt by the regulars for this apparition, alternately cringing and ludicrously grand, is most admirably handled. Then a third Outsider – another pair of Outsiders, in fact – appears, of quite a different order: Johnny Hobnails, who drives the tractor which trundles fruit-boxes back and forth, is let out to work by a local asylum, and his chum Tiny is almost more frighteningly odd than he.

The establishment, so to speak, is here represented only by the foreman, Spens, a sharply drawn example of the harassed incompetent, and by the puzzling figures, which remain pretty shadowy, of the owner and his daughter, whose remoteness is established but very little else. Rudkin's interest is in fact directed almost wholly to the spirit of destruction arising out of this situation – arising regularly out of it, we are given to understand, every year. The atmosphere of unspecified menace intensifies. Roche hovers, appears and disappears, is mocked and reviled. Johnny Hobnails conceives an affinity, part hero-worship, part sexual attraction, for Larry the student, and out of his rambling babble of the Blood of the Lamb shapes a passionate warning to the boy to go. The weather breaks. A helicopter sprays the orchard as the men pick: a parallel with radioactive fall-out is illiterately hinted at by the uneasy group. Then, in a slowly built scene of great power, they turn on Roche. Decapitated, his trunk scored with the sign of the Cross, he is hurried out of sight. The pears are picked; night has come; the men go, two by two; a solitary pitchfork impales the earth, glimmering alone in the moonlight.

Strong stuff, you see: an expression of atavistic forces which override sense and sensibility in all of us at times but show through most readily in the slow, the stupid, the trivial, the animal. Rudkin's play is powerful, but confused; what is not in doubt is his ear for significance in insignificant speech, his feeling for hysteria, and his ability to turn the dramatic screw.

Giles Cooper, too, in nearly all his work, shows us the dark side of the moon, but does so in an altogether more sophisticated way, choosing nearly always semi-sophisticated *milieux*: in EVERYTHING

IN THE GARDEN a suburb, portrayed, in terms of its attitudes of mind and turns of phrase, with alarming naturalistic accuracy. Here are a husband and wife; they have achieved a comfortable house, a garden to be proud of. She is always looking for more; he is always pointing out that he has to earn the money. With his job, his home comforts (which include his wife), and his garden, he is more or less content. She is bored, and has no imagination. All their friends, bar one, who is in any case not so much a friend as a confusing feature of the landscape, a commercial artist who lives in their world but mocks it, are in the same case. From this point the play abandons naturalism and plunges into fantasy – fantasy presented with an absolutely straight face. Enter another Outsider – a Polish Jewess who has been forced to live as these modest folk never have and runs a high-class London brothel in which all the apparently modest wives are only too pleased to pass the time and earn vast sums of money.

Out of their husbands' reactions to this singular turn of events Cooper makes a comic crescendo of horrifying force, in which one after another the loosely held convictions of slack-minded materialists vanish like dew in the morning sun. In fact, he seems to have lost his nerve, for after leading his tame suburbanites, threatened from outside the herd, to another ritual murder, he tries to give his central figure a turn of conscience. Has, in effect, tried twice to do so, for he has written two endings to this play, of which the second is printed here. In the first, the actor playing the principal husband was made suddenly to break out of his part in disgust. This Pirandellian dodge satisfied nobody; Cooper thought again, and arrived at the present version, in which the wretched man is allowed a few belated qualms, no more.

Even Shakespeare got into difficulties with his endings. Cooper's problem in no way vitiates the exquisite elegance of his play nor the sting of his satire. In terms of construction there is a beautiful spareness in each scene. All the dialogue is active, there is hardly a merely expository line in the whole play. The moment at which the husband discovers great wads of banknotes in his drawing-room is one of the most stiflingly comic in modern drama. The illiberal parrot-stupidity of the middle-middle-classes everywhere is never hammered home but always showing through. The squat old Polish madam's line,

'Nothing is disgusting unless you are disgusted', makes even them (or at least the men, for Cooper's women are indeed more deadly) shiver for a moment at the realization of just how disgusting they really are. The counterpointed party conversation, in which the women talk about having children and the men reminisce about war, is a dazzling exercise in technique and an appalling summary of civilized values (*vide* the most popular features in the best Sunday papers). The other Outsider, the artist, who pays the price for his effortless nonconformity, remains a rather dim figure it is true; but then Cooper's interest, like Rudkin's in its very different context, is in the split personality of conformity, not in the relatively simple and more easily admirable qualities of those who go their own way.

In this at least – in not making their nonconformist their hero – Rudkin and Cooper have the edge on Arnold Wesker. If a dramatist or a novelist identifies himself too readily with his central character, he will soften the core of his work; and in this respect, for all the brilliance of his dramatic contrivance, Wesker still has far to go. But for all three, conformity is the enemy; and while the theatre can still fight effectively on that front more power to its raddled old elbow.

J. W. LAMBERT

ARNOLD WESKER

Chips With Everything

TO JOHN DEXTER
who has helped me to understand the theatre of
my plays and directed them all when most others
said they would fail

CHARACTERS

Conscripts

ARCHIE CANNIBAL 239
WINGATE (Chas) 252
THOMPSON (Pip) 276
SEAFORD (Wilfe) 247
ANDREW McCLORE 284
RICHARDSON (Ginger) 272
COHEN (Dodger) 277
SMITH (Dickey) 266
WASHINGTON (Smiler) 279

Officers

CORPORAL HILL
WING COMMANDER
SQUADRON LEADER
PILOT OFFICER
P.T. INSTRUCTOR, FLT SGT

GUARD
NIGHT CORPORAL
FIRST CORPORAL
SECOND CORPORAL
AIRMAN

The song 'The Cutty Wren', which appears on page 41, is reprinted from *If I had a Song*, a collection of children's songs published by the Workers' Music Association, 136A Westbourne Terrace, London W2.

ACT ONE

SCENE ONE

An R.A.F. hut.

[Nine new conscripts enter. They are subdued, uncertain, mumbling. CORPORAL HILL *appears at door, stocky, Northern, collarless man. He waits till they notice him, which they gradually do till mumbling ceases, utterly – they rise to attention. After a long pause]*

HILL: That's better. In future, whenever an N.C.O. comes into the hut, no matter who he is, the first person to see him will call out 'N.C.O.! N.C.O.!' like that. And whatever you're doing, even if you're stark rollock naked, you'll all spring to attention as fast as the wind from a duck's behind, and by Christ that's fast. Is that understood? *[No reply.]* Well, is it? *[A few murmurs.]* When I ask a question I expect an answer. *[Emphatically]* Is that understood!

ALL *[shouting]*: Yes, Corporal!

HILL: Anyone been in the Air Cadets? Any of the cadets? Anyone twenty-one or more then? Nineteen? *[Two boys,* ANDREW *and* DICKEY, *raise their hands. To one]* Month you were born?

ANDREW: July, Corporal.

DICKEY: May, Corporal.

HILL *[to Dickey]*: You're senior man. *[To Andrew]* You're assistant. Shift your kit to top of hut. Not now – later.

*[*HILL *scrutinizes the rest. He lays his hand on the two smallest – Dodger and Ginger.*

These small boys, these two, they're my boys. They'll do the jobs I ask them when I ask them; not much, my fires each day, perhaps my bunk – my boys. But they won't do my polishing – I do that myself. No one is to start on them, no one is to bully them, if they do, then they answer to me. *[Pause.]* You can sit now.

[Reads out list of names, each recruit rises and sits as called. Boys sit on their beds, waiting; HILL *paces up and down, waiting his time. Then]*

Right, you're in the R.A.F. now, you're not at home. This hut, this place here, this is going to be your home for the next eight scorching weeks. This billet here, you see it? This? It's in a state now, no one's been in it for the last four days so it's in a state now. [*Pause.*] But usually it's like a scorching palace! [*Pause.*] That's the way I want it to be cos that's the way it's always been. Now you've got to get to know me. My name is Corporal Hill. I'm not a very happy man, I don't know why. I never smile and I never joke – you'll soon see that. Perhaps it's my nature, perhaps it's the way I've been brought up – I don't know. The R.A.F. brought me up. You're going to go through hell while you're here, through scorching hell. Some of you will take it and some of you will break down. I'm warning you – some of you shall end up crying. And when that happens I don't want to see anyone laughing at him. Leave him alone, don't touch him.

But I'll play fair. You do me proud and I'll play fair. The last lot we 'ad 'ere 'ad a good time, a right time, a right good scorching time. We 'ad bags o' fun, bags o' it. But I will tear and mercilessly scratch the scorching daylights out of anyone who smarts the alec with me – and we've got some 'ere. I can see them, you can tell them. I count three already, you can tell them, by their faces, who know it all, the boys who think they're GOOD. [*Whispered*] It'll be unmerciful and scorching murder for them – all. Now, you see this wireless here, this thing with knobs and a pretty light that goes on and off? Well that's ours, our wireless for this hut, and for this hut only because this hut has always been the best hut. No other hut has a wireless. I want to keep that. I like music and I want to keep that wireless. Some people, when they get up in the morning, first thing all they want to do is smoke, or drink tea – not me, I've got to have music, the noise of instruments.

Everyone's got a fad, that's mine, music, and I want to be spoilt, you see to it that I'm spoilt. Right, if there's anyone here who wants to leave my hut and go into another because he doesn't like this 'un, then do it now, please. Go on, pick up your kit and move. I'll let 'im. [*No movement.*] You can go to the Naafi now. But be back by ten thirty, cos that's bleedin' lights out. [*Moves to door, pauses.*] Anyone object to swearing? [*No reply. Exit.*]

[*Stunned. A boy rushes in from another hut.*]

BOY: What's your'n say?

SMILER [*imitating*]: My name is Corporal Hill, I'm not a happy man.

BOY [*imitating a Scotsman*]: My name is Corporal Bridle – and I'm a bastard!

SCENE TWO

The Naafi.
　　[*One boy strumming a guitar*]

WILFE:　　　Dear mother come and fetch me
　　　　　　Dear mother take me home
　　　　　　I'm drunk and unhappy
　　　　　　And my virginity's gone.

　　　　　　My feet are sore and I'm weary
　　　　　　The sergeant looks like dad
　　　　　　Oh, a two bob bit would buy me a nip
　　　　　　And a Naafi girl in my bed.
　　　　　　Now Eskimo Nell has gone back to the land
　　　　　　Where they know how to – Eight weeks!
　　　　　　EIGHT STUPID WEEKS, MOTHER!

CHAS: I've left two girls at home, two of them, and I've declared passionate love to them both – both. Poor girls, promised I'd marry them when it was all over. They'll miss me.

WILFE: Wouldn't be so bad if my mother could hear me, but she's as deaf as a bat.

PIP: Bats are blind.

WILFE: Oh dear me, bats are blind, deary, deary me fellows.

PIP: Look old son, you're going to have me for eight painful weeks in the same hut, so spend the next five minutes taking the mickey out of my accent, get it off your chest and then put your working-class halo away because no one's going to care – O.K.?

CHAS: Where are you from then?

PIP: My father is a banker, we idolize each other. I was born in a large country house and I'm scorching rich.

CHAS: You're going to do officer training then?

PIP: No! My father was also a general!

WILFE: Oh my father was a general
    And I'm a general's son
    But I got wise to the old man's lies
    And kicked him up his you know, you
    know, you know, you know what I mean.
    Now Eskimo Nell has gone back to the land –
    EIGHT STUPID WEEKS, MOTHER!

SMILER: Give over, Wilfe, give over.

GINGER: Well roll on Christmas, roll on I say.

DODGER: So what then? You'll be back after four days, and then four more weeks of this –

GINGER: But I'll be married.

DODGER: You'll be what?

GINGER: I'm getting married two weeks from tomorrow –

CHAS: Bleedin' daft to get married. I got two girls back home, one's blonde and one's dark – it's the Jekyll and Hyde in me. Married? Bleedin' daft!

PIP: You mean you can actually think of better things to do than produce babies?

CHAS: You shut your classical mouth you, go away, 'oppit! 'Oppit or I'll lay you down. I haven't liked you from the start.

PIP: Oh sit down, there's a good boy, I wouldn't dream of fighting you.

SMILER: You don't mind being a snob, do you?

PIP: One day, when I was driving to my father's office, the car broke down. I could have got a taxi I suppose, but I didn't. I walked. The office was in the City, so I had to walk through the East End, strange – I don't know why I should have been surprised. I'd seen photographs of this Mecca before – I even used to glance at the *Daily Mirror* now and then, so God knows why I should have been surprised. Strange. I went into a café and drank a cup of tea from a thick, white, cracked cup and I ate a piece of tasteless currant cake. On the walls I remember they had photographs of boxers, autographed, and they were curling at the edges from the heat. Every so often a woman used to come to the table and wipe it with a rag that left dark streaks behind which dried up into weird patterns. Then a man came and sat next to me – WHY should I have been surprised? I'd seen his face before, a hundred times on the front pages of papers reporting a strike. A market man, a porter, or a docker. No, he was too old to be a docker. His eyes kept watering, and each time they did that he'd take out a neatly folded handkerchief, unfold it and, with one corner, he'd wipe away the moisture, and then he'd neatly fold it up again and replace it in his pocket. Four times he did that, and each time he did it he looked at me and smiled. I could see grains of dirt in the lines of his face, and he wore an old waistcoat with pearl buttons. He wasn't untidy, the cloth even seemed a good cloth, and though his hair was thick with oil it was clean. I can even remember the colour of the walls, a pastel pink on the top half and turquoise blue on the bottom, peeling. Peeling in fifteen different places; actually, I counted them. But what I couldn't understand was why I should have been so surprised. It wasn't as though I had been cradled in my childhood. And then I saw the menu, stained with tea and beautifully written by a foreign hand, and on top it said – God I hated that old man – it said 'Chips with everything'. Chips with every damn thing. You breed babies and you eat chips with everything.

[*Enter* HILL.]

HILL: I said ten thirty lights out, didn't I? Ten thirty I said. I want to see you move to that hut like wind from a duck's behind –

WILFE: And O Jesus mother, that's fast mother, that's eight weeks and that's fast!

HILL: That's fast, that's fast, into the hut and move that fast. Into the hut, into the hut, in, in, into the hut. [*Looks at watch. Pause.*] Out! I'll give you . . .

SCENE THREE

Parade Ground: morning.

HILL: Out! I'll give you sixty seconds or you'll be on a charge, one, two, three, four – come on out of that hut, twenty-five, twenty-six, twenty-seven, twenty-eight. AT THE DOUBLE! Now get into a line and stop that talking, get into a line. A straight line you heaving nig-nogs, a straight line.

This is the square. We call it a square-bashing square. I want to see you bash that square. Right, now the first thing you've got to know, you've got to know how to come to attention, how to stand at ease and easy, how to make a right turn and how to step off.

Now to come to attention you move smartly, very smartly, to this position: heels together. STOP THAT! When I was born I was very fortunate, I was born with eyes in the back of my neck and don't be cheeky. Legs apart and wait till I give the command SHUN. When I give the command SHUN, you will move sharply, very sharply, to this position. Heels together and in a line, feet turned out to an angle of thirty degrees, knees braced, body erect and with the weight balanced evenly between the balls of the feet and the heels.

Shoulders down and back level and square to the front.

Arms hanging straight from the shoulders.

Elbows close to the sides.

Wrists straight.

Hands closed – not clenched.

Back of the fingers close to the thighs.

Thumbs straight and to the front, close to the forefinger and just behind the seam of the trousers. Head up, chin in, eyes open, steady and looking just above their own height. Come on now, heels together, body erect and evenly balanced between the balls of the feet and the heels – you didn't know you had balls on your feet did you – well you have, use them.

Stand up straight there – keep your mouth shut and your eyes open and to the front. Right, well, you are now standing – somewhat vaguely – in the position of attention.

To stand at ease you keep the right foot still and carry the left foot to the left so that the feet are about – do it with me – so that the feet are about twelve inches apart. At the same time force the arms behind the back, keeping them straight, and place the back of the right hand in the palm of the left, thumbs crossed, fingers and hands straight and pointing towards the ground. At the same time transfer the weight of the body slightly to the left so as to be evenly balanced. Keep your arms straight and don't bend at the waist. [*Inspects them.*] Right hand inside your left, *your* left not his. Try to make your elbows meet.

When you hear me give the command SQUAD, I want you to jump to that position, smarten up, as if you were going somewhere. We'll try it – stand easy, relax, just relax, but keep your hands behind your back, don't slouch, don't move your feet and don't talk – just relax, let your head look down, RELAX! IF YOU DON'T RELAX I'LL PUT YOU ON A CHARGE!

Squad, squad – SHUN! As you were, I want you to do it together. Squad – SHUN! As you were. Squad – SHUN! STAND AT EASE!

To make a Right Turn: keeping both knees straight, turn through ninety degrees to the right swivelling on the heel of the right foot and the toe of the left raising the toe of the right and the heel of the left in doing so. Keeping the weight of the body on the right foot, on completion of this movement the right foot is flat on the ground, the left leg to the rear and the heel raised – both knees braced back and the body in the position of attention. Bring the left foot into the right, good and hard, and for the time being I want that left knee good and high, slam your foot in good and hard and keep still.

Squad, squad – SHUN.

Turning to the right – RIGHT TURN.

All right you creepy-crawly nig-nogs, moon men that's what you are, moon men. I want it done together. As you were.

Squad, turning to the right – RIGHT TURN.

Now, to Step Off. When I say by the front – quick march, I don't want your pretty left foot forward anyways, like this, no, it's got to be scorching smart, like a flash of greased lightning. ONE!

Like this [*Petrified stance of a man about to step off.*] ONE! Like that, and I want that left hand up as high as you can get it and your right level with your breast pocket.

Now, on the word – MARCH – I want you only to take a step forward, *not* to march. I want you only to take a step forward, just pretend, got that? Some dimwitted piece of merchandise is sure to carry on. Now then, watch it. SQUAD – by the front – quick MARCH!

[*Sure enough two boys march off and collide with those standing still, and one in the front marches off out of sight.*]

Stop that laughing. I'll charge the next man I see smile.

[*Stands, watching the other one disappear.*]

All right, Horace, come back home. [*Airman returns, sheepishly.*] You nit, you nit, you creepy-crawly nit. Don't you hear, don't you listen, can't you follow simple orders, CAN'T YOU? Shut up! Don't answer back! A young man like you, first thing in the morning, don't be rude, don't be rude. No one's being rude to you.

Stop that laughing. I'll charge the next man I see smile. [*To Smiler*] You, I said wipe off that smile. I said wipe it off.

SMILER: I'm not smiling, Corporal, it's natural, I was born with it.

HILL: Right then, don't ever let me see that face frown or I'll haul you over the highest wall we've got. [*Approaching one of the two marching ones*] You. If you'd been paying attention you might 'ave done it correctly, eh? But you weren't, you were watching the little aeroplanes, weren't you? You want to fly? Do you want to reach the thundering heavens, my little lad, at an earlier age than you imagined, with Technicolor wings? KEEP YOUR EYES ON ME. [*To all*] You better know from the start, you can have it the hard way or you can have it the easy way, I don't mind which way it is. Perhaps you like it the hard way, suits me. Just let me know. At ease everyone. Now, we'll try and make it easier for you. We'll count our way along. We'll count together, and then maybe we'll all act together. I want everything to be done together. We're going to be the happiest family in Christendom and we're going to move together, as one, as one solitary man. So, when I say 'attention' you'll slam your feet down hard and cry 'one'. Like this. And when I say 'right turn' you'll move and bang your foot down and cry 'one-pause-two'. Like this. Is that clear? Is that beyond the intellectual comprehensibilities of any of you? Good! SQUAD – wait for it – atten-SHUN!

SQUAD: ONE!

HILL: As you were, at ease. Did I say slam? Didn't I say slam? Don't worry about the noise, it's a large square, no one will mind. Squad – atten-SHUN.

SQUAD: ONE!

HILL: As you were. Let's hear that 'one'. Let's have some energy from you. I want GOD to hear you crying 'ONE, ONE, ONE – pause TWO!' Squad – atten-SHUN!

SQUAD: ONE!

HILL: Right TURN!

SQUAD: ONE – pause – TWO!

HILL: By the left – quick – MARCH!

[*The boys march off round the stage, sound of marching and the chanting of* 'One, One, One – pause – Two! One, One, One – pause – Two!']

SCENE FOUR

Sound of marching feet. Marching stops. The lecture hall.
　　[*Boys enter and sit on seats. Enter the* WING COMMANDER, *boys rise.*]

WING COMMANDER: Sit down, please. I'm your Wing Commander. You think we are at peace. Not true. We are never at peace. The human being is in a constant state of war and we must be prepared, each against the other. History has taught us this and we must learn. The reasons why and wherefore are not our concern. We are simply the men who must be prepared. You, why do you look at me like that?

PIP: I'm paying attention, sir.

WING COMMANDER: There's insolence in those eyes, lad – I recognize insolence in a man; take that glint out of your eyes, your posh tones don't fool me. We are simply the men who must be prepared. Already the aggressors have a force far superior to ours. Our efforts must be intensified. We need a fighting force and it is for this reason you are being trained here, according to the best traditions of the R.A.F. We want you to be proud of your part, unashamed of the uniform you wear. But you must not grumble too much if you find that government facilities for you, personally, are not up to standard. We haven't the money to spare. A Meteor, fully armed, is more important than a library. The C.O. of this camp is called Group Captain Watson. His task is to check any tendency in his officers to practical jokes, to discountenance any disposition in his officers to gamble or to indulge in extravagant expenditure; to endeavour, by example and timely intervention, to promote a good understanding and prevent disputes. Group Captain Watson is a busy man, you will rarely see him. You, why are you smiling?

SMILER: I'm not, sir, it's natural, I was born like it.

WING COMMANDER: Because I want this taken seriously, you know, from all of you. Any questions?

WILFE: Sir, if the aggressors are better off than us, what are they waiting for?

WING COMMANDER: What's your name?

WILFE: 247 Seaford, sir.

WING COMMANDER: Any other questions?

[*Exit. Enter* SQUADRON LEADER. *The boys rise.*]

SQUADRON LEADER: Sit down, please. I'm your squadron leader. My task is not only to ensure respect for authority, but also to foster the feelings of self-respect and personal honour which are essential to efficiency. It is also my task to bring to notice those who, from incapacity or apathy, are deficient in knowledge of their duties, or who do not afford an officer that support which he has a right to expect or who conduct themselves in a manner injurious to the efficiency or credit of the R.A.F. You are here to learn discipline. Discipline is necessary if we are to train you to the maximum state of efficiency, discipline and obedience. You will obey your instructors because they are well trained, you will obey them because they can train you efficiently, you will obey them because it's necessary for you to be trained efficiently. That is what you are here to learn: obedience and discipline. Any questions? Thank you.

[*Exit. Enter* PILOT OFFICER. *The boys rise.*]

PILOT OFFICER: Sit down please. I'm your pilot officer. You'll find that I'm amenable and that I do not stick rigidly to authority. All I shall require is cleanliness. It's not that I want rigid men, I want clean men. It so happens, however, that you cannot have clean men without rigid men, and cleanliness requires smartness and ceremony. Ceremony means your webbing must be blancoed, and smartness means that your brass – all of it – must shine like silver paper, and your huts must be spick and span without a trace of dust, because dust carries germs, and germs are unclean. I want a man clean from toe nail to hair root. I want him so clean that he looks unreal. In fact I don't want real men, real men are dirty and nasty, they pick their noses – and scratch their skin. I want unreal, super-real men. Those men win wars, the others die of disease before they reach the battlefields. Any questions? You, what are you smiling at?

SMILER: I'm not, sir, it's natural. I was born like that.

PILOT OFFICER: In between the lines of that grin are formed battalions of microbes. Get rid of it.

SMILER: I can't, sir.

PILOT OFFICER: Then never let me hear of you going sick.

[*Exit. Enter* P.T. INSTRUCTOR, FLIGHT SERGEANT.]

P.T.I.: As you were. I'm in charge of physical training on this camp. It's my duty to see that every minute muscle in your body is awake. Awake and ringing. Do you hear that? That's poetry! I want your body awake and ringing. I want you so light on your feet that the smoke from a cigarette could blow you away, and yet so strong that you stand firm before hurricanes. I hate thin men and detest fat ones. I want you like Greek gods. You heard of the Greeks? You ignorant troupe of anaemics, you were brought up on tinned beans and television sets, weren't you? You haven't had any exercise since you played knock-a-down-ginger, have you? Greek gods, you hear me? Till the sweat pours out of you like Niagara Falls. Did you hear that poetry? Sweat like Niagara Falls! I don't want your stupid questions!

[*Exit.*]

PIP: You have babies, you eat chips and you take orders.
CHAS: Well, look at you then, I don't see you doing different.
 [*They march off. Sound of marching feet.*]

SCENE FIVE

Sound of marching feet and the men counting. The hut. Billet inspection.
 [ANDREW, *the hut orderly, tidying up. Enter the* PILOT OFFICER]

ANDREW [*saluting*]: Good morning, sir.
PILOT OFFICER: Haven't you been told the proper way to address an officer?
ANDREW: Sorry sir, no sir, not yet sir.
 [PILOT OFFICER *walks around.* ANDREW *follows awkwardly.*]
PILOT OFFICER: There's dust under that bed.
ANDREW: Is there, sir?
PILOT OFFICER: I said so.
ANDREW: Yes, you did, sir.
PILOT OFFICER: Then why ask me again?
ANDREW: Again, sir?
PILOT OFFICER: Didn't you?
ANDREW: Didn't I what, sir?
PILOT OFFICER: Ask me to repeat what I'd already said. Are you playing me up, Airman? Are you taking the mickey out of me? I can charge you, man. I can see your game and I can charge you.
ANDREW: Yes, you can, sir.
PILOT OFFICER: Don't tell me what I already know.
ANDREW: Oh, I wouldn't, sir – you know what you already know. I know that, sir.
PILOT OFFICER: I think you're a fool, Airman. God knows why the Air Ministry sends us fools. They never select, select is the answer, select and pick those out from the others.
ANDREW: What others, sir?
PILOT OFFICER: Don't question me!

ANDREW: But I was only thinking of –

PILOT OFFICER: You aren't paid to think, Airman, don't you know that? You aren't paid to think. [*Long pause.*] No, it's no good trying that line. [*Sits.*] Why pretend? I don't really frighten you, do I? I don't really frighten you, but you obey my orders, nevertheless. It's a funny thing. We have always ruled, but I suspect we've never frightened you. I know that as soon as I turn my back you'll merely give me a V sign and make a joke of me to the others, won't you? And they'll laugh. Especially Thompson. He knows you're not frightened, that's why he's in the ranks. But I'll break him. Slumming, that's all he's doing, slumming. What's your name?

ANDREW: Andrew McClore, sir.

PILOT OFFICER: I don't suppose Thompson's really slumming. There *is* something about you boys, confidence, I suppose, or cockiness, something trustworthy anyway. I can remember enjoying the Naafi more than I do the Officers' Mess. What was your job?

ANDREW: Electrician, sir.

PILOT OFFICER: My father was an electrician. He used to play the piano. He really played beautifully. Tragic – my God – it was tragic.

ANDREW: Had an accident, sir?

PILOT OFFICER: That would be your idea of tragedy, wouldn't it? My father never had that sort of accident; he couldn't, he owned the factory he worked for. It's the other things that happen to people like him. The intangible accidents. No, his fingers remained subtle till he died, and he touched the keys with love whenever he could, but no one heard him. That was the tragedy, Andrew. No one heard him except – four uncaring children and a stupid wife who saw no sense in it. God, Andrew, how I envied that man. I could have bought so much love with that talent. People don't give love away that easily, only if we have magic in our hands or in our words or in our brush then they pay attention, then they love us. You can forget your own troubles in an artist's love, Andrew; you can melt away from what you were and grow into a new man. Haven't you ever wanted to be a new man? [*Places hand on McClore's knee.*]

ANDREW: Don't do that, please, sir.

PILOT OFFICER [*change*]: Don't ever rely on this conversation, don't ever trust me to be your friend. I shall not merely frighten you, there are other ways – and you will need all your pity for yourself. I warn you not to be fooled by good nature, we slum for our own convenience.

[*Enter a* FLIGHT SERGEANT.]

FLIGHT SERGEANT: When is – I beg your pardon, sir.

PILOT OFFICER: You can take over now, Flight. [*Exit.*]

FLIGHT SERGEANT: When is this place going to be straight?

ANDREW: Pardon, Sergeant?

FLIGHT SERGEANT: *Flight* Sergeant!

ANDREW: Sorry, FLIGHT Sergeant.

FLIGHT SERGEANT: When is this place going to be straight, I asked?

ANDREW: I've just straightened it, Serg – or Flight – or Flight Sergeant.

FLIGHT SERGEANT: You what? If I come in here tomorrow and I can't eat my dinner off that floor I'll have you all outside on fatigues till midnight. Have you got that?

ANDREW: Yes, Flight Sergeant.

FLIGHT SERGEANT: Well, keep it. Tight! Tight! Tight, tight –

['Tight, tight, tight', *mixes to sound of marching feet, men counting.*]

SCENE SIX

The billet at night. The boys are tired. Beds are being made, brasses, shoes, webbing attended to.

ANDREW: And then he says:'I shall not merely frighten you, there are other ways, and you will need all your pity for yourself.' Man, I tell you it was him was frightened. A tall meek thing he is, trying to impress me.

HILL: It's not him you want to be frightened of, it's royalty. Royalty! I hate royalty more than anything else in the world. Parasites! What do they do, eh? I'm not in this outfit for them, no bloody fear, it's the people back 'ome I'm here for, like you lot. Royalty –

PIP: Good old Corporal Hill, they've made you chase red herrings, haven't they?

ANDREW: And he had something to say about you too, Pip Thompson. He said you were slumming, laddie, slumming; he said: 'Thompson knows you're not frightened, that's why he's in the ranks – but he's slumming.'

PIP: So he thinks you're not frightened? He's right – you're not, are you? But there *are* other ways – he's right about that too.

DODGER: You know, I've been looking at this hut, sizing it up. Make a good warehouse.

GINGER: A good what?

DODGER: Warehouse. It's my mania. My family owns a pram shop, see, and our one big problem is storage. Prams take up room, you know. Always on the look-out for storage space. Every place I look at I work out the cubic feet, and I say it will make a good warehouse or it won't. Can't help myself. One of the best warehouses I ever see was the Vatican in Rome. What you laughing at? You take a carpenter – what does he do when he enters – what does he do when he enters a room, eh? Ever thought about that? He feels how the door swings open, looks straight across to the window to see if the frame is sitting straight and then sits in the chair to see if it's made good – then he can settle down to enjoy the evening. With me it's pregnant women. Every time I see pregnant women I get all maternal. You can have your women's breasts all you want and her legs. *Me*, only one spot interests me – one big belly and we've made a sale. Can't help it – warehouses and pregnant women.

DICKEY: Hey, Cannibal my dear associate, what are you so engrossed in?

CANNIBAL: It's a book about ideal marriage, now leave me be.

DICKEY: Why you dirty-minded adolescent you – put it away.

DODGER: Here, let's have a read.

[*He and some others crowd round to read on.*]

PIP: 252 WINGATE! – give me a hand with this bed, will you, please.

CHAS: Why I bloody help you I don't know, not at all I don't.

PIP: Because you like me, that's why.

CHAS: *Like* you? Like *you*? You're the lousiest rotten snob I know.

PIP: And you like snobs.

CHAS: Boy, I hate you so much it hurts. You can't even make a bed properly.

PIP: It was always made for me.

CHAS: There you go. See what I mean. Boasting of your bleedin' wealth and comfort. Well, I don't want to know about your stinking comforts, don't tell me, I don't want to hear.

PIP: Oh, yes you do. You love to hear me talk about my home. We have a beautiful home, Charles, twenty-four rooms, and they're all large and thick with carpets.

CHAS: Modern?

PIP: No, built in the time of George III.

CHAS: I don't want to know.

PIP: They started to build it in 1776 when George Washington was made commander-in-chief of the American colonists and the great-grandfathers of the Yanks were issuing the Declaration of Independence. A jubilant period, Charles – exciting. Did you know that while my great-great-grandfather was trading with the East India Company in the land of the strange chocolate people, bringing home the oriental spoils, the American grandfathers were still struggling to control a vast land at a time when there was no communication? But they didn't struggle long. Each time my great-grandfather came home he heard more bad news about those traitorous Americans. Returning from India in 1830, with a cargo of indigo, he heard, twenty-three years after everyone else, that the steamboat had been invented. Terrible news. Returning in 1835 with a cargo of teak they told him about the strange iron horse that ran on wheels. Terrible, terrible, news. Returning in 1840 with a cargo of coriander he was so enraged that he refused to believe it possible to send messages through the air, and so he died without ever believing in the magic of the telegraph. What do you think of that, Charles boy? Still, my favourite relative was his father, a beautiful boy, the kind of boy that every aunt wanted to mother and every cousin wanted to marry. The only thing was he was incredibly stupid, much more than you, Charles, and strangely enough he was called Charles also. My family talk about him to this very day. You see, the fact was that very few people ever realized he was so stupid because he was such a handsome boy and very rarely spoke. And because of his silence everyone thought he was very wise, and this was so effective that he increased our family fortune by double. [*Nearly everyone is listening to him by now.*] You want to know how? Well, it was like this. Shortly after the shock of losing America, the English were disturbed by another event – another shock that rocked the whole of Europe and set my family and all their friends shaking. One day, the French kings and princes found themselves bankrupt – the royalty and the clergy never used to pay any taxes, you see they left that on the shoulders of the middle class and the commoners, and yet they still managed to become bankrupt. So what did they do? They called a meeting of all the representatives of all the classes to see what could be done – there hadn't been such a meeting for over a century, what a party! What a mistake! because, for the first time in a long while, the commoners not only found a means of voicing their discontent over the paying of taxes, but they suddenly looked at themselves and realized that there were more of them than they ever imagined – and they weren't fools. Now, they voiced themselves well, and so loudly that they won a victory, and not simply over the tax problem, but over a dozen and one other injustices as well. Big excitement, jubilation, victory! In fact, they found themselves so victorious and so powerful that they were able to cut off the heads of poor Louis XVI and Marie Antoinette and start what we all know as the French Revolution.

CHAS: What about Charlie, the silly one?

PIP: Patience, my handsome boy, don't hurry me. Now, my family had a lot of interests in France and its royalty, so they decided to send this beautiful boy out to see what was happening to their estates and fortunes. And do you think he did? Poor soul, he couldn't understand what the hell was happening. The royalty of all Europe was trembling because of what the French did to Louis and Marie, and he just thought he was being sent on a holiday. To this day we none of us know how he escaped with his life – but, not only did he escape with his life, he also came back with somebody else's life. A French princess! And would you believe it, she was also a simpleton, a sort of prototype deb with a dimple on her left cheek. Her family had given her all their jewels, thinking that no one would touch her, since she was so helpless, and indeed no one did. No one, that is, except our Charles. He met her on his way to Paris in a Franciscan monastery and asked her to teach him French. There were her relatives being beheaded one by one and there was she, chanting out the past tense of the verb 'to be'. You can guess the rest, within four weeks he was back in England with a lovely bride and four hundred thousand pounds'-worth of jewellery. They built a new wing to the house and had seven children. The rooms glitter with her chandeliers, Charlie boy – and – well, just look at the way your mouth is gaping – you'll get lockjaw.

HILL: Don't you tell stories, eh? Don't you just. I bet you made that one up as you went along.

PIP: That's right, Corporal, the French Revolution was a myth.

CHAS: Tell us more, Pip, tell us more stories.

PIP: They're not stories, Charlie boy, they're history.

CHAS: Well, tell us more then.

PIP: What's the use?

CHAS: I'm asking you, that's what's the use. *I'm asking you.*

[PIP *picks up his webbing to blanco. The others withdraw and pick up what they were doing.* CHARLIE *is left annoyed and frustrated.* HILL *takes a seat next to the fire and plays a mouth-organ. In between sounds he talks.*]

HILL: I was pleased with you lads today. You're coming on. When you did those last about turns I felt proud. You might even be better than the last lot we had. Know that? And by Christ that last lot were good. But there's one of you needs to buck up his ideas, I shan't mention names.

SMILER: I try, Corporal.

HILL: Well, you want to try harder, my son. Look at you.

SMILER: I look at myself every day, Corporal.

HILL: That stupid smile of yours, if only you didn't smile so much. Can't you have an operation or something? I'll go bleedin' mad looking at that for another five weeks.

DODGER: Oh, my gawd, listen to this! Listen what it says here. 'Between two hundred and three hundred million spermatozoa are released at one time of which only one succeeds in fertilizing the female ovum.' Jesus! All them prams!

34

GINGER: Give us a good tune, Corp, go on.

HILL: You're my treasure, aren't you, eh, Ginger lad? Don't know what I'd do without you. What shall I play for you, you name it, I'll play it.

GINGER: Play us the 'Rose of Tralee'.

HILL: You want the 'Rose of Tralee', my beauty? You shall have it then.

[CORPORAL HILL *plays, the boys rest, work, write letters, and listen.*]

GINGER: When's the Christmas Eve party?

DODGER: Tomorrow a week, isn't it?

HILL: Uh-huh.

[*Continue sound of mouth-organ – change to*]

SCENE SEVEN

The Naafi. Christmas Eve Party.

[*The rock-'n-'roll group play vigorously. The boys jiving, drinking, and singing. Officers are present.*]

WING COMMANDER: Look at them. Conscripts! They bring nothing and they take nothing. Look at them. Their wild dancing and their silly words – I could order them at this moment to stand up and be shot and they'd do it.

SQUADRON LEADER: You're drinking too much, Sid.

WING COMMANDER: Civilians! How I hate civilians. They don't know – what do they know? How to make money, how to chase girls and kill old women. No order, no purpose. Conscripts! They bring their muddled lives and they poison us, Jack; they poison me with their indifference, and all we do is guard their fat bellies. I'd sacrifice a million of them for the grace of a Javelin Fighter, you know that?

SQUADRON LEADER: Don't let them see you scowl. Smile, man, smile. It's a Christmas Eve party. We're guests here.

SMILER [*to Wilfe*]: Go and offer the Wing Commander a drink, then, go on.

WILFE: Leave off, will you, man? All evening you have been pester-
ing me. What do I want to go giving officers drinks for?

SMILER: Go up to him and say 'with the compliments of our hut,
sir', go on.

WILFE: I'll pour a bottle on you soon if you don't leave off.

SIMLER: Your fly button's undone.

WILFE: Where? Smiler, I'll bash you – you tantalize me any more
this evening and I'll bash that grin right down to your arse, so help
me, I will.

SIMLER: Listen to him. Wilfe the warrior. Do you talk like this at
home? Does your mummy let you?

WILFE: Now why do you talk to me like that? Why do you go on
and on and on? Do I start on you like that? Take this away, will you
boys, take him away and drown him.

SMILER: Go after one of them Naafi girls, go on, Wilfe. Go and find
out if they're willing.

CANNIBAL: Naafi girls! Camp bloody whores, that's all they are.

DICKEY: Well, he's woken up. Cannibal has spoken, come on, me
ole cocker, say more.

CANNIBAL: Who's for more drinks?

DICKEY: Good old Cannibal! He uttered a syllable of many dimen-
sions. The circumlocircle of his mouth has moved. Direct yourself
to the bar, old son, and purchase for us some brown liquid. We
shall make merry with your generosity.

CANNIBAL: I don't know where he gets the words from. He lies in
his bed next to me and he talks and he talks and he sounds like an
adding-machine.

DICKEY: You're under-educated, my old son – you're devoid of
knowledgeable grey matter. You should've gone to a technical
school like me; we sat in study there and ate up books for our
diluted pleasure. We developed voluble minds in that technical
college and we came away equipped with data. Data! That's
the ticket – the sum total of everything. Direct your attention to
the bar I say, and deliver us of that inebriating liquid, my
hearty.

CANNIBAL: Ask him what he means. Go on, someone! I don't know.
He lies on his bed next to me and he talks and he mumbles and

talks and he mumbles. One night he woke up and he shouted: 'Kiss me, Mother, kiss your dying son.'

DICKEY: You lie in your teeth, O dumb one. Buy the drinks.

CANNIBAL: And another night he crept up to me and he was crying. 'Let me in your bed,' he moaned, 'let me get near you, you're big and warm.'

DICKEY: You're lying, Cannibal. Don't let me hear more of your lies.

CANNIBAL: Shall I tell them how you pray at nights?

[DICKEY *throws his beer over Cannibal and they fight.*]

WING COMMANDER: Separate those men! Hold them! Stop that, you two, you hear me, an order, stop that! [*They are separated.*] Undisciplined hooligans! I won't have fighting in my camp. Is this the only way you can behave with drink in you? Is it? Show your upbringing in your own home where it grew but not here, you hear me? Not here! This is Christmas Eve. A party, a celebration for the birth of our Lord, a time of joy and good will. Show me good will then. I will not, will not, will not tolerate your slum methods here. This is a clean force, a clean blue force. Go to your huts, stay there, stay there for the rest of the evening and don't wander beyond ten feet of your door. Disobey that order and I shall let out the hell of my temper so hard that you'll do jankers the rest of your National Service.

[DICKEY *and* CANNIBAL *leave. On the way,* DICKEY *trips over, and* CANNIBAL *helps him to his feet.*]

WING COMMANDER: They don't even fight seriously – a few loud words, and then they kiss each other's wounds. God give us automation soon.

SQUADRON LEADER: You suffer too much, Sid.

WING COMMANDER: Nonsense! And forget your theories about my unhappy childhood. Mine is a healthy and natural hatred.

SQUADRON LEADER: I haven't time to hate – it takes me all my time to organize them.

WING COMMANDER: Look at them. What are they? The good old working class of England. Am I supposed to bless them all the time for being the salt of the earth?

SQUADRON LEADER: They provide your food, they make your clothes, dig coal, mend roads for you.

WING COMMANDER: Given half the chance you think they would? For me? Look at them, touching the heights of ecstasy.

PIP: They're talking about us – the officers.

CHAS: What are they saying?

PIP: They're saying we're despicable, mean, and useless. That fight disturbed the Wing Commander – we upset him.

ANDREW: Don't say 'we' and imagine that makes you one of us, Pip.

PIP: Don't start on me, Andy, there's a good man.

ANDREW: Don't do us any favours.

PIP: Don't start on me, Andy, there's a good man. I don't have to drop my aitches in order to prove friendship, do I?

ANDREW: No. No, you don't. Only I've known a lot of people like you, Pip. They come drinking in the pub and talk to us as though we were the salt of the earth, and then, one day, for no reason any of us can see, they go off, drop us as though that was another game they was tired of. I'd give a pension to know why we attract you.

WING COMMANDER: What do you know about that one, Jack, the one with the smart-alec eyes and the posh tones?

SQUADRON LEADER: Thompson? Remember General Thompson, Tobruk, a banker now?

WING COMMANDER: So that's the son. Thompson! Come here, Airman.

PIP: Sir?

WING COMMANDER: Enjoying yourself?

PIP: Thank you, sir.

WING COMMANDER: Gay crowd, eh?

PIP: I imagined you would dislike conscripts, sir.

WING COMMANDER: I haven't met you before, Thompson; your father impressed me but you don't.

PIP: Is that all, sir?

WING COMMANDER: I can have you, boy. I can really have you – remember that.

CHAS: What'd he want, Pip, what'd he say?

PIP: He wouldn't dare. Yes, he would. He's going to test you all. The old fool is really going to play the old game. I wonder what method he'll choose.

WILFE: What d'you mean, old game, what old game?

PIP: How he hates you; he's going to make an announcement. Listen how patronizing he'll be. Whatever happens, do as I tell you – don't question me, just do as I tell you.

ANDREW: If you have a war with that man, Pip, don't use me as fodder, I'm warning you.

PIP: Help, Andy, I'm helping, or do you want to be made fools of?

WING COMMANDER: Silence everybody, your attention please, gentlemen – Thank you. As you all know we hoped, when we organized this gay gathering for you, that we'd have a spot in the evening when everyone would get up and do a turn himself. A dirty recitation, or a pop song. I'm sure that there's a wealth of native talent among you, and now is the chance for you to display it in all its glory, while the rest of us sit back and watch and listen. My officers are always complaining of the dull crowds we get in this camp, but I've always said no, it's not true, they're not dull, just a little inhibited – you – er know what inhibited means, of course? So now's the time to prove them wrong and me right. You won't let me down, will you, lads? Who's to be first? Eh? Who'll start?

PIP: Very subtle, eh, Andy?

WILFE: Will someone tell me what's going on here? What's so sinister about a talent show?

WING COMMANDER: The first, now.

PIP: Burns, Andrew –

ANDREW: Burns?

PIP: Your bloody saint, the poet –

ANDREW: I know he's a poet but –

PIP: Recite him, man, go on, get up there and recite.

ANDREW: Recite what? I –

PIP: In your best Scottish accent now.

ANDREW: Hell, man [once there] I – er – Burns. A poem.
    [Recites it all, at first hesitantly, amid jeers, then with growing confidence, amid silence.]

    This ae nighte, this ae nighte,
        Every nighte and alle,

Fire and fleet and candle-lighte,
And Christe receive thy saule.

When thou from hence away art past,
Every nighte and alle,
To Whinny-muir thou com'st at last;
And Christe receive thy saule.

If ever thou gavest hosen and shoon,
Every nighte and alle,
Sit thee down and put them on;
And Christe receive thy saule.

If hosen and shoon thou ne'er gav'st nane
Every nighte and alle,
The whinnes sall prick thee to the bare bane;
And Christe receive thy saule.

From Whinny-muir when thou art past,
Every nighte and alle,
To Purgatory fire thou com'st at last;
And Christe receive thy saule.

If ever thou gavest meat or drink,
Every nighte and alle,
The fire sall never make thee shrink;
And Christe receive thy saule.

If meat and drink you ne'er gav'st nane,
Every nighte and alle,
The fire will burn thee to the bare bane
And Christe receive thy saule.

This ae nighte, this ae nighte,
Every nighte and alle,
Fire and fleet and candle-lighte,
And Christe receive thy saule.

[*Ovation.*]

WING COMMANDER: Come now, something more cheerful than that. How about a song – something from Elvis Presley.

[*Band and boys begin pop song.*]

PIP: Not that, not now.

WING COMMANDER: Lovely, yes, that's it, let's see you enjoying yourselves.

PIP: Don't join in, boys – believe me and don't join in.

WILFE: What *is* this – what's going on here?

WING COMMANDER: Look at them – that's them in their element.

PIP: Can't you see what's happening, what he's thinking?

WING COMMANDER: The beer is high, they're having a good time.

PIP: Look at that smug smile.

WING COMMANDER: Aren't they living it up, just, eh? Aren't they in their glory?

PIP: He could lead you into a swamp and you'd go.

WING COMMANDER: Bravo! Bravo! That's the spirit! Make merry – it's a festive occasion and I want to see you laughing. I want my men laughing.

[*Loud pop song. Pip moves to guitarist and whispers in his ear. Boy protests, finally agrees to sing* 'The Cutty Wren', *an old peasant revolt song. Boys join in gradually, menacing the officers*]

ALL:

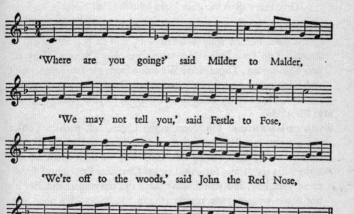

'Where are you going?' said Milder to Malder,

'We may not tell you,' said Festle to Fose,

'We're off to the woods,' said John the Red Nose,

'We're off to the woods,' said John the Red Nose.

'What will you do there?' said Milder to Malder.
'We may not tell you,' said Festle to Fose.

'We'll shoot the cutty wren,' said John the Red Nose,
'We'll shoot the cutty wren,' said John the Red Nose.

'How will you shoot him?' said Milder to Malder.
'We may not tell you,' said Festle to Fose.
'We've guns and we've cannons,' said John the Red Nose,
'We've guns and we've cannons,' said John the Red Nose.

'How will you cut her up?' said Milder to Malder.
'We may not tell you,' said Festle to Fose.
'Big hatchets and cleavers,' said John the Red Nose,
'Big hatchets and cleavers,' said John the Red Nose.

'How will you cook her?' said Milder to Malder.
'We may not tell you,' said Festle to Fose.
'Bloody great brass cauldrons,' said John the Red Nose,
'Bloody great brass cauldrons,' said John the Red Nose.

'Who'll get the spare ribs?' said Milder to Malder.
'We may not tell you,' said Festle to Fose.
'Give them all to the poor,' said John the Red Nose,
'Give them all to the poor,' said John the Red Nose.

WING COMMANDER: Quite the little leader, aren't you, Thompson? Come over here, I want a word with you in private. Stand to attention, do your button up, raise your chin – at ease. Why are you fighting me, Thompson? We come from the same side, don't we? I don't understand your reasons, boy – and what's more you're insolent. I have every intention of writing to your father.

PIP: Please do.

WING COMMANDER: Oh, come now. Listen, lad, perhaps you've got a fight on with your father or something, well that's all right by me, we all fight our fathers, and when we fight them we also fight what they stand for. Am I right? Of course I'm right. I understand you, boy, and you mustn't think I'm unsympathetic. But it's not often we get your mettle among conscripts – we need you. Let your time here be a truce, eh? Answer me, boy, my guns are lowered and I'm waiting for an answer.

PIP: Lowered, sir?

WING COMMANDER: You know very well what I mean.

[WING COMMANDER *and* OFFICERS *leave*.]

HILL: Well, a right mess you made of that interview. If there's any repercussions in our Flight, if we get victimized cos of you, boy, I'll see you –

PIP: Don't worry, Corp, there won't be any repercussions.

CHAS: Well, what in hell's name happened – what was it all about?

SMILER: This party's lost its flavour – let's go back to the hut, eh? I've got a pack of cards – let's go back and play cards.

CHAS [of pip]. Talk to him is like talking to a brick wall. PIP!

SCENE EIGHT

The Naafi.

PIP: You've got enemies, Charles boy. Learn to know them.
    [*The others have gone.*]

CHAS: Enemies? I know about enemies. People you like is enemies.

PIP: What do *you* mean when you say that, Charles?

CHAS: Oh, nothing as clever as you could mean, I'm sure.

PIP: Come on, dear boy, we're not fighting all the time, are we? You mustn't take too much notice of the way I talk.

CHAS: You talk sometimes, Pip, and I don't think you know that you hurt people.

PIP: Do I? I don't mean to.

CHAS: And sometimes there's something about your voice, the way you talk – that – well, it makes me want to tell you things.

PIP: You were telling me about enemies you like.

CHAS: You're embarrassed.

PIP: You were telling me –

CHAS: Now why should I embarrass you?

PIP: – enemies you like.

CHAS: No, about people you liked who were enemies. There's a difference. I'm surprised you didn't see the difference.

PIP: Go on.

CHAS: Go on what?

PIP: What do you mean?

CHAS: Mean?

PIP: What you just said.

CHAS: Well, I said it. That's what it means.

PIP: Oh, I see.

CHAS: I do embarrass you, don't I?

PIP: A bit. Are you an only child, Charles?

CHAS: I got six brothers. You?

PIP: Four brothers.

CHAS: What I meant was people say things meaning to help but it works out all wrong.

PIP: You could have meant a number of things, I suppose.

CHAS: Words do mean a number of things.

PIP: Yes, Charles.

CHAS: Well, they do.

PIP: Mm. I'm not sure why we started this.

CHAS: Well, you said we got enemies, and I was saying –

PIP: Oh, yes.

CHAS: There, now you've lost interest. Just as we were getting into conversation you go all bored.

PIP: Don't nag at me, Charles.

CHAS: Charlie.

PIP: Oh, I can't call you Charlie – it's a stupid name.

CHAS: Now why did you have to say that? Making a rudeness about my name. Why couldn't you leave it alone. I want to be called Charlie. Why couldn't you just call me Charlie? No, you had to criticize.

PIP: All right, Charlie then! Charlie! If you don't mind being called Charlie you won't ever mind anything much.

CHAS: You're such a prig – I don't know how you can be such a barefaced prig and not mind.

PIP: I'm not a prig, Charles, that's so suburban – a snob perhaps but nothing as common as prig, please. Tell you what, I'm a liar.

CHAS: A liar?

PIP: Yes – I haven't got four brothers – I'm an only son.

CHAS: So am I.

PIP: You? Yes – I might've guessed. Poor old Charlie. Terrible, isn't it? Do you always try to hide it?

CHAS: Yes.

PIP: Not possible though, is it?

CHAS: No. Funny that – how we both lied. What you gonna do when they let us out of camp?

PIP: When is it?

CHAS: Next Friday.

PIP: Oh, go into the town, the pictures perhaps.

CHAS: Can I come?

PIP: Yes, I suppose so.

CHAS: Suppose so! You'd grudge your grandmother a coffin.

PIP: But I've just said you could come.

CHAS: Yes, dead keen you sounded.

PIP: Well, what do you want?

CHAS: Don't you know?

PIP: Oh, go to hell!

CHAS: I'm sorry, I take it back, don't shout. I'll come – thanks. [*Pause.*] If I was more educated you think it'd be easier, wouldn't it, between us?

PIP: What do you mean 'us'?

CHAS: Let me finish –

PIP: For God's sake don't start wedding me to you –

CHAS: Just let me –

PIP: And don't whine –

CHAS: You won't let me –

PIP: You are what you are – don't whine.

CHAS: Let me bloody finish what I was going to say, will you! You don't listen. You don't bloody listen.

PIP: I'm sorry –

CHAS: Yes, I know.

PIP: I'm listening.

CHAS: Oh, go to hell – you –

PIP: I'm sorry, I take it back, don't shout, I'm listening.

CHAS: I didn't say *I* thought it'd be easier if I was more educated – I said *you'd* think it'd be easier, I thought *you'd* think it. And I was just going to say I disagreed – then you jumped.

PIP: Yes, well, I thought – yes, well, you're right Charles, quite right. It's no good wanting to go to university –

CHAS: Facts, that's all it is.

45

PIP: Like me and work – manual labour. The number of intellectuals and artists who are fascinated by manual labour. Not me though, Charles. I haven't the slightest desire to use my brawn, prove myself a man, dirty my nails.

CHAS: And facts don't mean much to me either.

PIP: It's dull, repetitive, degrading.

CHAS: Intelligence counts, not facts. Stick your education, your university. Who cares why Rome was built.

PIP: Van Gogh with the miners; Hemingway, hunting.

CHAS: Even if I knew all about that it wouldn't make it any easier.

PIP: God, how I despise this yearning to be one of the toilers.

CHAS: I knew someone who used to wear a bowler cos he thought it made him look educated.

PIP: The dignity of labour!

CHAS: But it wouldn't make it any easier –

PIP: The beauty of movement!

CHAS: Not between us –

[*They smile.*]

SCENE NINE

The hut.

SMILER: What shall it be – poker, pontoon?

WILFE: I'm for bed.

SMILER: 'I'm for bed', little boy is tired.

WILFE: You can go on man – nothing seems to affect you.

CANNIBAL: What happened? They kick you out too?

SMILER: We got sick – you game for poker?

DICKEY: The squalor overcame you, eh? Ah, well, welcome back to the delinquents.

[*Enter* HILL.]

HILL: Well, I've got a right bunch, haven't I, a real good crowd, that's a fact.

GINGER: Come off it, Corp – you know we're O.K. on the square.

DODGER: That's all that counts, isn't it, Corp?

HILL: My boys – even them, my own little boys let me down.

SMILER: It's poker, Corp, you playing?

HILL: I shan't say anything now because you're away home in two days – but when you come back it's rifle drill and bayonet practice – and that's tough, and if you slack – I'm warning you – no more easy life, it'll be back to normal for you all.

DODGER: Play us a tune, Corp.

HILL: You don't deserve no tunes – a kick up the arse you deserve, the lot, where it hurts, waken you up.

[CHARLES, SMILER, PIP, *and* DICKEY *sit down to play. The others lie in their beds, and* HILL *plays the mouth-organ.*]

GINGER: There's a bloody great moon outside. Dodge, you seen it? With a whopping great halo.

DODGER: Nippy, too. Who wants some chocolate? My uncle has a sweet shop. [*Produces dozens of bars.*]

DODGER: Ginge, what trade you going to apply for?

GINGER: Driver – I'm going to get something out of this mob – it's going to cost them something keeping me from civvy street. Driving! I've always wanted to drive – since I don't know how long. A six BHP engine, behind the wheel controlling it–nyaaaaaaarr. I dream about it. I dream I'm always in a car and I'm driving it, but I got no licence. I always know I've never driven a car, but somehow it comes easy to me and I've never got a ruddy licence. I'm always being chased by cops – and I keep dreaming it, the same dream. I got no licence, but I'm driving a car and the police are after me. What'll I dream about when I can drive a car, I wonder.

DODGER: You won't. Stands to reason you won't need to; when you got the real thing you don't pretend. How about some tea? Ginger, my cock, make some tea on the stove and we'll eat up these biscuits also.

CANNIBAL: Dreams is real you know, they may be pretending in your sleep, but they're real. I dreamt my girl was a prostitute once and when I see her next day she looked like one and I give her up.

DODGER: What's wrong with prostitutes? We need them, let's keep them I say. Nationalize them. Stuck in clubs like poor bleedin' ferrets.

47

WILFE: Don't it make you sick, eh? Don't it make you sick just – these eight weeks, these two years, the factory – all of it? Don't it make you just bleedin' sick? I SAID SICK, MOTHER, SICK! Poor dear, she can't hear a word.

[*Pause. Mouth-organ. Warm hut.*]

CANNIBAL: I'm going to get in that Radar-Plotting lark. All them buttons, them screens and knobs. You have to learn about the stars and space for that.

DICKEY: That's astronomy, my fine fellow. The code of the heavens. Radar! Radar is the mystic digits of sound-waves; you have to have an enlightened degree of knowledge for that. Cannibal, my son, you're not arrogant enough, not standard enough for that. But I could – oh yes, I could rise to the heights of radar. I've put in for that.

SMILER: I think I'll go into Ops. Bring the planes in. Operations calling DI7, are you receiving me, are you receiving me – over! DI7 calling flight-control, I'm receiving you – left jet gone, I said gone, think I'll have to make a forced landing, stand by for emergency. Nyaaaaaaah passssssssss, brrrrrrrrrr – we'll all learn a trade and then 'oppit – nyaaaaaaaaaaaa. . . .

[*Pause.*]

ANDREW: I like us. All of us, here now. I like us all being together here. In a way you know I don't mind it, anything. Old Corp and his mouth-organ – all of us, just as we are, I like us.

[*Pause. Mouth-organ. Warm hut.*]

GINGER: We've run out of coke you know – water won't ever boil.

PIP: Then we'll pinch some.

DICKEY: What?

PIP: That's all right with you isn't it, Corp? You don't mind a little raiding expedition?

HILL: You think you'll get in the coke yard? You won't, you know, mate; there's a wire netting and a patrol on that.

PIP: We'll work out a plan.

CHAS: Oh, knock it off, Pip, we're all in bed soon.

PIP: Think we can't outwit them?

DODGER: You won't outwit them, mate, they've got it all tied up neat, not them, me old *lobus*.

PIP: If you can't outwit them for a lump of coke, then they deserve to have you in here for a couple of years.

HILL: I know what you are, Thompson – you're an agent provocative.

WILFE: I'm game, how do we do it?

GINGER: We could snip the wire and crawl through.

PIP: No. We want to raid and leave no sign.

ANDREW: What do we put it in?

DICKEY: Buckets.

DODGER: Too noisy.

PIP: Buckets with sacking at the bottom. How high is the netting?

HILL: About six feet. You'll need a ladder.

WILFE: Take it from the fire hut near by.

CANNIBAL: What if there's a fire?

WILFE: Let it burn.

PIP: No, no risks. Efficient, precise, but humane. They happen to be the only qualities for absolute power. That's what we want – absolute success but without a price. Coke in ten minutes, with no one caught and no one but us the wiser. Trust me?

SCENE TEN

A large square of wire netting.
> *[A* GUARD *walks round it. Boys are in the shadows.]*

PIP: Now watch him – he walks round slowly – we can make three moves for each round except the last one and that requires speed. I want the first three stages started and finished between the time he disappears round the first corner and before he turns the third. If he changes his course or hurries his step or does anything that means one of us is caught, then we all, all of us make an appearance. He can't cop the lot. Right? *[All exeunt.]*
> *[*GINGER *dashes to wire, and places chair – dashes to other side of stage.* PIP *runs to chair, jumps up and over.* DODGER *runs to take chair away and joins Ginger. The* GUARD *appears and carries on*

round. DODGER *runs back, places chair.* WILFE *runs to chair with another, jumps on it, and drops chair into Pip's hands, runs off.* DODGER *runs on, and withdraws chair. The* GUARD *appears, and continues.* DODGER *runs on with chair again.* ANDREW *runs with buckets to chair, jumps up and passes them to Pip.* GINGER *runs to take chair away.* GUARD *appears, and continues. In like process, two buckets are returned 'full' of coke. In the last stage,* PIP *jumps back over netting, leaving chair.* GINGER *and* DODGER *appear with two stools.* DICKEY *dashes on to top of two stools, leans over wire and reaches down for chair, which he throws to Andrew.* DODGER *and* GINGER *run off with two stools.* GUARD *appears, and continues. This scene can be, and has to be, silent, precise, breathtaking, and finally very funny.*]

SCENE ELEVEN

The hut again.
  [*Mouth-organ.* DODGER *pouring out tea, drinking, eating. Silence.*]

DICKEY: Yes. Yes – very satisfactory. Very pleasing. I wouldn't've thought we could do it.

CHAS: No more you wouldn't have done it without Pip.

DICKEY: Do I detect in young Charles the ineffable signs of hero worship?

CHAS: You'll detect black and blue marks, that's what you'll detect.

DICKEY: I think we've got a love affair in our midst.

CHAS: Just because I respect a man for his nerve? You gone daft?

DICKEY: No, I think my mental balance is equilibralized, it's you I fear for my Charlie boy. First you start off baiting young Thompson here and now you can't take your eyes off him.

PIP: Don't act the goat, Dickey.

DICKEY: I'm correct in my observations though aren't I, Lord Thompson?

PIP: No observation you make is correct, Dickey, you just remember other people's.

DICKEY: But you have a marvellous mind, don't you?

CHAS: He has.

DICKEY: Now there's a question. Would we have pinched the coke without Pip's mind?

HILL: You always need leaders.

PIP: Always!

HILL: Well, don't you always need leaders?

PIP: Always, always!

HILL: Yes, always, always!

PIP: Always, always, always! Your great-great-grandfather said there'll always be horses, your great-grandfather said there'll always be slaves, your grandfather said there'll always be poverty and your father said there'll always be wars. Each time you say 'always' the world takes two steps backwards and stops bothering. And so it should, my God, so it should –

WILFE: Easy, Airman, easy.

GINGER: Hey, Dodge – come and look outside now. Have you ever seen a halo as big as that! – look at it.

DODGER: Means frost.

ANDREW: This ae nighte, this ae nighte,
              Every nighte and alle,
            Fire and fleet and candle-lighte,
              And Christe receive thy saule.

SLOW CURTAIN

ACT TWO

SCENE ONE

The hut, dark early morning.
[Enter night GUARD.]

GUARD: Hands off your cocks and pull up your socks, it's wake to the sun and a glorious day. *[Pulls off blankets of one near by.]* Rise, rise, rise and shine – Christmas is over. CHRISTMAS IS OVER. *[Exit.]*
[There have been moans and movements. Return to silence. Enter HILL. Pause.]

HILL: CHRISTMAS IS OVER, he said.
[Moans and movements.]
It's over, done, finished. You're 'ome. You're 'ome again and it's rifles today. Rifles and a stricter routine. You've been slacking. I've warned you and told you and today is judgement day, especially for you, Smiler – today is especially judgement day for you. You too, Airmen Wilfe Seaford, and Archie Cannibal, you shan't be passed. I intend making you the smartest squad in the glorious history of flying – and I will. But you – A/C2 Thompson – you're too good for me, too smart. The Wing Commander and all the officers in charge of this camp have got their guns on you and they're aiming to throw the book at you – the whole, heavy scorching book, so you beware and guard your mouth. I've heard, I know – so guard your mouth. CHRISTMAS IS OVER. *[Exits.]*

WILFE: Christmas is over and don't we know it. Rouse yourself, Smiler, or you'll get us all in the cart.

SMILER: Leave off.

WILFE: Rouse yourself, I say – I aren't suffering cos of you. Get up or I'll turn you under your bed.
[No reply. WILFE does so. SMILER rises from under the rubble and angrily fights with Wilfe till separated by others.]

ANDREW: Cut it out or I'll lay you both.

DICKEY: Its the basic animal rising to undiluted heights in them. A nasty morning, my boys, a nasty morning, nasty tempers, and a nasty undiluted life.

CANNIBAL: And you can shut your undiluted mouth for a start, too. I'm not stomaching you the rest of the time.

DICKEY: What side of the bed did you rise from?

CANNIBAL: I'm fit for you, so don't worry.

[*Enter* HILL *with rifles.*]

HILL: Come and get them. Don't grab them, don't drop them, and don't lose them. We start with them first thing after breakfast and I intend to train you so hard that you'll not be happy unless they're in bed with you.

[*Exit. Immediately, half the boys start playing cowboys and Indians, dropping behind beds and crawling on the floor, firing them at each other,* 'BANG. BANG.' *Enter* HILL.]

HILL: The next man to pull that trigger, his feet won't touch the ground.

[SMILER *clicks one unintentionally.*]

You – I've wanted to pounce on you, Smiler.

SMILER: It slipped, Corp – an accident.

HILL: You say accident, I say luck. I'm charging you, Smiler, just a little charge, a few days' jankers to start with – that's all.

PIP: Why don't you charge us all, Corporal?

HILL: YOU SHUT UP. You, I've warned. All of you, I've warned. The joke's over, the laughing's done. Now get ready. [*Exit.*]

DODGER: We used to have a master who'd crack a joke, and then look at his watch to see we didn't laugh too long.

HILL: All right, get fell in, the lot of you.

SCENE TWO

The parade ground.

[*The men in threes.*]

HILL: The first thing is – not to be afraid of it. It won't hurt you and if you handle it correctly you can't hurt it. [*Only one boy laughs.*] I know you think they're nice, boys. With one of them in your hand you feel different, don't you, you feel a man, a conquering bloody hero? You want to run home and show your girl, don't you? Well, they're not toys – you can kill a man wi' one o' them. Kill 'im! Your napkins are still wet – you don't really understand that word 'kill', do you? Well, you can be killed. There! Does that bring it home to you? A bullet can whip through your flesh and knock breath out of *you*. Imagine yourself dying, knowing you're dying, you can feel the hole in your body, you can feel yourself going dizzy, you can feel the hot blood, and you can't breathe. You want to breathe but you can't, the body you've relied on all these years doesn't do what you want it to do, and you can't understand it. You're surprised, you're helpless, like those dreams where you're falling – only dying isn't a dream because you know, you know, you know that you're looking at everything for the last time and you can't do a bloody thing about it, that's dying. And that's a rifle. So don't let me catch anybody aiming it at anybody – loaded or not. Now, you hold it here, just below the barrel, pushing it out slightly to the right and forward, with the butt tucked well in at the side of your feet – so – well in firm, straight, at ease – and at the command to 'shun' I want that rifle brought smartly in at the precisely same moment. So. Atten-shun! Together, and your hand holding firmly on to that rifle. I don't want that rifle dropped – drop that rifle and I want to see you follow it to the ground. Right. Squad – atten-shun!

SQUAD: One!

[SMILER *drops gun.*]

HILL: Leave it! Smiler, you nasty squirming imbecile! Can't you hear me? Can't you hear anything? Don't anything go through your thick skull? Look at you. Slob! Your buttons, your blanco, your shoes – look at them. They're dull. You're dull! You're like putty. What keeps you together, man? You're like an old Jew – you know what happens to Jews? They go to gas chambers. Now pick it up. Squad – atten-shun!

SQUAD: One!

HILL: Now to slope and shoulder arms, you make three movements. Watch me, follow me and you won't make a mess of it. I'll do it

54

slowly and I'll exaggerate the movements. Shoulder ARMS! One pause, two pause, three. Slope ARMS! One pause, two pause, three. Again [*Repeats.*] Now – you do it. Squad! Shoulder ARMS!

SQUAD: One pause, two pause, three.

HILL: Slope ARMS!

SQUAD: One pause, two pause, three.
[*Repeats order.*]

HILL: You're no good, Smiler, you're no good. Shoulder ARMS! Smiler, one pace forward march. The rest, about turn. By the left, quick march.

[*The squad march off, all except* SMILER. *The wall of the guardroom drops into place as scene changes to*]

SCENE THREE

The guardroom.
[SMILER *at the slope. Enter* HILL *and two other corporals.*]

FIRST CORPORAL: This him?

HILL: That's him.

SECOND CORPORAL: What's your name, lad?

SMILER: Smiler.

SECOND CORPORAL: I said your name, lad.

SMILER: 279 A/C2 Washington, Corporal.

FIRST CORPORAL: Washington, is it? You mustn't lie then, ha-ha! If you mustn't lie, then tell us, is your mother pretty? Is she? Answer me, lad. Do you know it's dumb insolence not to answer an N.C.O.? We'll make that six day's jankers, I think. Answer me, lad.

SMILER: Yes. She was.

FIRST CORPORAL: Have you ever seen her undressed? Eh? Have you, lad? Have you seen her naked?

SECOND CORPORAL: Wipe that smile off your face, lad.

SMILER: I'm not smiling, Corporal, it's natural, I was born like it.

FIRST CORPORAL: Arguing with an N.C.O. We'll make that nine days' jankers.

HILL: All right Smiler, order arms, slope arms, order arms, slope arms, slope arms, slope arms.

[*The two corporals walk round him.*]

FIRST CORPORAL: You're a slob, Smiler.

SECOND CORPORAL: A nasty piece of work.

FIRST CORPORAL: You're no good, lad.

SECOND CORPORAL: No good at all. You're an insult.

FIRST CORPORAL: Your mother wasted her labour.

SECOND CORPORAL: Your father made a mistake.

FIRST CORPORAL: You're a mistake, Smiler.

SECOND CORPORAL: A stupid mistake.

FIRST CORPORAL: The Queen doesn't like mistakes in her Air Force.

SECOND CORPORAL: She wants good men, Smiler, men she can trust.

FIRST CORPORAL: Stand still, boy. Don't move. Silent, boy. Still and silent, boy.

HILL: That'll do for a taster, Smiler. That'll do for the first lesson. Tomorrow we'll have some more. We'll break you, Smiler, we'll break you, because that's our job. Remember that, just remember now – remember – About TURN! By the left – quick march, eft – ite, eft – ite. Remember, Smiler, remember.

[*Exit.*]

SCENE FOUR

WING COMMANDER'S *office.*

[*With him at a table are* SQUADRON LEADER *and* PILOT OFFICER.]

WING COMMANDER: Just remember who we're dealing with – remember that. I don't want a legal foot put wrong – I just want him broken in.

PILOT OFFICER: Not broken in, sir, but loved – he's only lost temporarily, for a short, natural time, that's all.

WING COMMANDER: Bloody little fool – sowing seeds of discontent to semi-educated louts; what do they understand of what he tells them?

SQUADRON LEADER: Gently, Sid, anger'll only make it easier for him to be stubborn.

PILOT OFFICER: Leave it to me, sir. I think I know how to do it, I think I know the boy very well.

WING COMMANDER: I know the boy, by Christ I know him, I've known them all and I've broken them all.

[HILL *marches Pip into the room and goes.*]

PIP: You called me to see you, sir.

WING COMMANDER: Take your hat off, blast you, Thompson, take it off, lad, in front of an officer.

SQUADRON LEADER: Please sit down, won't you, Thompson, sit down and be at ease for a little while; we'd simply like a chat with you.

WING COMMANDER: Your square bashing is coming to an end. We're concerned about you. We have to find you something to do. It has to be decided now.

SQUADRON LEADER: I think, Wing Commander, if you'll excuse me, it would be more correct to say that Personnel must decide that in London, but we can recommend from here, isn't that the case? We are on the spot, so we can recommend.

PILOT OFFICER: We see, Thompson, that you've put down administration orderly as your first and only choice. A very strange choice.

WING COMMANDER: A damn fool choice, boy, your brains, your carriage and background, damn perversity!

SQUADRON LEADER: You know what administration orderly implies, don't you, son?

WING COMMANDER: Anything and everything – waste, absolute waste.

SQUADRON LEADER: Anything from dishwashing to salvage, from spud-bashing to coal-heaving.

[*Pause.*]

PILOT OFFICER: Listen Pip, excuse me, sir?

WING COMMANDER: Yes, yes, carry on.

PILOT OFFICER: Let's drop the pretence. We're the same age and class, let's drop this formal nonsense. The Air Force is no place to carry on a family war, Pip. This is not a public school, it's a place where old boys grow into young men, believe me. Don't force me to start listing all your virtues and attributes. We're not flatterers, but don't let's be falsely modest either – that's understood between us, I'm sure. God, when I think of what I did to try and get out of coming into this outfit – two years wasted I thought. But waste is what you yourself do with time – come on man, if people like us aren't officers, then imagine the bastards they'll get. This is a silly game, Pip – why look, you're even sulking. Admin orderly! Can you see yourself washing dishes?

PIP: It might be a pretence to avoid responsibility.

PILOT OFFICER: You, Pip? Come now! It may be that you want to prove something to yourself. I don't know, why don't you tell us?

PIP: Your tactics are obvious, please don't insult my intelligence. I do not feel obliged to explain my reasons to you.

WING COMMANDER: You'll do what you're told.

PILOT OFFICER: It's not a question of obligation, no one's forcing –

PIP: I have no wish to –

PILOT OFFICER: But there's no one forcing you –

PIP: I said I have no wish to –

PILOT OFFICER: But-no-one-is-forcing-you –

PIP: I have no wish to explain anything to you I say.

    [Pause.]

WING COMMANDER: Corporal Hill!

    [Enter HILL.]

HILL: Sir?

WING COMMANDER: The men in your squad are slobs. Their standard is low and I'm not satisfied. No man passes out of my camp unless he's perfect – you know that. Pull them together, Corporal Hill, fatigues, Corporal Hill. They're a wretched bunch, wretched, not good enough.

HILL: Yes, sir [Exit from room.]

    All right, fall in, the lot of you.

    [Boys enter.]

You're slobs, all of you. Your standard is low and I'm not satisfied. No man passes out of my hut unless he's perfect, I've told you that before. You're a wretched bunch – a miserable, wretched bunch, and since you're not good enough, it's fatigues for you all. Squad will double mark time.

[*They do so for one minute. Exeunt at the double. The Inquisition resumes.*]

WING COMMANDER: Carry on, P.O.

PILOT OFFICER: Right, Thompson, I have some questions to ask you. I don't want clever answers. You wish to be an administration orderly?

PIP: That is correct, sir.

PILOT OFFICER: Doesn't it occur to you that that very act, considering who you are, is a little – revealing? It's a rather ostentatious choice, isn't it?

PIP: It could be viewed like that.

PILOT OFFICER: You enjoy mixing with men from another class. Why is this? Do you find them stimulating, a new experience, a novelty, do you enjoy your slumming?

PIP: It's not *I* who slum, sir.

PILOT OFFICER: I suppose you feel guilty in some way for your comfortable and easy upbringing; you feel you must do a sort of penance for it.

PIP: A rather outdated cause to be a martyr for, don't you think, sir?

PILOT OFFICER: Possibly, Thompson, possibly. You enjoy their company, though, don't you?

PIP: I enjoy most people's company.

PILOT OFFICER: Not ours, though.

PIP: Certain standards are necessary, sir.

PILOT OFFICER: A very offensive reply, Thompson – it's almost a hysterical reply – a little too desperately spoken, I would say. But look, we haven't stiffened, we aren't offended, no one is going to charge you or strike you. In fact we haven't really taken any notice. We listen to you, we let other people listen to you but we show no offence. Rather – we applaud you, flatter you for your courage and idealism but – it goes right through us. We listen but we do not hear, we befriend but do not touch you, we applaud but we do not act. To tolerate is to ignore, Thompson. You will not really become an administration orderly, will you?

PIP: What I have written, stays.

PILOT OFFICER: You will not be a foolish, stiff, Empire-thumping officer – no one believes in those any more. You will be more subtle and you will learn how to deal with all the Pip Thompsons who follow you. I even think you would like that.

PIP: What I have written stays. You may recommend as you please.

PILOT OFFICER: Yes, we shall put you up for officer training.

[OFFICERS *exeunt. Scene changes to*]

SCENE FIVE

The Square. A dummy is hanging. It is bayonet practice for the squad.

HILL: Even officers must go through this. Everyone, but everyone must know how to stick a man with a bayonet. The occasion may not arise to use the scorching thing but no man passes through this outfit till he's had practice. It's a horrible thing, this. A nasty weapon and a nasty way to kill a man. But it is you or him. A nasty choice, but you must choose. We had a bloke called Hamlet with us once and he had awful trouble in deciding. He got stuck! I don't want that to be your fate. So! Again, hold the butt and drop the muzzle – so. Lean forward, crouch, and let me see the horriblest leer your face can make. Then, when I call 'attack' I want to see you rush towards that old straw dummy, pause, lunge, and twist your knife with all the hate you can. And one last thing – the scream. I want to hear you shout your lungs out, cos it helps. A hoard of screaming men put terror in the enemy and courage in themselves. It helps. Get fell in, two ranks. Front rank will assume the on-guard position – ON GUARD! Run, scream, lunge.

[HILL *demonstrates it himself. One by one, the men rush forward at the dummy, until it comes to* PIP. *He stands still.*]

I said attack. Thompson, you, that's you. Are you gone daft? I've given you an order – run, scream, you. Are you refusing to obey? A/C Thompson I have ordered you to use your bayonet. You scorching, trouble-making, long-haired, posh-tongued, lump of aristocracy – I'll high jump you, court martial you. I'll see you rot in every dungeon in the force. Oh, thank your lucky stars this ain't the war, my lad; I'd take the greatest pleasure in shooting you. You still refuse? Right – you men, form up a line behind this man; I'll need you all for witnesses. A/C2 Thompson, I am about to issue you with a legitimate order according to Her Majesty's rules and regulations, Section Ten paragraph five, and I must warn you that failing to carry out this order will result in you being charged under Section ten paragraph sixteen of the same book. Now, when I say attack, I want to see you lower your gun in the attack position and race forward to lunge that dummy which now faces you. Is that order understood?

PIP: Yes, Corporal.

HILL: Good. I am now about to give the command. Wait for it and think carefully – this is only practice and no one can be hurt. Within ten seconds it will all be over, that's advice. Attack.

[*Silence. No movement.*]

Squad – slope ARMS! A/C2 Thompson – I'm charging you with failure to obey a legitimate order issued by an N.C.O. in command under Her Majesty's Air Force, and may God help you, lad.

[*All march off except* THOMPSON.]

SCENE SIX

[*Enter* ANDREW.]

ANDREW: Idiot.

PIP: You?

ANDREW: Who the hell is going to be impressed?

PIP: You, Andrew?

ANDREW: Yes, Andrew! I'm asking you – who the hell do you think is going to be impressed? Not me. The boys? Not them either. I've been watching you, Pip – I'm not impressed and neither are they.

PIP: You don't really think I'm interested in the public spectacle, Andy, you can't? No, no I can see you don't. Go off now. Leave me with it – I've got problems.

ANDREW: No one's asking you to make gestures on our behalf.

PIP: Go off now.

ANDREW: Don't go making heroic gestures and then expect gratitude.

PIP: Don't lean on me, Andy – I've got problems.

ANDREW: I don't think I can bear your martyrdom – that's what it is; I don't think I can bear your look of suffering.

PIP: I'm not suffering.

ANDREW: I don't know why but your always-acting-right drives me round the bend.

PIP: I'm not a martyr.

ANDREW: It's your confident cockiness – I can't stand your confident cockiness. How do you know you're right? How can you act all the time as though you know all right from wrong, for God's sake.

PIP: Don't be a bastard Jock.

ANDREW: I'm trying to help you, idiot. The boys will hate any heroic gesture you make.

PIP: Andy, you're a good, well-meaning, intelligent, person. I will die of good, well-meaning, and intelligent people who have never made a decision in their life. Now go off and leave me and stop crippling me with your own guilt. If you're ineffectual in this world that's your look-out – just stay calm and no one will know, but stop tampering with my decisions. Let *them* do the sabotaging, they don't need help from you as well. Now get the hell out – they wouldn't want you to see the way they work.

[*Exit* ANDREW.]

SCENE SEVEN

PILOT OFFICER: It goes right through us, Thompson. Nothing you can do will change that. We listen but we do not hear, we befriend but do not touch you, we applaud but do not act – to tolerate is to ignore. What did you expect, praise from the boys? Devotion from your mates? Your mates are morons, Thompson, morons. At the slightest hint from us they will disown you. Or perhaps you wanted a court martial? Too expensive, boy. Jankers? That's for the yobs. You, we shall make an officer, as we promised. I have studied politics as well, you know, and let me just remind you of a tactic the best of revolutionaries have employed. That is to penetrate the enemy and spread rebellion there. You can't fight us from the outside. Relent boy, at least we understand long sentences.

PIP: You won't impress me with cynicism, you know.

PILOT OFFICER: Not cynicism – just honesty. I might say we are being unusually honest – most of the time it is unnecessary to admit all this, and you of all people should have known it.

PIP: I WILL NOT BE AN OFFICER.

PILOT OFFICER: Ah. A touch of anger, what do you reveal now, Thompson? We know, you and I, don't we? Comradeship? Not that, not because of the affinity of one human being to another, not that. Guilt? Shame because of your fellow beings' suffering? You don't feel that either. Not guilt. An inferiority complex, a feeling of modesty? My God. Not that either. There's nothing humble about you, is there? Thompson, you wanted to do more than simply share the joy of imparting knowledge to your friends; no, not modesty. Not that. What then? What if not those things, my lad? You and I? Shall I say it? Shall I? Power. Power, isn't it? Among your own people there were too many who were powerful, the competition was too great, but here, among lesser men – here among the yobs, among the good-natured yobs, you could be king. KING. Supreme and all powerful, eh? Well? Not true? Deny it – deny it, then. We know – you and I – we know, Thompson.

PIP: Oh, God –

PILOT OFFICER: God? God? Why do you call upon God? Are you his son? Better still, then. You are found out even more, illusions of grandeur, Thompson. We know that also, that's what we know, that's what we have, the picture you have of yourself, and now that we know that, you're really finished, destroyed. You're destroyed, Thompson. No man survives whose motive is discovered, no man. Messiah to the masses! Corporal Hill! [Exit.]

HILL [off stage]. Sir?

SCENE EIGHT

[*Enter* HILL.]

HILL: I have instructions to repeat the order, Thompson. The powers have decided to give you another chance. I don't know why, but they know what they're doing, I suppose. When I give the order 'attack' I want you to lean forward, run, thrust, and twist that blade in the dummy. Have you understood?

PIP: Yes, Corporal.

HILL: Run, thrust and twist that blade – good. ATTACK.

[PIP *pauses for a long while, then with a terrifying scream he rushes at the dummy, sticking it three times, with three screams.*]

SCENE NINE

The hut.

[CHARLES *and* PIP.]

CHAS: What they say, Pip? What they want you for, what did they say? Hell, look at your face, did they beat you? Did they make you use the bayonet? They did, didn't they? I can tell it from your face. You're crying – are you crying? Want a cigarette? Here, have a cigarette. The others have all gone to the Naafi, it's New Year's Eve, gone for a big booze-up. Bloody fools – all they do is drink. I think I'll give it up, me. Well, what did they say, man – talk to me? You know why I didn't go to the Naafi – I – I was waiting for you. It seemed fishy them calling you in the evening, so I waited to see. Pip? I'm telling you I waited for you. I wanted to tell you something, I want to ask you a favour; I've been meaning all these last days to ask you this favour. You see – you know me, don't you, you know the sort of bloke . . . I'm – I'm, I'm not dumb, I'm not a fool, I'm not a real fool, not a bloody moron and I thought, well,

I thought maybe you could, could teach me – something, anything. Eh? Well, not anything but something proper, real.

PIP: Ask someone else – books, read books.

CHAS: Not books! I can't read books, but I can listen to you. Maybe we'll get posted to the same place, and then every evening, or every other evening, or once a week, even, you could talk to me a bit, for half an hour say. Remember how you talked that night about your grandfathers, about all those inventions and things. Well, I liked that, I listened to that, I could listen all night to that. Only I want to know about something else, I want to know about – I don't even know how to put it, about – you know, you know the word, about business and raw materials and people working and selling things – you know, there's a word for it –

PIP: Economics.

CHAS: Enocomics – that's it.

PIP: Economics not enocomics.

CHAS: Ee-mon-omics.

PIP: No, Ee –

CHAS: Ee

PIP: Con

CHAS: Con

PIP: Om

CHAS: Om

PIP: Ics.

CHAS: Ics.

PIP: Economics.

CHAS: Economics. There, about that, could you? I'd listen, you could draw diagrams and graphs; I wasn't bad at maths.

PIP: Someone else, Charles, not me, someone else.

CHAS: There you go. You're a hypocrite – a hypocrite you are. You take people to the edge. Don't you know what I'm asking you, don't you know what I'm really asking you?

PIP: Ask someone else.

CHAS: But I want to be with you – I want to. Ah, you give me a pain in the neck, you do, you're a coward. You lead and then you run away. I could grow with you, don't you understand that? We could do things together. You've got to be with someone, there's got to be someone you can trust, everyone finds someone and I found you – I've never asked anyone before, Jesus, never –

PIP: Ask someone else.

CHAS: Someone else. Someone else. It's always someone else, you half-bake you, you lousy word-user you. Your bleedin' stuffed grandfathers kept us stupid all this time, and now you come along with your pretty words and tell us to fend for ourselves. You clever useless leftover you. Oh, you're cocky, aren't you – Ask someone else. The truth is – you're scared, aren't you? You call us mate, but you're a scared old schoolboy. The pilot officer was right, you're slumming. You're a bleedin' slummer –

PIP: And he also said 'we will listen to you but we will not hear you, we will befriend you but not touch you, we will tolerate and ignore you'.

CHAS: Well, what did that mean?

PIP: We'll do anything they want just because they know how to smile at us.

CHAS: You mean *I'll* do what they want, not you boy. You're one of them – you're just playing games with 'em, and us mugs is in the middle – I've cottoned on now. [*Long pause.*] I'll do what *you* want, Pip.

PIP: Swop masters? You're a fool, Charles, the kind of fool my parents fed on, you're a fool, a fool –

[*Fade in the sound of marching feet and the Corporals repeating the insults they heaped upon Smiler and change to*]

SCENE TEN

A roadway.

[SMILER *has run away from camp. He is desperate, haggard and tired. Mix:* 'You're a fool, Charles' *to* 'You're a slob, Smiler' 'A nasty piece of work' 'You're no good, lad', *etc., rising to crescendo –*]

SMILER: LEAVE ME ALONE! Damn your mouths and hell on your

stripes – leave me alone. Mad they are, they're mad they are, they're raving lunatics they are. CUT IT! STUFF IT! Shoot your load on someone else, take it out on someone else, why do you want to pick on me, you lunatics, you bloody apes, you're nothing more than bloody apes, so damn your mouths and hell on your stripes! Ahhhhh – they'd kill me if they had the chance. They think they own you, think that anyone who's dressed in blue is theirs to muck about, degrade. YOU BLOODY APES, YOU WON'T DEGRADE ME! Oh my legs – I'm going home. I'll get a lift and scarper home. I'll go to France, I'll get away. I'LL GET AWAY FROM YOU, YOU APES! They think they own you – Oh my back. I don't give tuppence what you say, you don't mean anything to me, your bloody orders nor your stripes nor your jankers nor your wars. Stick your jankers on the wall, stuff yourselves, go away and stuff yourselves, stuff your rotten stupid selves – Ohh – Ohhh. Look at the sky, look at the moon, Jesus look at that moon and the frost in the air. I'll wait. I'll get a lift in a second or two, it's quiet now, their noise is gone. I'll stand and wait and look at that moon. What are you made of, tell me? I don't know what you're made of, you go on and on. What grouses you? What makes you scream? You're blood and wind like all of us, what grouses you? You poor duff bastards, where are your mothers? Where were you born – I don't know what grouses you, your voices sound like dying hens – I don't know. That bloody lovely moon is cold, I can't stay here. I'll freeze to death. That's a laugh, now that'd fool them. Listen! A bike, a motor-bike, a roaring bloody motor-bike. [*Starts thumbing.*] London, London, London, London, LONDON! [*The roar comes and dies.*] You stupid ghet, I want a lift, can't you see I want a lift, an airman wants a lift back home. Home, you bastard, take me ho'ooooome. [*Long pause.*] Now they'll catch me, now they'll come, not much point in going on – Smiler boy, they'll surely come, they're bound to miss you back at camp – eyes like hawks they've got – God! Who cares. 'Stop your silly smiling, Airman' – 'It's not a smile, Corp, it's natural, honest, Corp. I'm born that way. Honest Corp, it's not a smile. . . .'

[*Enters hut.*]

SCENE ELEVEN

The hut.

[CHARLES and PIP as we left them. SMILER is now with them.]

SMILER: The bastards won't believe it's natural. Look at me, me!

[A very broken SMILER stands there. SMILER turns to PIP for help. Pip approaches him and takes him gently in his arms. They sway a moment.]

SMILER: Wash my feet for me.

[SMILER collapses. PIP lays him on the ground. He is about to remove his shoes –]

CHAS: Leave him. I'll do it.

[CHARLES doesn't know what to do to begin with. Surveys SMILER. Then – picks him up and lays him on his bed, looks at him; thinks; takes off his shoes and socks.]

CHAS: His feet are bleeding.

[Takes a towel and pours water from pot on it; washes Smiler's feet; a long unconscious moan from SMILER; clock strikes midnight; sound of boys singing 'Auld Land Syne'. CORPORAL HILL's voice, loud.]

HILL *[off stage]*: You pass out with the band tomorrow – rifles, buttons, belts, shining, and I want you as one man, you hear me? You'll have the band and it'll be marvellous; only you Smiler, you won't be in it, you'll stay behind a little longer, my lad – HAPPY NEW YEAR.

[Silence. One by one the rest of the men come in, returning from the Naafi. They make no sound, but their movements are wild and drunk. No sound at all – like a TV with sound turned off, till they see Smiler.]

DODGER: Look at his feet. The rotten bastards, look at his feet.

ANDREW: What'd he do?

CHAS: Tried to hop it.

ANDREW: Couldn't make it?

CHAS: Walked for miles and then came back.

CANNIBAL: They had it in for him, you've got no chance when they got it in for you.

GINGER: He's staying behind, you know? I reckon they'll make him do another two weeks of this.

DICKEY: Give me the chance, just give me one chance and I'd have them. Five minutes in civvy street and I'd have them chasing their own tails.

WILFE: Ah, you wouldn't, man – you talk like this now but you wouldn't, and you know why? Cos you'd be just as helpless there, you'd be just as much wind and nothing there, man. 'Just gimme the boss,' you'd say, 'just gimme him for one hour in uniform and I'd teach him what a man is.' That's all you'd say, civvy street, the forces – it's the same, don't give me that.

GINGER: What about Smiler's stuff?

CANNIBAL: I'll do it.

CHAS: No, you won't, I'm doing it.

CANNIBAL: All right, all right, then. Blimey, what's gotten into you? Jumping at me like that – I don't much want to do my own buggers, let alone his. Takes all the guts out of you, don't it. Look at him, lying there like a bloody corpse. His feet are cold.

DODGER: He's like a baby. Sweet as a sleeping baby. Have you ever watched a baby sleep? It always looks as though it's waiting for something to happen, a grown-up seems to be hiding away but a nipper seems to trust you, anyone. He's done it, ain'tee, eh? He's really had it –

CHAS: For Christ's sake, give over – you talk like he was dead or something. Come on, help cover him.

[*As many as possible manoeuvre Smiler so that his jacket and trousers come off, with the least disturbance. This action is done lovingly and with a sort of ritual.* DODGER *takes a comb to Smiler's hair and* CHARLES *gently wipes a towel over his face. Then they tuck him in bed and stand looking at him. Unknown to them the* PILOT OFFICER *has been watching them.*]

PILOT OFFICER: Beautiful. Tender and beautiful. But I'm sorry, gentlemen, this man is needed in the guardroom.

[*Enter* HILL.]

HILL: Squad – shun!

[*The men slowly come to attention, except* CHARLES, *who, after a pause, moves to his bed and sits on it. One by one the other boys except* PIP, *also sit on their beds in defiance.*]

PILOT OFFICER: Corporal – take that smiling airman to the guard-room.

CHAS: YOU'LL LEAVE HIM BE!

PILOT OFFICER: And take that man, too.

GINGER: You won't, Corporal Hill, will you?

PILOT OFFICER: And that man, take the lot of them, I'll see them all in the guardroom.

PIP: You won't touch any of them, Corporal Hill, you won't touch a single one of them.

PILOT OFFICER: Do you hear me, Corporal, this whole hut is under arrest.

PIP: I suggest, sir, that you don't touch one of them. [PIP *and the* PILOT OFFICER *smile at each other, knowingly, and* PIP *now begins to change his uniform, from an airman's to an officer's.*] We won't let him will we Charles – because you're right. Smiler has been badly treated and you are right to protect him. It's a good virtue that loyalty. You are to be commended, Charles, all of you; it was a brave thing to do, protect a friend. We lack this virtue all too often, don't you agree, sir? These are good men, sometimes we are a little hasty in judging them – don't you agree, sir, a little too hasty? These are the salt of the earth, the men who make the country really. Don't worry, Charles, nor you, Ginger, nor you, Andrew – none of you, don't worry, you shan't be harmed – it was a good act. We like you for it, we're proud of you, happy with you – you do agree, don't you, sir? These are men we need and these are the men we must keep. We are not hard men, Charles – don't think ill of us, the stories you read, the tales you hear. We are good, honest, hard-working like yourselves and understanding; above all we are understanding, aren't we, sir? There, that's a good fit, I think. [*The* PILOT OFFICER *hands a list over to Pip.* PIP *reads out the list.*]

PIP: 239 A/C2 Cannibal – [CANNIBAL *rises to attention*] administration orderly, posted to Hull. [*Stands at ease. Same procedure for others.*]

252 A/C2 Wingate – administration orderly, posted to Oxford.

247 A/C2 Seaford – administration orderly, Cyprus.

284 A/C2 McClore – typing pool, Malta.

272 A/C2 Richardson – administration orderly, Aden.

277 A/C2 Cohen – administration orderly, Halton.

266 A/C2 Smith – administration orderly, Lincoln.

279 A/C2 Washington – put back three weeks to flight 212 – decision of employ will be made at a later date.

Squad – Squad, SHUN.

[*Sudden loud sound of brass band playing the R.A.F. March Past.*]

SCENE TWELVE

Music of March Past. The Parade Ground. Passout Parade. The men march into position. A flagpole is moved in.

HILL: Squad atten-shun! Shoulder arms! Right turn! By the left quick march! Lift your heads, raise them, raise them high, raise them bravely, my boys. Eft-ite, eft-ite, eft-ite, eft. Slope that rifle, stiffen that arm – I want to see them all pointing one way, together – unity, unity. Slam those feet, slam, slam, you're men of the Queen, her own darlings. SLAM, SLAM! SLAM! Let her be proud. Lovely, that's lovely, that's poetry. No one'll be shot today, my boys. Forget the sweat, forget the cold, together in time. I want you to look beautiful, I want you to move as one man, as one ship, as one solid gliding ship. Proud! Proud! Parade, by centre, quick march, saluting to the front.

[*Men salute to audience, return back to face* WING COMMANDER. *Music stops.* WING COMMANDER *on a rostrum. Officers around him.*]

WING COMMANDER [*a long, broad, embracing smile*]: I am satisfied. Good. Good men. One of the best bunch I've had through my gates. Smart, alert, keen. Two years of service in Her Majesty's Air Force lie ahead of you, I am confident of the service you will give, you have turned out well, as we expected, nothing else would have done, just as we expected. God speed you.

[GINGER *comes to attention. Lays rifle on ground. Steps forward to flagpole and takes ropes in his hands.*]

HILL: Parade about turn.

[*Men now facing audience again.*]

SQUADRON LEADER: Parade, for colour hoisting. PRESENT ARMS!

[*Ginger very very slowly hoists the R.A.F. colours. Let it be a tall pole. 'The Queen' is played, and there is a*]

SLOW CURTAIN

DAVID RUDKIN

Afore Night Come

TO JOHN HOLMSTROM
to whom I owe much

CHARACTERS

SPENS, *foreman*
JEFF, *teddy boy*
LARRY, *student*
JUMBO, *worker*
GINGER, *worker*
ALBERT, *worker, Ginger's father*
TAFFY HUGHES, *worker*
MRS TREVIS, *woman*
JIM, *worker*
ROCHE, *tramp*
JOHNNY ('Hobnails') CARTER, *tractor driver*
TINY, *his mate*
MR HAWKES, *owner*
GLORIA, *his daughter*

ACT ONE

The Black Country. Early autumn. Morning. A clearing in an orchard. Proscenium arch disguised by shed-fronts with practical doors. By trees, piles of fruit crates.

> [*Enter* LARRY *and* JEFF. *They look around them. Sounds of road traffic and rooks cawing not far away.*]

SPENS [*off*]: You there! [*Enters.*] You looking for a job?

JEFF: Man in a cape said we was to come down here.

LARRY: Man with a Land Rover.

JEFF: Said report to Mr Spens.

SPENS: That's me. Who were it? Gaffer?

JEFF: Told you. Man in a cape.

LARRY: Up at the barn.

SPENS: Black cape, were it? That'm Hawkes. Gaffer. [*To Larry*] You looking for a job, too?

LARRY: That's right, sir.

SPENS: Student? Bloody see it, and all. Where you come from, then?

LARRY: West Heath.

SPENS: Over by Brummagem? Come on the bus, then, did you?

LARRY: Cycled.

> [SPENS *shows surprise. Turns to Jeff.*]

JEFF: Saw the advert in the paper –

SPENS: Ted, am you? Bloody Teddy Boy?

JEFF: Why?

SPENS: They trousers.

JEFF: Ain't left school yet.

SPENS: Take the mickey out on you if you are. Must have someone to take the mickey out on. How come you get brought here, then?

JEFF: Same as him.

SPENS: How far?

JEFF: Headless Cross.

SPENS: Where?

75

JEFF: Headless Cross. Other side of Redditch. Got a church with a hollow spire.

[SPENS *writes in notebook with stub.*]

SPENS: Headless . . . Cross. . . .

LARRY: There's someone else, sir, too. He's walking down.

SPENS: Another worker?

JEFF: Yeah.

SPENS: Student?

JEFF: Looks about fifty. Cut himself shaving.

LARRY: Irish.

JEFF: Don't half reek.

SPENS: Irish. Christ, not a-bloody-gain. They'm hopeless, Irishmen. Bloody hopeless. Come one day, gone the next. Unre-bloody-liable. This'm a man's job, fruit-picking. Man's job. O.K., O.K., come on, the two on you. Picked fruit afore, have you?

[*They go to shed down right; disappear into it.*]

JEFF [*going*]: Don't look too difficult. . . .

SPENS: That'm what they all say. . . .

[*Door closes. Stage empty. Voices variously off.*]

JUMBO: Hello, Ginge.

GINGER: Hello, Jumbo.

JUMBO: Where are you, Ginge?

GINGER: I be here. Where'm you, then, Jumbo?

JUMBO: Here. Hello, Albert!

ALBERT [*sour*]: 'lo, Jumbo.

GINGER: Hello, Albert.

ALBERT: 'lo, Ginger, lad.

GINGER: Where be you, Albert?

ALBERT: Be here, Ginger. Where be you?

GINGER: I be here, Albert.

ALBERT: Where you got to, Jumbo?

JUMBO: Top of this bleeding pear-tree, Albert. Where are you?

ALBERT: Top of this bleeding pear-tree.

GINGER: Hello, Taff.

TAFFY: Hello. Who is that calling?

GINGER: It'm Ginger, Taff.

TAFFY: Hello, Ginger. Where are you?

GINGER: I be here, Taff.

TAFFY: Jumbo with you?

GINGER: Yeah. Jumbo'm with me.

TAFFY: Hello, Jumbo.

JUMBO: Hello, Comrade. Having fun?

TAFFY: Am I fuck!

[MRS TREVIS *appears from shed down left and crosses to pile of crates. Her job: to line and stack empty crates. This she does. Enter from shed down right* JEFF, LARRY, *and* SPENS *carrying three fruit buckets.*]

SPENS: Here. Fruit buckets. Wear her round your neck, see? Arms through, first. Then head. . . .

[JEFF *succeeds.* LARRY *tangles.* SPENS *leaves third bucket down.*]

No. What you got for arms, lad? Straps be adjustable, see? Don't do to have them too long, either. Cut your head off, else. Morning, Mrs Trevis.

MRS TREVIS: Morning.

SPENS: Big hole down there at the end of the row. Know what'm in there?

JEFF: You tell us.

SPENS: Students. Them as pulled their heads off last year through having their straps too long. That right, Mrs Trevis?

MRS TREVIS: Ah.

[LARRY *struggling still.* SPENS *helps.*]

SPENS: Bloody pen-pusher. See that. Hands like a woman's. O.K., O.K., boy, they'm best at it. Mrs Trevis here, best man I got in the orchard. That right, Mrs Trevis?

MRS TREVIS: Ain't taking a bit of notice, Spens.

SPENS: And don't go dropping the pears in the boxes. Her'm not stones. Place her in. Gentle. Like her were eggs. And don't go putting her in any boxes that bain't lined. Else what'm Mrs Trevis bloody here for? Hmm. Look at you. Low shoes again. Bloody sandals. I don't know.

MRS TREVIS: Get rheumatism, you will, in the long grass. Get arthritis.

SPENS: What they call you?

LARRY: Lewis.

SPENS: Got a Christian name, have you?

LARRY: Larry.

SPENS: Wants to know what to call you, Larry. Reckon I s'll forget, though. Call you any bloody thing when I gets going. You s'll bring rubbers tomorrow, boy. If you come. [*To Jeff*] What they call you at home?

JEFF: What?

SPENS: I wants to know what you'm bloody called.

JEFF: Fiske. Jeff.

SPENS: Fish?

JEFF: Fiske.

    [SPENS *writes in notebook.*]

SPENS: Fish. Horrible name. You under twenty-one?

JEFF: Told you. I ain't left school.

SPENS: Only gets paid half on it, under twenty-one. Till we get on piecework.

JEFF: When we going on piecework?

SPENS: Soon as we get this lot for Doncaster done. O.K. Along the rows, then, the two on you. Trousers. And you. Leonard, whatever you'm bloody called –

LARRY: Larry.

SPENS: Six hundred boxes to fill afore night come, Doncaster. Six hundred. That right, Mrs Trevis?

MRS TREVIS: You can say that again.

SPENS: Six bloody hundred. [SPENS *sends off Larry and Jeff.*] Okay, Leonard; you go along with Ginge and Jumbo there. Not you, Trousers; you go along over here, with Jim and old Albert. . . .

    [*They go where they are told.*]

[*calling to Jeff*] and don't get shooking them boughs! I s'll shoot any bugger as I catch shooking them boughs! Will, and all. You s'll get a pair of steps later. . . . I told gaffer. 'No more students, Mr Hawkes,' I says, 'they'm worse than useless.' 'But Spens,' he says, 'we're short of labour. We shall have to advertise.' And that kid of his, that horrible daughter of his in the jodhpurs, Gloria, says: 'Oh, Daddy. You'll have to advertise for some students, Daddy –' 'No, Mr Hawkes!' I says, 'no! We had them last year. . . .' Remember over at Ashbold's, Mrs Trevis?

MRS TREVIS: Do, and all. Awkward trees, over at Ashbold's.

SPENS: Students fell down them, Mrs Trevis. All day, remember? Thumping students falling down they bloody trees.

MRS TREVIS: I fell down them, and all.

SPENS: And look at the way they bruised the fruit all over. Some-one'll suffer. I told him. I says to him: 'With all due respect, Mr Hawkes . . .' Look at them. Look at them now. Just look at them, Mrs Trevis. Down there with old Albert, shooking them bloody boughs . . . Hey! Trousers! Don't you get shooking them boughs! Give you what for if I catch you shooking them boughs. Will, and all. [*Exit.*]

[*Enter* JUMBO. MRS TREVIS *finishes, pauses.*]

MRS TREVIS: Go and have my cup of tea, now. [*Exit.*]

[*Enter* GINGER. *They empty buckets; sit; relax.* JUMBO *smokes – through holder.*]

JUMBO: Bastard heat.

[*Enter* LARRY.]

You've copped it this place, kid. Work till all hours.

LARRY: No union?

JUMBO: Unions? What's the use of a fucking union? Stop the fruit growing, can they? All right for the miners and factory workers: coal don't grow when their backs is bloody turned. Whole year's work, these bleeding trees!

GINGER: Ah, Jumbo. Got something there. Go into a shop up in Brummagem. 'Pound of pears, please.' Do have no idea on the labour that pound of pears cost.

JUMBO: Damn all doing, either, when you do get home. Saving flop down, knackered. Got us on the cheap, old bloody Hawkes.

GINGER: Been married a twelve-month, too, I have, Larry. 'a'n't taken the missus up to Brummagem, only the once. See *South Pacific*, that were. And once to Malvern. In the whole on a twelve-month.

JUMBO: Daresn't get caught by the green bleeding earth.

GINGER: Don't wait for no one. Got to hang on to her. See what I mean?

[*Enter* JEFF *and* ALBERT *to crates.*]

JEFF: Saving up for a machine.

ALBERT: What for you want one, then?

JEFF: Have races on. Ton it.

ALBERT: Where you do your ton, then, Trousers? Back garden?

JEFF: Swive off, Albert. On the road.

ALBERT: Not on the road, Trousers. You'm making it up.

JEFF: Heard me, didn't you?

[*Enter* JIM *to crates.*]

    Here. Jim. You seen us, ain't you? Jim? Racing up to Brum of a night? Bloody good road, Brummagem. All bends in it. Corners.

JIM: Have done, Trousers.

JEFF: See? Birds won't look at you, Albert, only you got a machine. Ticket to bloody marriage.

ALBERT: Don't do no good a-speeding on main road, Trousers. Have accident. What on all the others, then?

JEFF: Other what?

ALBERT: Drivers.

JEFF: Swive off, will you? Don't get no less chance than we do, do they?

[*Pause.*]

JUMBO: Roll on winter. Worth it, then, kid. Sit back by the fire with all the money you've earned, and enjoy your bloody self. Long evenings, winter.

[*Enter* MRS TREVIS *with lining papers.*]

ALBERT: How many midsummer blooms you got there? And bleeding bitter pip?

JUMBO: Bad trees down our way, Albert.

[*Enter* TAFFY HUGHES *to crates.*]

GINGER: Trees gone bitter since last year.

TAFFY: Gone bloody rotten, the whole orchard.

JEFF: Here, Albert. Mate of mine. Sid, his name is. Gets thirty pound a week up in Brum. Crane driver. One of the new sites there. Thirty pound a week. Imagine. Got a smashing machine. Did have.

[*Pause.*]

GINGER: And you don't want these uns in either, Larry. Knobbly all over, see?

LARRY: I didn't know.

TAFFY: Bitters.

LARRY: What makes them go like that?

GINGER: Christ knows. Did try to investigate it, though.

JUMBO: That right, Mrs T.? Tried to investigate what makes them bitter pip?

MRS TREVIS: Ain't found nothing. [*To Larry, whom she eyes*] You at college?

LARRY: Why?

JEFF: Going up, him and his bird, see, Albert. To the new Locarno in Hurst Street. Dance hall. Fifty an hour, he was doing. Knocked a woman down. Walking right across the road, she was: books in her arm. Didn't read no more. Machine though. Twisted shambles, it was. Buckled to buggery, Sid's machine. Fifteen stitches. Cuts all over. Had one eye out. Come home from hospital all changed. Work of art.

MRS TREVIS: Nothing sticks like education.

LARRY: Nothing, indeed.

TAFFY: Hey, and you don't want these uns in either Larry, you, know. Twisted types. Bloody perverts, I call them.

JUMBO: You would.

MRS TREVIS: Hey! This ain't a pear. It'm Mr K. Look! You can see his bloody rotten awful face.

JUMBO. Throw it away. Spoil the sample.

MRS TREVIS: They been on to you about the Russians? Bloody Communists, them are.

JIM: He'm Conservative. All you students'm bloody Conservative.

JUMBO: Communist, ain't you, Taff?

MRS TREVIS: Sexomaniac. Lift the lid off him, it all comes out.

JUMBO: Artist and all. Ain't you, Taff? Pictorial.

MRS TREVIS: Proper Welsh.

JUMBO: Got pictures in all the Gents' between here and Merthyr.

TAFFY: Dowlais.

JUMBO: What?

TAFFY: Dowlais.

JUMBO: Communist, ain't you, Taff?

GINGER: You do swop husbands and wives at the week-ends in Wales, though; don't you, Taff?

TAFFY: Husbands and wives?

GINGER: I seen it in the paper.

TAFFY: I'll be a grandfather long before you're a father, even. And I'm only five years older, you know. You should never have married a woman that wears a black nightdress, Ginge; I'm sorry.

GINGER: How do you know what colour my missus' nightdress am?

TAFFY: No, Larry. Never you marry a woman that wears a black nightdress.

LARRY [*awkward*]: I'll remember.

[TAFFY *notices tone, studies him.*]

GINGER: How s'll it be, then, Taff, you being a granfer?

TAFFY [*offering cigarettes*]: Have a foul Anchor, Larry.

GINGER: How s'll it be?

TAFFY: Love's Labour's Lost, I call your marriage.

GINGER: How'm you a-going to, then? Change into a woman, am you?

TAFFY: Yeah. Cut her off, tuck her inside; I could do with a change.

[*Enter* SPENS.]

SPENS: Come on you lot! Six hundred bloody boxes to fill afore night come; and you ain't got a dozen on them done. What'm the matter with you, then? Eh?

[*Workers stamp out cigarettes, start to look busy.*]

Ain't paid to stand here bloody nattering all day. Let's have some fruit off.

JUMBO: Flaming pears. I dreams about them.

SPENS: How long you been here, Jumbo?

JUMBO: Too bloody long.

SPENS: Out in the open here. Nice and healthy.

JUMBO: Rather be inside. Pack it in yet, I will; you see.

TAFFY: Heard that before.

JUMBO: Go back to travelling saleshood, you see if I don't.

TAFFY: Travelling debt-collector, more like.

JUMBO: Respectable job, debt-collecting! Respectable! Saving in the week. Women. Friday night, Saturday and Sunday; that was the time to call. When they got the money. Not in the week. Women. Do anything rather than pay. Any bloody thing. With all respects, Mrs Trevis. . . .

MRS TREVIS: Ain't heard nothing, Jumbo.

JUMBO [*miming*]: 'Would you like a cup of tea? Perhaps you'd like a biscuit with it? I'll get you a biscuit, if you'd like one.' 'No, madam, I came about the washing machine. . . .' 'Oh. Oh, dear. It's the old man, you know. Been ill. Oh, proper poorly. Been away from work. Not that I'm too good myself. My spine. Would you like to feel . . .?' 'No, madam. About the washing machine. . . .' 'Would you like a cup of coffee? Sure? Mind you, we've had the decorations done. Like to see? Nice pattern, isn't it? Yes. This is my room. Isn't it nice? Aren't the walls lovely? Oh, dear. Look at the time. Got to go out now. I'll have to change. You don't mind. . . ?'

> [ROCHE *has entered meanwhile where Larry and Jeff first appeared. He is shabby, in tramp's garb, with leather bag. On his head, draped, a tea-cloth; over his eyes, dark glasses. He stands, not seen, listening.*]

SPENS: What'm you here for, then, Jumbo, if it'm like that?

> [*One by one they notice Roche. Pause.* ROCHE *advances.*]

ROCHE: Good morning to you. Allow me to introduce myself. My name is Roche.

SPENS: Roach? Got a hawk in the orchard, now we got a bleeding fish.

ROCHE: It's not spelled that way. It's not spelled that way at all.

SPENS: How am it bloody spelled, then?

ROCHE: R-o-c-h-a. . . .

SPENS: You got it arse about face, man. . . .

ROCHE: R-o-c-h-a. . . .

SPENS: What? . . .

ROCHE [*flaring*]: I know how to spell my own name! Don't think I don't know how to spell my own name! It's a fine name. An early Norman name. It means a rock. I'm from Limerick.

SPENS: Where?

ROCHE: Limerick. The kingdom of Munster. Ireland.

JUMBO: Fuck the Irish!

SPENS: Might have knowed. You'm a dirty-looking sod. All you Irish'm filthy dirty. Filthy dirty tongues, too, the bloody lot on you. . . .

> [*Writes in notebook.* ROCHE *peers.*]

ROCHE: An Eh at the end of it, not an Ah in the middle. . . .

SPENS: A what?

ROCHE: Eh for elephant.

SPENS: A for what?

ROCHE: You English have always persecuted us. You English have always deliberately misunderstood us. The Saxon mind detests the poetry of the Gaelic soul. Detests and loathes it.

SPENS: You looking for a job?

ROCHE: I saw the advertise-ment. Male workers.

SPENS: You any good?

ROCHE: I'm very good.

SPENS: You any good at this?

ROCHE: I done finer.

SPENS: It'm strenuous.

ROCHE: I done worse.

SPENS: You'm not a student, you'm bloody fifty!

ROCHE: I am, but!

[*Laughter.*]

Ay! Laugh at me, if you will. The laugh will be on the other side of your faces before this day is out.

SPENS: What studying then?

ROCHE: Humanity. I am a poet. I write, in a way.

SPENS: Hear that? Got a poet in the orchard with us, now. Bloody Shakespeare.

JUMBO: What you reckon to Shakespeare, then, Pat? Critically speaking.

ROCHE: I think him good. Very good.

JEFF: I like Macbeth.

[SPENS *takes up third bucket.*]

SPENS: O.K., O.K. Get this bleeding bucket on you, then. And take that tea-cloth off your head. . . .

[ROCHE *downs bag; with alacrity struggles with bucket.* TAFFY, JUMBO *exeunt.* LARRY *follows.*]

And they eyeglasses. You look bloody loony. What'm they for?

ROCHE: To protect my eyes against the day.

SPENS: Think this'm the French Rivi-bloody-eera, do you? What'm the tea-cloth for?

ROCHE: To protect my head against the rain.

ALBERT: Bain't raining, Shakespeare.

ROCHE [*mysteriously*]: Ah!

[SPENS *straightens Roche out.* ROCHE *seizes his bag, quivering to go.*]

SPENS: Get down among they bloody trees, then; along with Albert, here. And Trousers.

ROCHE: Sir.

[*Exeunt* JEFF *and* ALBERT, ROCHE *following.*

JEFF: Come along, Shakespeare. We s'll show you what to do.

[*Exit* GINGER.]

SPENS [*calling after Roche*]: Think it'm a-going to rain, do you? [*Pause.*] Thinks as it'm a-going to bloody rain. . . . [*Glances at sky. Pause.*] I don't know. Do with some more empties to line, Mrs Trevis, couldn't you? [*Pause.*] Told Johnny Hobnails to bring some down from the yard when he come for the next load.

MRS TREVIS: Pity about Hobnails, isn't it, Spens? Nice eyes.

SPENS: Reckon as some'at'm keeping him up the yard. Short of lining papers, too, Mrs Trevis, bain't you?

MRS TREVIS: Could do with some more bottoms, Spens. Plenty of sides. No bottoms.

SPENS: Plenty of bottoms in this orchard, if you knows where to look for them. Ah, don't take a bit of notice on me, Mrs Trevis. Sometimes I bloody forgets you'm here.

MRS TREVIS: Ain't heard a single word, Spens. . . .

[SPENS *inspects fruit in crates. Slings some out.*]

MRS TREVIS: Did you smell him, Spens?

SPENS: Who? [*Pause.*] Ah. Irish'm' all the same. Should hear them when they gets going, too. Bloody blasphemous bastards.

MRS TREVIS: Sends all their rubbish over here, Spens. Paying us out for what we done to them in ancient times.

SPENS [*howling*]: Don't get shooking them bloody boughs! Shoot any bugger as I catch shooking them bloody boughs; will, and all!

[*Enter* ROCHE. *Proceeds to empty quarter-bucket of pears into crate, heavily.*]

. . . What'm the steps for? Climb up them, now you got them. . . .

[*Sees Roche*] What you think you'm on? Eh? Stone-breaking?

ROCHE: Maybe.

SPENS: You'm asking for trouble. More used to stones too, I reckon. Been in prison, ever, Shakespeare?

ROCHE: Maybe.

SPENS: Always tell a man as has been in prison. Written on his face. And you'm a student!

ROCHE: I told you. Till the day I die.

SPENS: What on, then? Human bloody nature?

ROCHE: There's queer things happens in the world.

MRS TREVIS: You can say that again.

ROCHE: Mighty queer.

MRS TREVIS: I been in Worcester afore now, and think I seen my sister. I hollers out, and she turn round: and she'm someone else.

ROCHE: I tell you. I seen a witch once. In Bromsgrove, it was. She had the very face of a witch. Gnarled, and black-a-vised, and ageless old. And warts on the wrists of her. 'Sir!' says she to me, 'sir, you are a man of strength and nobility. You have poetry in your veins. A fine man, you are. A humane man ...'

SPENS: Reckon her needs her bloody crystal dusting. I seen a witch, too. At Cross, in Worcester. Her had a pointed hat, and all. And a cat at her elbow. And a little black toad on the end of a crimson thread. ...

ROCHE [uncertain]: It's laughing at me you are. ...

SPENS: Think it'm a-going to rain?

ROCHE: Laughing ...

SPENS: Bloody am, you scarecrow! Witches and warlocks'm over and done with, Shakespeare! You'm finished.

ROCHE: You'll see. ...

SPENS: Your kind am done. ...

[Exit ROCHE. Pause.]

Don't you take no bloody notice on him, Mrs Trevis.

MRS TREVIS: I'll go and have my coffee now. ...

[Exit MRS TREVIS. Pause. Exit SPENS. Tractor stops near by off back; engine runs. Voices of JOHNNY and TINY off, above engine.]

JOHNNY: Further, Tiny! Further!

TINY: Can't do.

JOHNNY: Up along the boxes, Tiny: guide us!

TINY: Can't go no further, Johnny.

JOHNNY: Why?

TINY: Can't do. There'm a big hole in the way.

[*Engine switched off.*]

JOHNNY: What?

TINY: Big hole in the way. [*Pause.*] Have to carry them, Johnny.

JOHNNY: Sodding nuisance. [*Enter* JOHNNY.] O.K. Let's have them empties, any road. What hour am it?

[*Enter* TINY *with empties from trailer.*]

TINY: Don't know.

JOHNNY: Got a watch, haven't you?

TINY: Sh, Johnny. Trees got ears. Eyes. [*Looks at watch.*] Five and twenty to eleven, Johnny.

JOHNNY: Still, isn't it? Isn't it still?

TINY: Hot, though. Don't like it when it'm hot. It makes my head all sore. Don't like it raining, either.

JOHNNY: Isn't going to rain. Not a cloud in the sky.

[*Exit* TINY. JOHNNY *pauses, juggles with pears. Enter* TINY, *with empties; he stands, gazing in wonder.*]

TINY: Oh, you'm a marvel. It'm wondrous, the way you juggle with they pears. . . .

[JOHNNY *turns on Tiny, hurls pears at him, one by one, chasing him.* TINY *scuttles in genuine terror. Enter* LARRY *to boxes.* TINY *and* JOHNNY *pull up short, stop. Silence, stillness.* LARRY *and* JOHNNY *see each other. Pause.*]

JOHNNY: Hello.

LARRY: Hello.

JOHNNY: You new? You come today?

LARRY: I came this morning.

JOHNNY: Permanent?

LARRY: Only till – until they don't want me any more.

[TINY *exit for empties.*]

JOHNNY: Who am you then? What'm you called?

LARRY: What do they call you?

JOHNNY: No. Honest.

LARRY: Larry.

JOHNNY: John. Johnny for short. What they call you for short?

LARRY: Larry.

JOHNNY: What'm your real name, then?

LARRY: Larry.

JOHNNY: Come from Ireland, do you?

LARRY: Why?

JOHNNY: Your voice.

LARRY: No. I used to speak like you. I don't come from Ireland.

JOHNNY: Thought you come from Ireland. Go to college, do you, then?

LARRY: How did you guess?

JOHNNY: Like it, college?

LARRY: Yes.

JOHNNY: Why don't you scarper?

LARRY: Not before I get my degree.

JOHNNY: What's that?

[Enter TINY with empties.]

TINY: He's a student, Johnny. [To Larry] He's Johnny.

JOHNNY: He'm Larry.

TINY: I'm vague.

JOHNNY: Are you saved? Baptized, I mean. Am you, Larry? Baptized in the Blood of the Lamb?

TINY: It'm a marvel the way he juggles with they pears. Should see him juggle.

JOHNNY: We'm baptized. Both. In the Blood. How long you been here, did you say?

LARRY: Two hours. How long have you?

JOHNNY: Four years. Ever since I can remember.

TINY: His dad were blowed up in the war.

JOHNNY: Afore I were born.

TINY: His mother's someone else's mother, now. [To Larry] You'm not baptized. You'm marked with the mark of the beast.

JOHNNY: Teach you good and evil, do they?

TINY: At the University?

JOHNNY: Teach you to distinguish?

LARRY: I don't know about that.

JOHNNY: You'm lucky, though. Going to college. But we'm baptized. In the Blood.

[LARRY *makes to go.* JOHNNY, *by a strange movement, stands in front of him, halts him. Pause.*]

How do you like the hanging gardens?

LARRY: I do it for the money.

JOHNNY: He told the truth. [*To Tiny*] He told a true thing two times since we come here. That'm strange. Know something? I live with Tiny's folks. He's my cousin.

TINY: I'm not, Johnny. You told a lie.

JOHNNY: Cousin-german. I'm like you, Larry. Honest, I am. Tolerate it only for the money. I bloody hate it, to be confidential. Dark side of the moon, this place. There, where you and us come from, they got gardens. Am I right?

LARRY: We don't live there any more.

JOHNNY: Lupins, too. They'm proud that way, Black Country, don't you think so?

TINY: Only in June. They all go black, though, after, Johnny, the lupins: in the grime.

JOHNNY: Ever made them come up purple, did you? Know you how? Plant copper nails in, in the autumn. How long you here for, did you say?

LARRY: Three weeks. If.

TINY: Shouldn't send students. They don't last. They disappear. Oh, it'm utter, their disap-bloody-pearance. Saving for the cinders. The cinders was scattered far and wide. It'm a lovely ceremony.

JOHNNY: Courting, are you, Larry? [*Pause.*] You daft sod, am you courting? Asked you a question; reply to us! What the hell you come here for, only you don't answer us damn-all?

LARRY: I'm not courting.

JOHNNY: Or stay locked up, then, if you prefer? [*Pause.*] Going to have sons, are you? [*Pause.*] Tell us, though. Tell us some'at. If us went to a marriage, what colour should us wear?

TINY: Black, Johnny.

JOHNNY: With a white flower. Whiter than snow.

LARRY: You should wear something dark.

TINY: He'm telling you, Johnny. Black. With stripes.

JOHNNY: A red flower. Red. Like the Blood of the Lamb. We'm all washed whiter than snow in the Blood of the Lamb.

[*Enter* SPENS *with tarpaulin.*]

SPENS: Hello, Hobnails. Get they couplings seen to afore long. Don't like the look on them. Trailer come apart. [*Pause.*] Good trailer, mind. Reckon, though, as they bring their axles too far aforeways. Make her back-heavy. [*Pause.*] They loading for Doncaster, yet?

JOHNNY: B.R.S. bloke turned up just afore I come down, Spens.

SPENS: How'm it a-going up the yard, then?

JOHNNY: Slow. Had to stop three times, too, coming down. Empties kept falling off.

SPENS: I don't know. Can't seem to get organized today, somehow. Something'm wrong.

[TINY *flings down last empties.*]

JOHNNY [*stirring*]: Okay, Tiny. Let's have the fruit weighed. [*Moves on and off now with* TINY, *taking loaded crates to trailer. Sounds of weighing, off.*] How many boxes you reckon you got for us, Spens?

SPENS: Hundred. Hundred and twenty. . . .

[*Enter* MRS TREVIS]

MRS TREVIS: What you bring down the tarpaulin for?

SPENS: Eh? Keep them boxes dry. . . .

MRS TREVIS: Isn't going to . . .

SPENS: You shut up moaning, Mrs Trevis! You bloody line them: job you'm paid for; and shut up moaning. . . .

[MRS TREVIS, *surprised, shrugs; resumes.*]

How were that, Hobnails? How you say it were a-going up the yard?

JOHNNY: Slow. Know what gaffer done? Whole load of students come. Bloody bus-load. All kinds. Come up from Bromsgrove on the ten past ten. Know what he done: gaffer? Packed them off to Grimbley's. Says he don't want no Grimbley's done; and he pack them off to Grimbley's.

SPENS: Reckon he meant send them off to Ashbold's.

MRS TREVIS: Bloody awkward trees, Ashbold's.

JOHNNY: Grimbley's though. Isn't no one there.

TINY: He'm starkers, Mr Hawkes.

SPENS: I don't know. Reckon, though, every year, come picking-time, it'm the bloody same. Shambles. Pande-bloody-monium. Can't organize, Hobnails; that'm his trouble.

TINY: Shouldn't send students. They disappear.

SPENS: What weights you got on them, Hobnails?

JOHNNY: Thirty-eight, Spens. Twenty-eight the pears, and ten the box.

SPENS: Hope you have. . . .

MRS TREVIS [*confidentially*]: Pity about Hobnails. Isn't it, Spens?

SPENS: Ah. Doesn't know what to do with they types, Mrs Trevis. Should put them to sleep, or some'at, I reckon. Act of mercy.

MRS TREVIS: Nice eyes.

SPENS: Oh. He's a nice bloke, Mrs Trevis.

[*Enter* JEFF *to crates. Enter* ROCHE, *who carries majestically one pear.*]

ROCHE: Excuse me. This pear I have . . . [*Goes to crates.*]

[SPENS *goes into shed left.*]

Now would you say it was large enough, or would you say it was too small? Is it acceptable on any basis?

JEFF: Do what, Shakespeare?

ROCHE: Is this pear acceptable on any basis at all?

JEFF [*examining knowledgeably*]: It'll do. Don't want to put in the knobbly ones, Shakespeare, 'count of they'm bitter. Nor the twisted ones, neither. 'Count of they spoil the sample. And them red ones is midsummer blooms. O.K.?

ROCHE: But how am I to tell whether they're large or small? The segregation seems quite arbitrary to me.

JEFF: Just take the small ones, Shakespeare, and put them in the box for smalls.

ROCHE: Oh! [*Makes to exit with pear*] The segregation seems totally arbitrary to me. . . .

[*Enter* ALBERT.]

ALBERT: Here! You there!

ROCHE: Yes, foreman?

ALBERT [*laughing*]: Hear that, Trousers? Foreman, he bloody called me.

ROCHE: I'm sorry, sir. I didn't see.

ALBERT: Want any help?

ROCHE: With what, but?

ALBERT: That bloody pear you'm carrying!

[*His look on Roche is laughterless, fixed.* ROCHE, *with show of injured dignity, makes to go.*]

Foreman, he bloody called me. . . . [*Exit* ALBERT.]

[SPENS *enters from shed left with ladder. Exit* JEFF.]

SPENS: Here, Shakespeare! Grab a hold on this, then. This'll take you as near to heaven as you s'll ever get. . . .

[ROCHE *takes ladder. Exit.*]

JOHNNY: Chap from Pest Control's coming 's afters, Spens. Did you hear?

SPENS: Pest Control?

JOHNNY: 's afternoon.

SPENS: 's after-bloody-noon? Who said so? Reckon as he needs his bloody head testing, then. What do he want to spray for, and it a-going to rain?

JOHNNY: Rain, Spens?

TINY: It'm awful when it rains.

JOHNNY: Isn't a cloud in the sky.

SPENS: Wash all the spray off on them.

TINY: All down your neck, it goes, the rain does. And your arms.

SPENS: Half the fruit'm bloody picking, now.

JOHNNY: Helicopter'm ready, any road. I seen it up the yard.

TINY: It'm a marvel. Shining in the sunshine, helicopter. Like a fly.

SPENS: Didn't ought to spray when the blokes'm a-picking, Hobnails. Make them go all bald. Make all their hair come out. Make them so's they won't get no babbies.

MRS TREVIS: Dangerous stuff, that spray. Radioactive.

SPENS: Ah. Make an Hiroshima on us. Eh, don't you laugh, Hobnails. Proper bloody Hiroshima.

MRS TREVIS: Had a horrible dream last night, and all. Dreamed as the bloody bomb went off. And all my teeth was falling out in my mouth. Like nails, they was.

SPENS: Reckon you'm sickening for something, Mrs Trevis. Bloody warbles, or some'at. Pest Control. [SPENS *joins* MRS TREVIS *lining crates. Pause.*] Don't reckon much to old bloody Shakespeare, though. Him with the tea-cloth on his head. . . . He'm hopeless, Hobnails. He'm bloody hopeless. Puts them all in, too. Bitters; midsummers; bloody smalls, too.

[*Re-enter* ROCHE *with bucket in his hands.*]

Educated, though. That right, Shakespeare?

ROCHE: What?

SPENS: You'm educated.

ROCHE: Never.

SPENS: Bloody am.

[ROCHE *takes empty crate from stack, goes apart with it. Fills it meanwhile.*]

I got the measure on you. You'm on the bloody National Assistance.

[ROCHE *stands holding the filled crate; looks ill.*]

What for you want to come this place, then, if you'm getting paid already for doing bloody nothing? Eh? Irish'm all the same. Comes over here with their bloody chest complaints and gets paid for doing bloody nothing. . . .

[ROCHE *drops crate; pears spill. He puts hand to head; sways.*]

ROCHE: You'll see.

SPENS: What'm the matter with you now?

ROCHE: I have a headache.

SPENS: Bet you have. Good day's work would kill you.

ROCHE: To hear a man blaspheming out of him the way you do would give the Lord Almighty himself a headache. Holy God, but the climate is terrible close. Don't youse find it so?

JOHNNY: It'm warm, I grant you.

ROCHE: I had the most terrible accident. At the age of four. It was all the fault of a Black-and-Tan.

SPENS: Blackantan? What kind of bloody animal am that?

ROCHE: You might well ask. A convict, he was, from Manchester Gaol. Where he was serving a sentence for larceny with violence and petty rape. Sent over by the British to civilify us.

SPENS: Reckon he made a bad job of it.

ROCHE: Youse set the great example. Oh, this head I have on me this moment is something terrible.

SPENS: Why don't all you Irish stay at home, then, now you got your inter-bloody-dependence?

ROCHE: I think the true proportion of ether and air in my

constitution must be mortally disturbed. Do you believe, now, young man, in such a thing as the hypothetical ether?

JOHNNY: What's that, then?

ROCHE: The hypothetical ether. That was postulated by the ancients as the celestial counterpart of the lower air we humbler mortals breathe. In the human constitution, as you may, or may not, know . . .

SPENS: Get bloody weaving!!

[*Exit* ROCHE.]

How many you got on her now, Tiny?

TINY: Hundred and four, Spens.

SPENS: Hundred and four. Ah. [*Looks off at trailer. Considers. Looks at few full crates still to load. Enter* JEFF.] Be back afore lunch, will you, Hobnails?

JOHNNY: Have to be. How much more you reckon you got to come?

SPENS: Boat-loads. Six hundred boxes to fill afore night come. Hey! Look at this, Hobnails. Specimen here. Trousers, I bloody calls him. Teddy Boy, that so?

JEFF: No. I'm a bishop disguised.

SPENS: See it in your face, kid. Teddy Boy.

[*Enter* ROCHE *with bag; makes to depart across stage.*]

What you stopped off for, Shakespeare? You tired? You going home?

ROCHE: I'm going to take my Alka-Seltzer now.

SPENS: Your what?

ROCHE: My Alka-Seltzer. My friend in need.

JEFF: Good for you, ain't they, Alka-Seltzers?

ROCHE: Can you tell me, foreman, where I could find a glass of water?

SPENS: Hear that, Hobnails? Foreman, he bloody call me. What you want a glass of water for?

ROCHE: To dissolve my Alka-Seltzer.

JEFF: Make you fit, don't they?

SPENS: I's'll tell you what'll make you fit, Shakespeare. Fighting fit. . . .

TINY: That'm the lot, Johnny. Can we go now?

SPENS [*taking out book and stub*]: How many were it, Tiny?

94

TINY: Hundred and five, and four. Hundred and fifty-four, Spens.

SPENS [*writing*]: Hope you'm right. I s'd rope them over, Hobnails. Don't want all they crates to come a-falling off. Kill someone.

TINY: Empties come off.

SPENS: Hobnails said as empties come off.

[*Kicking Tiny off.*]

ROCHE: There's not a house in sight at all. Where do youse all live here? Holes in the ground, is that it?

SPENS [*deep in book*]: What kind of poetry you write, Shakespeare?

JEFF: Yeah; what kind of poems you write?

ROCHE: You'll see.

JEFF: Don't you sell none?

SPENS: Don't sell them, poets. Do all starve. That right, Shakespeare?

JEFF: Ain't they good enough?

SPENS: Tell us one of your poems, Shakespeare.

JEFF: I like poetry. Honest, I do.

SPENS: We'm all ears.

JEFF: Modern, I bet.

MRS TREVIS: All art's modern, these days.

JEFF: Dirty, I bet.

ROCHE [*flaring*]: Are you going to tell me whereabouts I can lay my hands on a tumbler of water, or are youse not?

[JEFF *sniggers*.]

MRS TREVIS [*admonishing*]: Spens. [*Pause.*]

SPENS: All right, then. Shakespeare. No need to get rattled. Go up the lane, see. Up the lane. And down on your left-hand side there'm a row of cottages.

ROCHE: I came that way. Itself. I saw no cottages.

SPENS: They'm hidden, Shakespeare. You s'll see them. A-down your left-hand side a-going down the lane. . . .

ROCHE: Thank you, foreman. . . . [*Exit with dignity.*]

SPENS [*calling*]: And mind out after that dog up there!

[*Suddenly off, sounds of vicious altercation between* JOHNNY *and* TINY.]

JOHNNY [*off*]: Oh, Tiny, Tiny, bloody hell, you got the weights on wrong! Weights for apples, them are. Pears we'm doing, and we weighed for bloody apples.

TINY [*off*]: I'm sorry, Johnny. Only there was apples last time, and they got me moithered. Them apples for South Africa.

JOHNNY: Fuck South Africa.

TINY: All muddled, Johnny.

JOHNNY: Lose us our job, you will.

TINY: I'm sorry, Johnny.

[*Engine revs up; tractor pulls away; is gone; silence.*]

SPENS: Shakespeare. Reckon as he won't come back, Trousers.

JEFF: Yeah. Reckon we seen the last of him.

MRS TREVIS: Hope so.

SPENS: You ain't much to write home about, Mrs Trevis, am you? Like a bloody mangold-worzel, any road.

MRS TREVIS [*packing to go*]: Ain't taking a bit of notice, Spens. Go and have my lunch now. . . .

SPENS: Two hours bloody lunch hour. I don't know. Reckon you gets it all ways, this world, you women. Franchise. Seats in buses. First off a sinking vessel.

MRS TREVIS: 'preciate the female sex, Spens, I don't think. See you. . . . [*Exit* MRS TREVIS.]

SPENS: All ways. Ah, Trousers. He s'll be a hopeless long time a-looking for they cottages. There bain't none. . . .

[*Exit* SPENS. *Enter severally to stacked crates* TAFFY, ALBERT, JIM, JUMBO, GINGER, *and* LARRY.]

TAFFY: Hey, Trousers. Where did your mate get to?

JEFF: Who? Shakespeare? Hopped it. Went after water to stir his healing powders.

TAFFY: Where did he go?

JEFF: Christ knows. Some cottages or other Spens says ain't there.

JUMBO: Oh. Oh, well, if that's so, I reckon we seen the last of him. Not that I minded the bloke.

JEFF: Yeah. 'Up the lane,' he says, 'and down your left-hand side. . . .'

ALBERT: Ah. He s'd be a hopeless long time a-looking for they, and all.

GINGER: Wander a-looking for them till the day he bloody die.

JEFF: His healing powders in his hand.

JUMBO: Poor Shakespeare. Reckon he gets the boot wherever he bloody goes.

TAFF: Yeah, wrapped up in a kindness, too. Isn't that Spens all over? The boot in a cloth of gold?

[*Pause.*]

JEFF: Dock it out on his wage, though, whatever.

ALBERT: Hadn't earned bugger-all. Didn't deserve no wage.

GINGER: Fruit were a-falling out the bucket at his shoes.

JEFF: Didn't wear no socks; did you notice?

JIM: Hadn't picked damn-all, hasn't earned damn-all.

JUMBO: Come off it, Jimither; give the bleeder a chance. He'd have got into it, given time.

GINGER: No call to give no bugger time, this place.

JUMBO: Weren't stupid, Ginge. Might be a bit touched, I grant you. But he weren't stupid. He'd had education.

ALBERT: What did he want a-doing here, then, Jumbo?

JUMBO: Earn a bit. Same as the most on us.

[*Pause.* LARRY *embarrassed.*]

LARRY [*manages*]: He didn't look very well, did he . . .?

JEFF: Didn't half go on, too. Did you hear him?

GINGER: Ah, Trousers. I reckons too as he talked too bloody much.

JEFF: Didn't get damn-all done. . . .

GINGER: Natter, natter. They bloody rile me, talkers. What were it he kept on saying? Irish Gaelic the language of bloody kings. I said to him, 'Ho, ho,' I said, 'Shakespeare: I bloody caught you there. 'count of there bain't no kings no more.' Saving on the pack of cards, like; know what I mean? Irish Gaelic the language of bloody kings.

[*Pause.*]

JUMBO: Poor bastard. All shaven smartish for his nice new job, and he don't get taking home no wage.

ALBERT: Perhaps he ha'n't got no home.

[*Pause. An unease spreads through them.*]

TAFFY: These tramps, though. Clever fuckers, sometimes, deep down you know. Wisdom of the whole bloody world, they carry, sometimes.

GINGER: Seed him shaking them tops down, did you? Seen him, Albert?

LARRY: He had a headache. . . .

JEFF: Had a headache!

LARRY: What's wrong with that?

JEFF: Wrong with what?

LARRY: He can have a headache. . . .

JEFF: I never said there was nothing wrong with having a headache. Just said he had a headache, that's all. What's wrong with saying he had a headache, then? Eh?

[*Enter* SPENS.]

SPENS: Get bloody moving!! Six hundred bloody boxes to fill afore night come, and you ain't got a quarter on them done. Come on, Jumbo. Taff. You want this job, or don't you? Eh? Ain't fit for nothing else, I reckon. Even this'm a-bloody-bove you.

[*Exeunt* JUMBO *and* TAFFY.]

And you, Leonard, Larkin, whatever you'm bloody called. Too Conservative to work with the workers, I reckon. . . .

[*Exit* LARRY.]

[*Calling*] They s'll inherit the earth, the workers! Blessed are the pieceworkers, for they shall inherit the earth! [*Pause.*] Trousers.

[*Exit* JEFF.]

[*Calling*] And don't you get shooking them bloody boughs, Trousers. Shoot any bugger as I catch shooking them boughs. Will, and all. [*Pause.*] Done worse afore now. That right, Albert? Ginge?

[*Unease again.*]

Bloody near . . . Gaffer were after us, that time. Remember? 'Where'm your slowest man?' he say. Remember? 'Find him. Find your slowest man. Chase him. . . .' [*Pause.*] Don't get no piecework, Jim, till these rows'm all done. Don't get half the money. Ain't worth it, day work. Am it? Gaffer say to me, 'Give pears preference. Give pears preference, Spens,' he say, 'but no piecework, till them Margarets'm all done. . . .'

[ALBERT *has gone.* JIM *follows. Pause.*]

How'm it a-going, then, Ginge? How's the missus keeping?

GINGER: Bit poorly, Spens.

SPENS: Ain't no sign on a babby, Ginge, am there? [*Pause.*] Reckon you s'll have to have another go, when night come. Get you on night work, else. I s'll show her how to play ludo. . . .

GINGER: You keep your bloody paws off her, Spens!

SPENS: Reckon her needs a-spraying, Ginge. Bloody two on you.

Dried blood, or some'at; fertilizer. Got a blight on you, I reckon, Ginge. Reckon as there'm some'at a-holding you back. . . .

[GINGER *exit.* SPENS *lights cigarette stub, glances up at sky; exit. Enter* LARRY. *Lights brighten; glare. Enter* ROCHE, *seeming unwell and remote.*]

ROCHE: There's a terrible silence fallen over the place. The birds are stopped. Oh, it is terrible; the heat of the day.

LARRY: Did you get some water?

ROCHE: The young man. The one they call Hobnails. . . .

LARRY: John. . . .

ROCHE: Found me water. It was very kind. [*Pause.*] It seems the foreman must have made some mistake. There's no cottages. He must have made some mistake. . . .

LARRY: How is your headache? Going?

ROCHE: It's a wee bit improved. Do you not find the climate terrible close?

LARRY: I think there's thunder coming.

ROCHE: Terrible deleterious close. Do you have headaches, at all?

LARRY: Sometimes I do. . . .

ROCHE: Are they neuritic or sinusitic, do you know? That is to say, would you be of the opinion that they were caused by the nerves or by the congestion of the cerebral tubes?

LARRY: Overwork.

ROCHE: That may well be. I used to suffer with the sinuses terrible bad. I still do. Ah. But it could be worse. There's no point at all in complaining. It could be a hundred times worse. A thousand times worse. Things could be a thousand times worse. Ten thousand times worse. Glory be to God, they could be a million times worse. [*Pause.*] Sure, there's no end to the disasters that could choose to unfurl themselves upon the world. Floods and cataclysms, revolutions and thunders and bloody wars, and lightnings on the field of battle, and nucular bombs and tongues of flame. Ah, things could be worse; and that's a fact. [*Pause.*] All your fortune stems from your nose. Did you know that?

LARRY: No.

ROCHE: Well, now, wait till I tell you. Do you suffer from your sinuses at all?

[LARRY *nods no.*]

The moment you do, take you a wee smear of Ultimatum ointment on the tip of your finger and apply it gently over the linings of the nose.

LARRY: Ultimatum.

ROCHE: Ultimatum. That's the stuff. Ah, there's some very precious bones in the body. And others, too, that's not so precious. Now would you, sir, or would you not, be of the opinion, so to say, that the metatarsal, for instance, could be classed a kind of – average bone?

LARRY: More than average. If you broke a metatarsal, you wouldn't be able to walk. The loss of a metacarpal wouldn't be so grave.

[*Pause.* ROCHE *blank.*]

ROCHE: I have a hammer toe. Ever since that day and moment I was thrust in the gutter by that Black-and-Tan, I have the hammer toe. And the course of my natural health has deviated ever since. It's a sad thing. [*Pause.*] Here. Here. I know you're not on the medical side, but you're a shrewd man, I can see that; I could tell that, from the way you looked up at the clouds there now. If you were to look at my tongue, now, could you determine at the sight of the colour of it, the shade of it, only, whether or not I was in passable health? [*Thrusts out his tongue.*]

LARRY: Your tongue is blue.

ROCHE: Lord bless us, is that so? Is that bad, do you know?

LARRY: I've no idea. I don't think so. At any rate, it isn't yellow. If it were yellow, you might have something to worry about.

ROCHE: Ah, well! It's not yellow. It's not yellow. That's a great relief, surely. [*Pause.*] Ah. If I could have half an hour of the dry heat. The half hour of it, only. I could set myself up, don't you see? I'll have to make myself strong again. Perhaps I might sleep awhile. Ah. Sleep awhile. I'll do that, so. I'll lay me down on the earth a wee space, and shut my eye. . . . [*Prepares to lie, using bag for pillow.*] Here now. Here's a nice wee place; in the shade. [*Covers bag with tea-cloth; lies, head front.*]

There. Ah. And, when I waken again, I'll show youse wonders. . . . [*Sleeps.*]

[*Pause.* LARRY *watches. Enter* JOHNNY, *silent, embarrassed.* TINY *hovers vaguely in background.*]

JOHNNY: Larry.... Go away.... Don't come this place no more.

TINY: Can't we go now, Johnny?

[ROCHE *groans in his sleep.*]

JOHNNY: Out on the tar road with you, Larry. Scarper.

ROCHE [*in his sleep*]: The wild flowers!

JOHNNY: Where from did you get them arms? And them eyes? Your mother and father?

[JOHNNY *and* LARRY *face each other,* ROCHE *lying between them,* TINY *hovering.*]

TINY: Johnny, can't we go now...?

ROCHE: The wild, wild flowers...!

JOHNNY: Get out on it, Larry. Far.

LARRY: What for?

JOHNNY: Damn-all the bloody thing you know?

TINY: Things happen.

JOHNNY: Going to have sons, am you?

ROCHE: Flowers is wonderful. A miracle. They'll grow in any place....

JOHNNY: Make sure. [*Makes to go.*] Be sorry you ever come this place, afore the day am done. Be sorry you was ever born.... [*Exit.*]

[TINY *lingers.*]

TINY: I seen ever so much blood in my time. [*Exit.*]

[LARRY *exit. Pause.* ROCHE *stirs mumbling out of sleep. Enter* JEFF *and* ALBERT *to crates.* ROCHE *sits up.*]

ALBERT: 'lo, Shakespeare.

JEFF: Hello, Shakespeare.

[ROCHE *scrambles guiltily to his feet; clutches bag protectively.* ALBERT *and* JEFF *empty.*]

ALBERT: Reckoned as you'd gone home.

JEFF: Yeah, Shakespeare. Thought you'd hopped it.

ROCHE: What call would I have to do that? I'm glad I took on the job. It'll set me up rightly against the winter days.

JEFF: Thought Spens give you your cards.

ROCHE: He did not.

JEFF: Bet you anything you like he will now.

ROCHE: What, so? I'll be away, if he does. To Italy or Spain, or one of them places.

[*Enter* GINGER *to crates. Enter* JIM.]

GINGER: Have a nice walk, then, Shakespeare? Enjoy your Alka-Seltzer?

JEFF: Good for you, ain't they?

ALBERT: Did you find the cottages, Shakespeare?

JIM: Ah, proper cottages.

ROCHE: It seems the foreman must have made some mistake.

ALBERT: Reckoned as perhaps, Shakespeare, you didn't like us no more.

[*Enter* JUMBO *and* TAFFY *to crates.*]

JUMBO: Well, well, well, if it ain't the playboy of the bleeding Western world.

TAFFY: Thought you'd had your lot, Paddy.

ROCHE: Perhaps you did. Perhaps I have. Perhaps I am gone. Perhaps I'm not. Ha! [*Makes to exit past Ginger and Albert.*]

JUMBO: No need to take it that way, Shakespeare.

[GINGER *and* ALBERT *block exit.*]

JEFF [*blocking Roche's attempt to pass him*]: Thought Spens sacked him. Thought we was never going to see him more.

TAFFY: Thought wet the bloody bed.

GINGER: Bloody tried, though, Spens did. Sack him.

TAFF: Yeah some subtle way. Out of consideration for his feelings.

GINGER: Bloody hint, it were.

TAFFY: Didn't take it, did he?

JEFF: He thought Spens made a mistake.

TAFFY: O.K. So he thought Spens made a mistake. So what's the worry? Happy, isn't he? So what's the bloody worry?

GINGER: Found them, though. Found they cottages. Reckon as bloody Hobnails told him where.

JUMBO: So what? I don't mind, Shakespeare. Stick up for a bloke done down. But I'm warning you all the same. Warning you. Get picking. I'm warning you. Get picking, Shakespeare. Spens won't keep you, only it's worth his while to.

TAFFY: He's got to get his boxes done.

JUMBO: If he don't get his boxes done, he don't get no commission; and Hawkes'll chew him. And if Mr Hawkes chews foreman, foreman'll chew us; and we s'll all get it. And we don't want to get no chewing on account of you ain't picked no pears.

ROCHE: But I have picked pears!

TAFFY: Fair's fair.

ROCHE: I've worked as hard as any of you.

[*Noises of scorn.*]

As hard as could any man in my condition.

JEFF: Natter, natter!

ROCHE: My health won't allow me to overreach myself. And there are things I can not do. If I bend over backways, for example, my eyes go out. [*Pause.*] What time is it?

JEFF: Half past nowhen, Shakespeare. Time you knowed better.

ROCHE: Oh. . . .

TAFFY: Quarter to one, Paddy. Quarter to lunchtime.

ROCHE: Thank you, sir.

[*Pause.* ALBERT, GINGER, JIM, JEFF *gather round Roche, jolting him, nudging him more and more with baskets.*]

GINGER: Spens'll sack you good and proper next time, any road. See if he doesn't.

ROCHE: What so? I'll be away, if he does. To some warmer and more congenial clime.

ALBERT: Won't get no pay, though, Shakespeare. Have to go home and starve.

GINGER: Missus'll beat you. Like mine do.

ALBERT: You married, Shakespeare?

ROCHE: That would be telling.

GINGER: Can't go home to the missus without no money, Shakespeare.

JIM: Sack, first day.

GINGER: Won't have you. Won't let you come to her.

ALBERT: Gaffer'll come after you.

JEFF: Flaming mad.

ALBERT: 'Where'm the slowest man, Albert?' he say to me. 'Bring him to me. We s'll send him home.'

JIM: Get rid on him.

ALBERT: Get some'at done, and get on piecework.

GINGER: Let some'at grow. Bain't hindered, no more.

JIM: Get rid on him.

GINGER: Don't go putting no bloody eye on us.

ALBERT: Chase him.

GINGER: Make sure he don't find no way back again. . . .

[*Enter* SPENS.]

SPENS: I'm fed up with the bloody lot on you! Asking for trouble, bloody asking for it! Think I can't see you, do you? I can see you. Got eyes in my backside, I can see you. [*Sees Roche.*] What do you think this am, then? Eh? United bloody Nations? Get on, the bloody lot on you. Not lunchtime, yet, you know. Ha'n't heard the horn go.

[*Workers, except* ROCHE, *disperse, exeunt severally.*]

Get bloody weaving, then, the lot on you! Telling you! There s'll be some fun, else, in this orchard, afore night fucking come!

[*Pause.* SPENS *looks at Roche a moment.*]

Reckon, Shakespeare, as you ought to go.

ROCHE: Ay. I know where I'm not welcome. [*Gathers possessions; is almost gone; pauses.*] You're much mistaken, but. Aha, foreman. In me you're much mistaken. Ah. I'd show you wonders. I'd be up and down them trees with the best of you. Ay, and out and along them branches, too. Sprightly as a gipsy.

SPENS: Reckon as you'm a paradox, Shakespeare. Thinks as you'm among us, and you'm bloody vanished. Thinks, then, as we'm rid on you, and then you'm in our midst a-bloody-gain.

ROCHE: There's not a tree in this orchard, but I'd strip it. Ah. Give me the chance, and I'll have the orchard that bare of pears, you'll say a plague of locusts had come and passed and gone. I'll have the trees that lonely and bereaved, they'll sprout and bloom again twiced in the one year for the sake of company. Twiced in the one year! I done it, see.

SPENS [*abstracted*]: What?

ROCHE: Estates. I done head gardener once. For Lord Derrycreave himself. There wasn't one gardener in the length and breadth of Ireland could equal me. I done wonders. I done the impossible!

[*Factory horn blows, off. Cheers off.*]

I done flowers. I had flowers growing in the starved wilderness there, in the poisoned mountains away beyond Killorglin and the Pass of Keimaneigh, where flowers had been afeared to grow!

[*Stage fills slowly meanwhile; workers come on, satchels on shoulders, bearing step-ladders. These, they stand in a bunch off-centre; buckets, they sling over ladders, or place on ground beneath. Some begin to smoke.*]

Dagh! This whole orchard, this whole estate is nothing but a postage stamp compared. And I'll be over it in a hop and a step, I tell you! A hop and a step, only!

[SPENS *writes.*]

SPENS: Bring your ladder, Shakespeare. [*Pause.*] You deaf or some'at?

ROCHE: I'll leave it by my tree.

SPENS: When I says a thing, I bloody means it!

ROCHE: I'll be using it again. . . .

SPENS: That'm what you think. Fetch it!

[ROCHE *defiantly exit.*]

All right, you lot. What'm you standing around for? Eh? Earth to open? Go off and have your dinners.

[*They go, taking lunch-tins, flasks, etc.* ALBERT, GINGER *share lunch-tin.*]

And back here, mind, at two minutes to two! Two minutes to!

[*Enter* ROCHE *labouring under ladder. Collides with other ladders, brings them crashing down above him. He is flattened.*]

What'm the bloody matter with you now?

ROCHE: Oh, dear. The ladders all fell down on top of me.

SPENS [*extricating him*]: I don't know. Reckon as you'm from another planet, Shakespeare. Do, and all. Ghost, or some'at. Bloody zombie. . . .

[*Rights ladders.* ROCHE *brushes himself.*]

ROCHE: Thank you, foreman.

[SPENS *tears page out of notebook, gives to Roche.*]

SPENS: Your wage. [*Exit.*]

[ROCHE *gapes at paper. Determines. Crumpling paper, exit after Spens. His voice is heard protesting off, into distance.*]

ROCHE: . . . Another chance . . . I want another chance . . . [*Further*] Another chance . . .

[*Silence. Stillness. Distant long rumble of thunder off.*]

ACT TWO

The same, as at end of preceding act.

    [*Voice of* SPENS, *off.*]

SPENS [*off*]: Okay, let's have you! Three minutes to bloody two. Let's have you!

    [*Enter during following, silent, to ladders* JUMBO, ALBERT, GINGER, JEFF, JIM, *and* TAFFY; *they hoist buckets. Enter* SPENS.]

Better look after yourselves this afternoon. God of war, now, Mr Hawkes. After the whole lot on us! And Pest Control. Spray the whole lot on you, Pest Control. Make your hairs come out. Make you so's you won't get no babbies. . . . Come on, then, Leicester, London, Leamington, whatever you'm bloody called. What time do you think this is? Reckon you'm too Conservative to eat your lunch with the workers.

    [*Enter* LARRY, *on whom attention.* . . .]

What you want to come here for, then, if you'm too good to work with us? Eh? [*Pause.*] Let's have you, then [*exit.*]

    [*Only Roche's ladder remains. They become aware of this.*]

JIM [*dolefully*]: He did have a teapot, Shakespeare. Weren't nothing in her, though. Empty. Didn't eat nothing, neither. Sat there: in the barn. Eyeing us a-eating our sandwiches. Folleying our hands up with his eyen, up from the package to our mouths and down a-bloody-gain.

JUMBO: Poor bastard.

ALBERT: Poor bloody bastard.

    [*General uncertainty, uneasiness, and hesitation.*]

JUMBO: Anyway. He ain't come.

TAFFY: Yeah. We said good-bye to him now.

JUMBO: He ain't here; he ain't come. Spens give him his cards good and proper this time, and he ain't bloody come. So you can all bleeding well shut your faces now, and leave him a-bloody-lone.

    [*Exeunt. Voice of* HAWKES *off.*]

HAWKES [*off*]: Spens! Spens! !

[*Enter* HAWKES *and* GLORIA.]

Spens!

GLORIA: Spens!

HAWKES: Spens!

[*Enter* SPENS, *buttoning up his flies.*]

SPENS: Oh. Mr Hawkes. Reckon as I didn't hear you first time.

HAWKES: Send a man down to the dusthouse, Spens: immediately. Those tyres needs doing.

SPENS: Tyres?

HAWKES: They cycle tyres. Send a man down to the dusthouse, Spens. That's all I ask. Send two men, Spens. I need the tyres. They must be done.

GLORIA: Slashed. That's what you mean, Daddy; isn't it? Slashed.

HAWKES: Give they preference, Spens. And go along with the men to show them where the knives are. . . .

SPENS: Where the knives are?

HAWKES: Where the knives are!

SPENS: But Doncaster, Mr Hawkes. Four hundred boxes . . .

HAWKES: Give tyres preference, Spens. That's all I ask.

GLORIA: We need the rubber to bind the trees!

SPENS: But they four hundred boxes, Mr Hawkes . . .

HAWKES: Down to the dusthouse, Spens! Immediately! Send two! Send three!

SPENS: All right, Mr Hawkes. If that'm how you want it. . . .

[*Exeunt swiftly* HAWKES *and* GLORIA.]

[*To himself*] Give tyres preference. . . . [*Moves away calling*] Taff . . . ! Taff . . . ! Job for you . . . ! Dusthouse . . . !

[*Exit* SPENS, *calling*]

Trousers . . . ! Job for you . . . ! Dusthouse . . . !

[*Enter* MRS TREVIS. *Without emptying fruit-bucket, drags empty crate down, flops on to it. Enter, to crates,* JUMBO.]

JUMBO: Hello, you painted Gorgon. Where *you* been?

MRS TREVIS: Where you think I bloody been? Picking. Tops. The tops as Shakespeare left.

JUMBO: I reckon we seen the last of him.

MRS TREVIS: I hope so.

JUMBO: Give him his cards. Never see him more.

MRS TREVIS: Leaving all his tops. Didn't pick a single fruit as was higher than his head, didn't Shakespeare. Afraid of bending over backways. Blind his self. Said so. Some'at to do with his eyes.

JUMBO: Not many empties lined, though. Am there?

MRS TREVIS: Not many nothings, Jumbo. No more boxes, neither. No more bottoms, no more sides; nothing. All gone. [*Takes out cigarettes.*] Have a coffin nail.

JUMBO: Ta.

[JUMBO *accepts. They light,* MRS TREVIS *peering guiltily around.*]

MRS TREVIS: Spens ain't looking, I hope? Never know with him. Standing up the end of the row, as like as not. A-watching us. See the gleam in his eye a bloody mile away. Like a star in the leaves.

[*They smoke.*]

JUMBO: Not that I minded the bloke. Shakespeare. But leaving his stuff; leaving his stuff undone – got to get your finger out. Paid for doing a job, you got to get your finger out.

[*Pause. They smoke.*]

Where did Hobnails get to? Seen him?

MRS TREVIS: He's still waiting.

JUMBO: What for?

MRS TREVIS: More empties. Won't come down here without none empties, Jumbo. Waste of time. Besides. There ain't none.

JUMBO: None what?

MRS TREVIS: None empties. Told you. All gone.

JUMBO: All gone? Where to?

MRS TREVIS: Cardiff.

JUMBO: Cardiff?

MRS TREVIS: Reckon as somebody cocked up the orders, Jumbo. Filled them all up with Pitmastons; over at Grimbley's. . . .

JUMBO: Thank Christ this ain't Grimbley's, that's all. . . . Pitmastons? Pitmaston's a bloody Christmas pear. Won't be ripe till October, November. . . .

MRS TREVIS: You can say that again. . . .

JUMBO: Bloody Christmas pear. Who done it?

MRS TREVIS: Students.

JUMBO: Who told them?

MRS TREVIS: Don't ask me. Anyway, they've gone, now. It's too late.

JUMBO: We'm ruined, Mrs T.

MRS TREVIS: Hawkes went up in flames when he was told.

JUMBO: Keep out of his way, we'd better.

MRS TREVIS: They've all been sacked. Students as picked them has all been sacked. Should have seen them waiting at the bus stop, going home. Like plucked birds, they was. Said as they'd been told to.

JUMBO: Ah. But by whom?

[*Enter* SPENS, *angry, with hayfork, which he leans against shed front.*]

SPENS: O.K., O.K., you two. Smoke break'm over, now.

[*Enter* JEFF *and* TAFFY, *burdened with armfuls of cycle tyres.*]

Mucked up bloody Cardiff, can't afford to muck up Doncaster. . . .

TAFFY: Hey. Stuff that for a game of soldiers. What about these tyres?

SPENS: Reckon as Doncaster got to be accomplished.

JEFF: Got to slash these tyres, though. . . .

TAFFY: Yeah. How about these tyres?

JEFF: Gaffer said to . . .

SPENS: I don't care the hell what gaffer said! Reckon as I won't give tyres preference. Reckon as Doncaster'm more im-bloody-portant, see? Bugger the gaffer!

TAFFY: Make up their minds. . . .

SPENS: O.K., Taff, Trousers. Fling them down. We s'll attend to them later.

[TAFFY *and* JEFF *fling tyres down.*]

JUMBO: Heard about Grimbley's then, Spens.

SPENS: Ah. Like to get my hands round bloke as done it, and all. Reckon as he thinks it'm some kind of joke, or some'at. Something's the wrong in this place. Every year, come picking time, it'm the bloody same. Shambles. Pande-bloody-monium.

[*Exit* JUMBO. *Exit* MRS TREVIS.]

Cardiff. Your home town, Taff, Cardiff, isn't it?

TAFFY: Dowlais.

SPENS: What?

TAFFY: Dowlais.

SPENS: Bloody Wales, anyway. . . .

[HAWKES *heard baying off.*]

HAWKES [*off*]: Spens! Spens!

GLORIA [*off*]: Spens!

SPENS: Christ . . . !

[*Enter* HAWKES *very excited. Enter* GLORIA.]

HAWKES: How's it going, Spens? How are you on my tyres?

SPENS: Just starting on them, Mr Hawkes.

HAWKES: Starting? Well, hurry, Spens. Hurry! The knives, too. Did you find the knives?

[SPENS *produces three short ugly knives.*]

HAWKES: Three? [*Takes knives from Spens; inspects; tries blades.*] Oh, get them sharpened, Spens! Send Ginger down to fetch the kniving-stone. [*Hands them back.*] Oh, this is terrible. . . .

SPENS: Sorry to hear about Grimbley's, Mr Hawkes . . .

HAWKES: Sorry! Can't you say no more? Oh, terrible things is happening this day. Terrible awful things, you've no idea. [*Pause.*] Send Ginger down to fetch the kniving-stone; and then get weaving right away. The sky, Spens. Don't you observe? It'm coming over dark. So get them weaving right away. . . . Come along, Gloria. . . .

[*Exeunt* HAWKES *and* GLORIA. *Enter* GINGER, ALBERT, *and* JIM *to crates.*]

SPENS: Where's Shakespeare?

JIM: What?

SPENS: Where's bloody Shakespeare got to, now?

JIM: Gone home, Spens.

SPENS: What!

GINGER: You gave him his cards, Spens. Didn't you? Heard you. . . .

ALBERT: Got rid on him. . . .

JIM: You . . .

[*Pause.*]

GINGER [*suddenly furious*]: Spens, what you done?

[*Pause.*]

SPENS: I give him another chance.

GINGER: You give the bugger . . .

SPENS: Who'm the bloody foreman here?

GINGER: Who has to get the picking bloody done?

ALBERT: Holding the whole lot on us up, Spens. He were hopeless . . .

JIM: Brought bad luck to the place. . . .

GINGER: Said so, yourself, Spens. [*Uncertain*] Didn't you?

SPENS: What'm the bloody worry, then? Eh?

GINGER: I knowed it.

SPENS: Get your babby, now, Ginge, won't you? Get some'at done?

GINGER: I knowed it. . . .

SPENS: Get on piecework, Jim? Scarpered? Gone, now, isn't he?

ALBERT: You bowed the knee to him, Spens.

GINGER: Good and proper.

SPENS: Get in they trees. . . .

GINGER: Got the last laugh on us, now, old Shakespeare has. A-laughing at us. . . .

SPENS: Get in among they trees. . . .

GINGER: Sitting on a dung-heap, now, Shakespeare, somewhere around; a-laughing his bloody head off, 'count of you give in to him, and he bloody betray you. . . .

SPENS: Get in among they bloody trees!

    [GINGER, JIM, *and* ALBERT *do not move.* SPENS *sees* MRS TREVIS, *who enters to crates; looks off towards her tree.*]

Who been leaving his bloody tops unpicked?

MRS TREVIS: Shakespeare.

SPENS: Who . . . ? Reckon as I told him to go, Mrs T. 'Get bloody miles away,' I says, 'so's I don't have to contemplate your flaming face no more!'

MRS TREVIS: He had a horrible face.

    [*Enter* TAFFY.]

SPENS: Ah, Taff. Shakespeare. Told him to go. And he s'd bloody argue, see. . . . [*Spies Ginger, Albert, and Jim still motionless.*] What you lot waiting for, then? Eh? Earth to open?

    [*Enter separately* JUMBO *and* JEFF.]

TAFFY: Yeah. Had his lot, though, this time.

ALBERT: He ha'nt. Shakespeare ain't gone.

GINGER: Spens give in to him.

MRS TREVIS: What?

JUMBO: Reprieved?

SPENS: Reckon as he persuaded me to give him another chance.

GINGER: Bow the knee to him, you bloody mean.

SPENS: He did argue. Can't work when you'm feeling poorly, Ginge. Reckon as he prevailed upon me.

TAFFY: Hit you in the teeth, Spens, with your own bloody kindness, more like.

SPENS: Get bloody picking!

[*No response.*]

O.K., Mrs Trevis. You get weaving again on they tops as got left undone. . . .

MRS TREVIS: Reckoned I'd never live to see the day a worker tricked you out of a triumph, Spens. The road Shakespeare gone and done . . . [*Exit* MRS TREVIS.]

GINGER: I knowed it. Should have got rid on him for sure, Spens.

SPENS: We have got rid on him, haven't we?

GINGER: You done it against me, Spens. To hinder all on us; and to hinder me. . . .

SPENS: Ballocks!

GINGER: To spite the workers, Spens, you done it. Undo our bloody labour.

SPENS: Superstitious bastard, Ginger: I know you.

TAFFY: I didn't like him any more than you, you know. . . .

JUMBO [*amused*]: Old bloody Shakespeare . . .

TAFFY: But you got to give a bloke a chance, that's what I say. Done Spens a fast one: O.K.; good for him. Good for Paddy who done Spens a fast one. But you got to give a bugger a chance, see? Besides. He's vanished, now. Bloody scarpered, in the heel of the hunt, so what's the bloody worry?

JUMBO: Yeah. You can all shut your faces now, and . . .

GINGER: Won't get no babby now . . .

TAFFY: Christ Jesus . . .

GINGER: I know it.

TAFFY: You know something, Ginger?

GINGER: That am true!

TAFFY: You want to know something?

GINGER: His hands'm the hands on a dead man. His voice am the voice on a dead man. He'm a dead, rotten, filthy, a-dirtying kind of thing. Don't drink nothing; don't eat nothing . . . what am he, then? What am he?

TAFFY: Always got to have someone to compensate you, Ginge. Got a bloody Oedipus, you have. Marital failures, the same the whole world over.

GINGER: What do he come here, for, then, Shakespeare? Eh?

JUMBO: He's gone.

ALBERT: Is he?

JIM: Perhaps he'm a-listening to us. Laughing.

SPENS: And youse'm a-giving him some'at to laugh at, amn't you? 'fraid on him, are you?

GINGER: Don't you go a-sneering at us, now. Come to Shakespeare and you, Spens, seems as he proved himself bigger!

SPENS: Get back in among they trees.

GINGER: I reckon he been a-wandering the earth years now. And everywhere he do go, the grass do wither at his feet. Everywhere he do tread, the earth do bloody die. Why don't someone make him die, then?

SPENS: Get back in among they bloody trees.

JUMBO: Let's wander, Taff.

TAFFY: Yeah. let's go. . . .

[*Exeunt* JUMBO *and* TAFFY. SPENS *takes hayfork.*]

SPENS: All on you! Come after you with this bloody hayfork, else. I tell you. I tell you. O.K., O.K., I'm telling you, now. If I sees Shakespeare ever again . . .

GINGER: Doesn't know where he am, though: do we?

SPENS: If I sees Shakespeare ever a-bloody-gain . . .

[*Silence. Exeunt all except* SPENS *and* JEFF. *Pause.*]

Where'm that Leominster got to, then? Eh? Him with the sandals.

JEFF [*laughs*]: Who? Rosie? Reckon as he were gone soft on Shakespeare, somehow. Bet you a million dollars.

[*Pause. Lightning flickers faintly twice.*]

SPENS: Go you down the dusthouse, Jeff. And bring that kniving-stone.

[*Exit* JEFF. SPENS *thrusts hayfork into stage; takes knives out of belt; feels blades; exit, knives in hand. Stage somewhat darkens, light turning unnatural, stormy. Enter, shivering,* JOHNNY *and* TINY, *with a few empty veneers, which they stack beneath tarpaulin.*]

JOHNNY: The gaffer'm on his flamy throne. He'm wild. Keep out of his way, we'd better. Come down for the fulls, then scarper up the yard. Then out the tar road, till the storm am done. . . .

[TINY, *then* JOHNNY, *see hayfork.* TINY's *face crumples; he hurries to Johnny, buries his head on Johnny's breast.*]

Remember, do you, onced upon a time? Our first day come? Thought they was like us. Had our first job, and was proud; remember?

TINY: We was proud.

JOHNNY: Come back down the orchard from the yard that afternoon, and . . .

TINY: Us done nothing!

[*Pause.*]

JOHNNY: I wanted to wash my hands. And wash my hands and wash them. I couldn't touch my food no more. . . . It were ham. . . . [*Pause.*] The Blood of the Lamb isn't no good. Not really. . . . [*Pause.*] I think Larry am a smashing bloke. [*Movement.*] Go out on the tar road, miles away. Come down for the fulls, and take him up the yard. . . .

TINY: No. . . .

JOHNNY: And out the tar road, till the storm am done.

TINY: No, Johnny. We got to keep our job.

JOHNNY: And not come back, though. How about that?

TINY: You won't leave me?

JOHNNY: Won't do.

TINY: No room, though. . . .

JOHNNY: Plenty. . . .

TINY: Not for the both on us, and you. . . .

JOHNNY: Then make some! Made up my mind. And not come back this place no more. Never. Imagine. . . .

TINY [*struck*]: Oh. . . .

JOHNNY: Not never again. You with me, Tiny? I want you with me. Couldn't dare it, daresn't, only you'm with me. You'm our cousin, remember? Cousin-german.

TINY: I'm not. Only Hawkes'll rave. He s'll rave, Johnny. Go up in flames, when he discovers. Turns into a dragon after dark, old Gaffer Hawkes; come ravening after us, his chops all slime. . . . [*Pause.*] I'm with you. [*Pause.*] What shall you tell Larry, though?

JOHNNY: Mmm?

TINY: To take him away, you got to tell him a reason. You got to tell him the true reason.

JOHNNY: No –

TINY: What they'm going to do!

JOHNNY: No, else his hands'm filthied with it any road. Knowing a thing and doing it am all the same.

TINY: Won't come with us, Johnny, only you tell him. Won't come away with us for nothing. Won't believe you, any road.

JOHNNY: Must do.

TINY: Won't, Johnny.

JOHNNY: Must believe me. He does do, Tiny. I tell him true. Doesn't I tell him true? He mustn't see.

TINY: How shall you get him to come away, then?

JOHNNY: I'll find a device. In my head.

TINY: Your head'm useless. There'm fuck-all in it. Bloody wheel, we'm on, this orchard. Bloody murders. . . .

JOHNNY [inspired]: I'll tell him a lie! I'll tell him. . . . [Pause. Inspired] Fantastimonious. . . .

[Looks at Tiny. Whispers to him, They share looks. TINY understands; shows anxiety, fear, doubt, resignation. Pause.]

TINY: Poor Shakespeare, though.

JOHNNY: We s'll go up, Tiny. And fetch the trailer down.

[Exeunt JOHNNY and TINY. Enter to crates GINGER, ALBERT, and JIM.]

GINGER: Ain't gone . . . I know . . . he'm hereabout. [Pause.] Never get rid on him. Shall we? Come to plague us: never shake him off. Hang on to us. Blight us. Never shake him free. . . .

[Pause.]

ALBERT: Thought I seen him, then. . . .

GINGER: Won't grow no more. . . .

ALBERT: Isn't that funny? Isn't that strange, Ginger? Up along the end of the row, there. . . .

GINGER: Orchard'll die. . . .

ALBERT: A-tween they trees. . . . Thought I seen him stand a-watching us . . . that white shawl a-flapping on his head . . . they two pits of darkness, where his eyen are. . . .

JIM: Bend over backways, his eyen do go out. . . .

GINGER: I heard him laugh . . . ! He s'll laugh no bloody more . . . ! Shakespeare . . . ? Shakespeare . . . ?

[*Enter to crates* LARRY. *Exeunt* GINGER, *then* ALBERT, *then* JIM. *Voices of* JUMBO *and* TAFFY *heard approaching off.*]

TAFFY: Bloody moral coward, Jumbo. . . .

[LARRY *lights a cigarette, lingers a moment or two during following, then exit. Light unsettled. Enter* JUMBO *and* TAFFY.]

JUMBO: Education, he had, too.

TAFFY: Climbed down backwards out of living.

JUMBO: Kind of different for us blokes, isn't it? I mean: wasn't made for thinking, blokes like us, Taff. Was we? Different for him.

TAFFY: Could have taken his life in his two hands, Paddy.

JUMBO: Couldn't have done no better, us two. My own life, isn't it? If I want to make a ruin of it; bloody shambles? My own?

TAFFY: Got to walk in the world.

JUMBO: Got things to look forward to, I have. Dark evenings, winter-time. Telly; bit of lead in my pencil; bit of money in my drawer, and a Mackeson's by my side. Bloody sight more than most people have in this horrible world. Isn't it?

TAFFY: I'm not complaining. I had no choice in the matter.

JUMBO: Some blokes. Just ain't the kind. For this job. Things between boxes and bloody trees. Sacrifices.

TAFFY: Whole world's a bloody human sacrifice. Slaughter-house, three-quarters of the bloody world, to feed the privileged. Lot of twittering zombies, human beings. Shakespeare was privileged, wasn't he? Working-class, I don't doubt it; but he was privileged. God give him a orb and golden sceptre. And he bloody smashed it. Reckon I didn't get no orb and golden sceptre. . . .

[*Enter* JEFF *with kniving-stone.* JUMBO *smokes through his holder.*]

JUMBO: Left your mark, though, Taff; between here and Merthyr. Bloody art galleries.

TAFFY: Not the same thing, drawing.

[*Pause.*]

JUMBO: I didn't want rid of Shakespeare. Kind of worried me; yeah. But I didn't want rid of him. Only he got to get down to it,

same as the rest of us. Wants to come down a bump in the bloody
world, slum it, get his finger out.

JEFF: Hear, hear.

JUMBO: For instance. Where was Shakespeare during the war? I seen
the Jerries try to kill our cities night upon night. And in the morning, what met your eyes? A bath; hanging out of a window.
Patterns of a staircase on a wall. Fire grates, three floors up; only
there weren't no floors. Seen a kid's hand once; all on its own, in
the dust. And people. That had been people, a minute before. And
Shakespeare; was in the little Emerald Isle. Cowering; in the little
innocent bloody Emerald bloody Holy Isle. . . .

[*Enter to crates, limping,* MRS TREVIS.]

JEFF: Yeah. What about the U-boats? I read about them.

JUMBO: The war was good for his kind. Got themselves set up.
Richest country in bloody Europe. They was neutral. I seen the
Cripples Hospital go up in fire. I was on A.R.P., and I seen the
cripples trying to crawl out the flames on their hands and arms. And
I seen the whole wall of the loony bin torn away like a page. And
the mad people; I seen them dancing inside up and down on their
beds. Think because I'm ignorant, I don't know nothing.

JEFF: I read about the U-boats in Winston Churchill's books.

JUMBO: Think because I don't know no long words, I'm ignorant,
and don't know nothing! And they was shaking hands with them
as was bloody doing it!

TAFFY: Yeah. Clapping their hands and laughing and saying now it's
bloody England's turn. Getting what she asked for after nineteen
twenty bloody three.

JUMBO: Not a care what happened the rest of the world, so long
as their own tiny toothache was bloody avenged. Need a good
bombing in Ireland, that's what I say. Real modern. Bring them up
to date a bit.

JEFF: I brought the kniving-stone. Shall I leave it?

TAFFY: Anywhere. Bloody Irish.

[JEFF *leaves the kniving-stone down by tyres.* MRS TREVIS *now hears
something; we do not.*]

MRS TREVIS: Hey. Listen. Aeryplane.

[*They look off, up.*]

JEFF: Pest Control.

TAFFY: Yeah. Look at the sky, though. Clouds all over.

[*Enter* SPENS, *knives in belt again.*]

JEFF: Going to pour down.

MRS TREVIS: Backways and foreways. Behind the hill, Spens. Over by Ashbold's. . . .

SPENS [*looking*]: You'm right, Mrs Trevis. He am, too.

[MRS TREVIS *clips bucket, studying sky.*]

MRS TREVIS: Isn't half going low.

JEFF: Graze the hill top, bet you a million dollars.

MRS TREVIS: Crash his self.

JEFF: Go up in flames. . . .

MRS TREVIS [*waving to pilot*]: Cooee! Cooee!

JUMBO: Spraying too. . . .

[*Exit* MRS TREVIS, *waving, cooeeing to pilot. Others watch for a moment.*]

TAFFY: Bloody waste of time, though; isn't it? Spraying. Raining heavens hard before you know where you are; and half the fruit is bloody picked, besides.

SPENS: Tell that to Gaffer Hawkes, then! [*Flaring*] What'm the matter with you lot, any road? None on you never seen no aeroplane afore? Eh? Her s'll blast you. Telling you. Blast you. When her come above you, turn your heads away. Mean it, Trousers. Burn your eyen out, else. Insecticide. Germicide. Bloody eyeicide. Unman you! All your hairs'll fall out in under a week. . . .

[*Off, horrified screech from* MRS TREVIS. *Crash of snapping branches; silence; thud on ground; silence; sound of ladder hitting ground, then of pears. On stage,* ALL *freeze. At last, enter, bloody, crawling on all fours,* MRS TREVIS.]

MRS TREVIS [*very feeble*]: Ohhh. . . .

[*Disorder.*]

SPENS: Mrs Trevis!

JUMBO: Ye Gods!

TAFFY: Christ Al-bloody-mighty!

SPENS: Mrs Trevis, you all right?

MRS TREVIS: Ohhh. . . .

JEFF: Broke something, have you?

MRS TREVIS: I'm all wounds ... I don't know. ...

SPENS: Stand up, then.

TAFFY: Here. ...

JUMBO: Easy does it, Mrs Trevis. ...

TAFFY: Easy, Mrs Trevis. ...

MRS TREVIS [*swaying*]: Ohhh. ... Ohhhh. ... That bloody plane.
[*Collapses. They hoist her again.*]
It was that as done it ... watching it, and I didn't look. ... Stepped
back to wave at the pilot. ...

TAFFY: The wages of pride. ...
[MRS TREVIS *gapes in pocket mirror.*]

SPENS: Reckon as you'd better go home, Mrs Trevis. ...

MRS TREVIS: Ohhh ... my face ... ! Ruined ... ! All bruised. ...
Ruined. ...

SPENS: You face'm just the bloody same. ...

JEFF: Have an X-ray, Mrs T., if I was you. Might be internal haemor-
rhage.

SPENS: Run along, Trousers, to Gaffer Hawkes, and tell him to bring
the van over. Take Mrs Trevis down to Bromsgrove.

JEFF: Where s'll I find him?

SPENS: Look for him!

MRS TREVIS: Martyrdom, this place. ...

SPENS: Tell him as Mrs Trevis'm fallen down a tree. Think she may
have broken some'at. ...
[*Exit* JEFF.]

MRS TREVIS: Be a saint soon. Penny a peep at the bleeding wonder. ...

TAFFY: Manage it as far as the barn, Mrs Trevis?
[TAFFY *and* JUMBO *haul her off.*]

MRS TREVIS: Oh. Where's my feet gone? My feet don't seem on the
end of my legs no more. My legs go through. The ground is going
up and down. ...

JUMBO: O.K., Mrs Trevis. We got you.

MRS TREVIS: Oh! Some'at went inside me, Jumbo. I heard some'at
go. ...

JUMBO: Reckon as Shakespeare left his mark on this orchard many a
long day. ...

[*Enter from other direction to that of Mrs Trevis's tree,* JIM *and* ALBERT, *who see what has happened.* SPENS *watches after exit; sees Jim and Albert.*]

SPENS: Better try, Jim, and get they tops down as Mrs Trevis didn't manage.

JIM: Don't like it when it'm raining, Spens. Do go all down your arms. No protection. Lift up your hands to pick fruit off, and rain do go all down your arms.

SPENS: One more bucket, Jim. Albert. One.

JIM: Why do we have to work in the rain, then, Spens? Why'm we kept at it when the rain am falling?

SPENS: Promise you. Shan't get no more picking now.

JIM: Pick up the fruit that fell in the night, and the wet grass do cut your hands a million times over. A million tiny times. Look at them, Spens. . . . [*Thrusts his hands before Spens' face*] Look! Ha'n't got no hands. Not a man's hands. Am they?

[SPENS *looks at them; then at Jim.* JIM *rather ashamedly drops hands. Enter* GINGER, *without bucket.* SPENS *sees him.*]

SPENS: Hello, Ginger. . . . [SPENS *takes knives out of belt.*]

GINGER: Spens.

[SPENS *gives Ginger knives.* JIM *watches.* GINGER *takes knives.*]
Trousers bring up the stone, did he?

[SPENS *gives him kniving-stone; looks up at sky; glances at* GINGER, *who meets his glance; exit.*

Slowly, at first, GINGER *begins to sharpen knives.* JIM *and* ALBERT *watch.*

First knife sharpened. GINGER *gives this to Albert.* ALBERT *takes, tries blade on finger; puts knife through belt; moves off. . . .*

Enter LARRY, *meeting Albert at exit. They pause, resume.* ALBERT *exit.* LARRY *comes to crates.* GINGER *aware of new presence.* JIM *unaffected.* LARRY *senses something.*

Second knife sharpened. GINGER *gives this to Jim.* JIM *takes, tries blade on finger, breathes in tensely, audibly; laughs a little; then sees* LARRY *watching and, quickly, with a glance at Ginger, which* GINGER *meets, shafts knife through belt, and exit quickly towards Mrs Trevis's tree, hoisting bucket. . . .*

Third knife sharpened. LARRY *replaces tarpaulin. . . .*]

GINGER: Larry....

[LARRY *comes down to Ginger.* GINGER *holds knife to Larry.*]

Feel that....

[LARRY *feels blade. It cuts him. Disturbed,* LARRY *returns knife.* GINGER *expressionless, takes it.* LARRY *sucks at finger.* GINGER *takes up tyre, slashes at it, with difficulty at first, becoming panicky, frenzied, until he has the rubber slashed. Pause.*]

Got a knife, have you?

[LARRY *nods no.* GINGER, *expressionless, puts knife in belt. Tractor approaches, off.*]

Trousers has....

[*Exit* GINGER. LARRY *watches. Tractor stops. Engine silent. Voices of* JOHNNY *and* TINY *off.* LARRY *seems not to hear at first.*]

TINY [*off*]: No, Johnny ... No ... There'm not enough room for him....

[*Enter* JOHNNY. LARRY *hears.* TINY *follows.*]

Them boxes ... we got to get them finished. I s'll have pains in my bones all winter long if I stay out in the rain.... There'm not enough room for him, any road....

JOHNNY [*embarrassed but urgent*]: Larry....

TINY: Trailer'm all piled high with Worcesters from across the way ... [*Sets to, hauling off crates.*]

JOHNNY: Come with us, Larry. We'm going. Come away....

TINY: Let's hurry, Johnny.... Orchard am full on them, now.... [TINY *exit with crate.*]

JOHNNY: You daft sod, Larry. You bloody daft sod! Don't know damn-all, you college blokes. Thinks as there'm nothing a-going to happen to you! Don't you!

[*Pushes him.* LARRY *makes to exit.*]

Listen to us!

[*Re-enter* TINY.]

TINY: Them boxes. They'm your responsibility. Can't leave them in the rain. The fruit won't keep....

JOHNNY: The aeroplane am come. Was part on this, onced upon a time. Last year. The year afore. When wasn't we?

TINY [*taking second crate off*]: Leave him, Johnny....

JOHNNY: Was on the wheel, them killings. Not never again. I say so. Have blood on my hands no more.... Larry, Larry, Larry, come away. We s'll take you. Keep you. Come away....

[TINY *re-enters, shuddering.*]

TINY: Ohhh.... It'm raining now.... I'll have my pains.... Johnny, hurry up and go.... I hear the swishing in the long grass.... Let's hurry up and go....

JOHNNY [*turning on Tiny*]: Thought you was with me....

TINY: I am with you....

JOHNNY: Thought you was with *me*....

TINY: Johnny, can't we go...?

HAWKES [*off, distant*]: Spens!!

GINGER
ALBERT } [*Off, severally distant, not quite together*]: Spens!
JIM

[TINY *takes off a third box.*]

LARRY: Shakespeare... Where's he? Where has he gone? Have you seen him? Haven't you seen him? Why hasn't he come back? Was he afraid?

JOHNNY [*bleak*]: I don't know about Shakespeare. He stirred them up. And now...

LARRY: Now....?

[JOHNNY *snatches up hayfork, aims it at Larry's face.*]

JOHNNY: What the hell am a hayfork doing in a orchard?

LARRY [*paralysed*]: It's something in your head. It's all something inside your head....

[TINY *has entered meanwhile.* JOHNNY *sees him, rushes to seize him.*]

JOHNNY: Show you... Larry....

TINY: Johnny, no....

JOHNNY [*dragging Tiny to Larry*]: See this... Larry... [*shows Tiny's watch.*]

TINY: No, Johnny; leave me go....

JOHNNY: Whose do you think this was! Think Tiny bought it, do you...?

TINY [*struggling*]: Them boxes....

JOHNNY: Look at it, Larry. Feast your eyes....

TINY: It'm my watch, Johnny. Mine....

JOHNNY: Whose were it, though? [*Shaking Tiny violently*] Describe to Larry whose it were! His face! And how you come by it. Describe!

TINY: You'm hurting me. . . .

[*Struggles free.* JOHNNY *relaxes.*]

Shame to think on it. Watch, rotting. Waste, else.

[*Pause.* TINY *exit. Aeroplane is heard.*]

JOHNNY: Spraying. That'm poison. . . . Rains'll wash it, though. . . .

[LARRY *deliberately takes off his bucket slowly.* JOHNNY *sees. Though this is what he has come to achieve, he suddenly seems incurious.*]

Coming with us, am you?

[*Pause.* LARRY *inscrutable.*]

LARRY [*at last*]: What would they do to you? When they found out you'd taken their victim away? What would they do to you then?

JOHNNY [*catching a menace in Larry's tone: uneasy*]: I won't come back no more.

LARRY: Where will you go?

JOHNNY: Out the tar road. Miles away.

[LARRY *approaches Johnny.*]

LARRY: Why do you want to make me afraid? Of something that isn't real? Something only inside your head? It's all some dream inside your head . . . !

JOHNNY: Larry, Larry, Larry, come away. . . .

LARRY: I'm not –

JOHNNY: Larry –

LARRY: Not with you –

JOHNNY: Why?

LARRY: Mad!

[*Pause.* LARRY *is struggling in himself.* JOHNNY *comes to him; folds his arms around him protectively.* LARRY *relaxes a moment, begins to enjoy the embrace, then with a violent gesture of repudiation and repugnance, thrusts him away, and makes to exit, trying to find words with which to answer Johnny's speech.*]

JOHNNY [*destroyed*]: Don't think I care what happens to you. One wheel I amn't on, any road. You. You. Larry Lewis. It'm only a wonder after all you'm anything. Don't you think so? You needn't have been. Not like the Word. Not like the sun and moon. Them are eternal. You just come. A father and mother met together; and you just come. Didn't know what you s'd look like, did they?

[LARRY *exit.* JOHNNY *howls after him. Pause. Enter* TINY.]

TINY: Couldn't you have told no better lie?

[*Pause.* JOHNNY, *kicking shed violently, exit.* TINY *follows. Enter, silent, to crates,* GINGER, ALBERT, *and* JIM, *with buckets. Long silence. Enter* JUMBO, TAFFY, *clothed against rain.*]

JUMBO: Hawkes give us a job. Down the farmhouse. Painting bloody beams.

[*Pause.* GINGER, ALBERT, *and* JIM, *in silence, don oilskins sit on ground, surround themselves with tyres, unaffected by storm which now begins. Enter* JEFF. JUMBO *and* TAFFY *hover, uneasy, showing discomfort in squalls and rain.* JEFF *between these states, but soon attains the stillness of the three with knives; using his own, a flick-knife, on tyres. Enter, limping, exhausted, bent,* ROCHE.]

JEFF: Look what's come.

JUMBO: Hello, Shakespeare.

JEFF: You come to help us?

[ROCHE *puts down bag. Still wears head-cloth and glasses.*]

Making your farewell appearance, Shakespeare?

JUMBO: Likes the company. Kind of congenial.

TAFFY: Audience, more like.

JUMBO: Where you been, then, Shakespeare? Having a little snooze?

ROCHE: I had a pure, clear dream. That I went walking along the lanes about this place. And I saw a field. There was young men in it, the likes of you. And I seen a man there. I thought it was myself. So in I went. The young men there, they were terrible anxious. For they were not sure, don't you see, not sure at all, whether or not they were supposed to pick the pears there. So I told them they were to pick the pears, and hurry, using the wicker boxes that were lying around them in untidy piles. . . . [*Pause.*] That was a strange dream. . . .

JEFF: Yeah, Shakespeare. Strange of you to dream that dream.

JUMBO: Mrs Trevis'm gone down to have an X-ray, Shakespeare. Fell off that tree you was picking from, and broke something. . . .

ROCHE: Is that so?

JUMBO: Serious.

ROCHE: Broke a bone, is it?

JUMBO: Several.

ROCHE: Oh. . . . It will take her an illimitable time to heal, and her in a plaster cast up to the neck of her a year or more. Especially, don't you know, some of them higher-class bones? A tendon, for instance; or a femur. . . .

TAFFY: Reckon some people are afraid to climb ladders, Jumbo. . . .
  [*Pause.* ROCHE *looks round for invitation to join work. None comes.*]

ROCHE: Ah. Quite so. Quite so; it would take more than the threats of a foreman the like of that one to get me gone. Wrongly dismissed, I said to him. Wrongly dismissed. . . .

JEFF: Wrongfully dismissed. . . .

ROCHE: So I come back, now, to do my daily dozen on them tyres. . . . [*Pause.*] Could I be helping youse at all with them tyres? [*Pause.*] Would it be in order, at all, for me to be assisting you?
  [ROCHE *kneels, touches Albert's tyres.*]

ALBERT: Out on it.

ROCHE: I'll just be . . .

JUMBO [*uneasy, warning*]: Shakespeare. . . .
  [*Disturbed pause.* ROCHE *looks to Jumbo and Taffy; finds only embarrassment, grim hardness on their faces. Moves towards Ginger.*]

ROCHE: Just assist youse in the small way I have. . . .

GINGER Heard us, didn't you?
  [ROCHE, *rudely shocked, retreats.*]

ROCHE: To take the bare look off me . . . Standing here, and youse working; and me with my two arms the one length . . . I have two arms!
  [JEFF *sniggers.*]
  The same as any one of you!

JEFF: Want to do something for us, Shakespeare? Do us a favour? [*Pause.*] Turn into a scab, and drop off.
  [*On a decision,* ROCHE *takes bag, lifts out teapot, begins to pack away as many pears as he can.*]

JUMBO: Going home?

ROCHE: The moment I draw my wage, I'll be away from this. Into the town.

JIM: Going to Brummagem, Shakespeare?

ROCHE: I'll not stay here, now that youse none of youse need me any more. . . . [*Struggles to fit last pear in.*]

JUMBO: You seen them working in them factories all day? All pale?

TAFFY: Yeah, they're all bent over, Paddy. The people in Birmingham are all bent over, from going up and down steep hills all bloody day.

[ROCHE *fits in last pear; struggles to pack teapot.*]

Short of teachers, though.

ROCHE: Ay. They are.

JUMBO: What could you teach, Shakespeare? Ballet dancing?

ROCHE: I taught in my time. Many things. For instance the Gaelic. The language of the kings. . . .

JEFF: Yeah. I speak that fluent.

ROCHE: You see? Youse didn't know that. I taught the Gaelic at the Ring. The Ring, in the county Waterford; where they have a Gaelic summer school. Every verb in the Gaelic tongue has the dual system of stems. One for the asseverative moods, and a separate stem for the oblique. You see, I have the photographic memory.

JEFF: Get a pair of socks, first –

TAFFY: Short of teachers, I said; not short of tramps.

[*Pause.* ROCHE *halted.* JUMBO *is laughing to himself, shaking his head, muttering 'Shakespeare' over and over to himself. Laughter grows, spreading.*]

ROCHE: Is the city too good for me, then? Is it? I tell you! It's writing a book I am. A book will explode in the face of all the earth! I am a Master of Arts.

[*More laughter.*]

I'll be a bricklayer, if need be! Ay. There must be thousands of houses building in Birmingham there; after the great war they had.

JUMBO: They?

[ROCHE *crams teapot on top of pears, leaves bag unclosed.*]

ROCHE: The moment the foreman comes, I'll be away.

JUMBO [*shaking Roche roughly by the shoulder*]: Plenty of Brummies out of jobs. Without looking for no Irish bastards to cater for.

Shoved yourselves off, didn't you? Out to bloody sea? Got your new Jerusalem? Crawl bloody home, then, to your own little emerald bog, and work there. Coming over here, with your bloody tuberculosis and venereal disease.

TAFFY: Yeah. You know something, Paddy? One prostitute in ten on the streets of this country comes from Southern Ireland. One in ten.

ROCHE: It was the English brought prostitution to Ireland in the first place.

TAFFY: And when you go over there, what do you see? Bloody newspapers, with articles and speeches by parish priests and cardinals, addressed to young Irish virginals, giving them advice on how to keep themselves pure and spotless when they come over here, to the land of sin and crime.

ROCHE: Ah, the English are a terrible high-sexed race. The lubricity of them, it's positively gi-normous.

TAFFY: Over here! What happens you? What's rotten in your young ones, that's what I want to know; turn into vermin no sooner than leave the holy island of saints and scholars. What's rotten in you?

ROCHE: I'd be taking no jobs from none of you. Seeing youse are so entitled. I'd not deprive you. I'll be away from this. Some other place. Your great, rotten, putrefying city. I seen you; crawling into your city in the morning time; like the maggots and grubs squirming and squeezing in and out of a side of rotten meat in a bin of garbage and the bin burning! A city of sin, thon! A city of terrible perversion and evil and sin. I need no telling; I need only be looking at the filth in their eyes. Ay! And the country around its edge is rightly named. The Black. The sphincter of the earth! [ROCHE *shakes with fury.*]

JEFF: Don't half look funny when you'm cross, Shakespeare.

[ROCHE *turns towards him.*]

Got no eyes ... No eyes, Shakespeare.... [JEFF *clutches knife, worried.*] Look stupid ... Look how horrible his face is, Ginge. Look how his flesh am all rotten. All diseased. Got leprosy, Shakespeare?

[ROCHE *stands before him, angry, powerless. Now, for first time, steady drone of helicopter, swooping, zooming; but not seeming to approach.*

Suddenly JEFF *whips off head-cloth.*]

ROCHE: Give me!

[JEFF *teases him as* ROCHE *impotently chases him.*]

My cloth! My head-cloth! The damp will destroy my head! I'll have my headache pains all over again. . . .

[JEFF *skites it off stage.*]

JEFF: Wind took it, Shakespeare.

[*Whips off Roche's glasses.*]

ROCHE [*in panic*]: My eyeglasses . . . give me!

[JEFF *treads on them; they are destroyed.*]

JEFF: Busted.

[ROCHE *looks round at workers; they are expressionless, slashing as before. Fear crosses his heart. He turns to Jumbo and Taffy.*]

JUMBO: Let's wander, Taff.

TAFFY: Yeah. Let's go.

JUMBO: Got a job, Taff. Haven't we?

TAFFY: Yeah. Got to hurry.

[ROCHE *clutches his bag.*]

Lot of work to do, Pat. Sorry.

ROCHE: Jumbo. . . .

JUMBO: Painting beams, Taff.

TAFFY: Yeah. Fast falls the eventide.

[TAFFY *and* JUMBO *make to go.* ROCHE *gapes at them, stupefied.*] Don't cross them, Paddy. That's all I say. You'll be all right. Don't you worry.

JUMBO [*motioning*]: Taff. . . .

TAFFY: Only don't cross them, that's all I say. . . .

ROCHE: Jumbo. Stay with me.

[*They are gone.*]

Welshman. . . . [*Pause.* ROCHE *turns to workers with sudden alarm, first touch of propitiation*] I'll be away from this, the moment I draw my wage. I'll be out from this, the moment I've drawn my wage and my insurance card. Youse are not bad men. Only a wee bit rough.

[*Enter* SPENS, *in army groundsheet, gumboots, to crates;* ROCHE *sees, marshals himself to approach. Enter* JOHNNY, *numbed.*]

SPENS: Hello, Hobnails. About bloody time, and all. [*Glances towards tractor.*] Bit on a load on her, this time, haven't you?

[*Enter* TINY *huddling in long black macintosh.*]

JOHNNY: Worcesters, Spens. From across the road.

TINY [*numbed, too*]: Too many. They s'll all fall down and kill me.

[TINY *and* JOHNNY *start to clear loaded crates.* SPENS *takes out book, looks round; sees Roche, but shows nothing; turns to others.*]

GINGER: Spens.

ALBERT: Spens.

JIM: Spens.

JEFF: Spens.

[SPENS *nods curt recognition, others continue work.* SPENS *looks at Roche again; as before; bends over book, protects his scribbling from rain.*]

ROCHE: Mr Foreman. . . .

[*No response.*]

Mr Foreman, sir. . . .

SPENS: Hear that, Ginge? Foreman, he bloody call me.

ROCHE: Concerning the small matter of my wage. . . .

SPENS: Hear that, Jim? Wage.

ROCHE: I'll be collecting. . .

[SPENS *back to his book. Pause.*]

I'll be collecting my wage. And then I'll be away, Mr Foreman. . . .

SPENS: Rope them over, will you, Hobnails?

[JOHNNY *and* TINY *go on and off with crates; say nothing.*]

ROCHE: Now that youse are all of a mind to dispense with my services, I'll be away. I'm in agreement with youse now!

[SPENS *crosses to where he can watch loading.*]

I'll be collecting my wage! I'll be content with the half my wage. My morning's wage. I'll be contented with that, don't you see, as it was after the morning you sacked me. . . .

[*All* SPENS' *attention on loading.*]

But with less than that, I'll not. . . .

SPENS: Stacking them six high, am you, Hobnails?

JOHNNY: Five. Six in the middle.

TINY: They s'll all fall down. And kill me.

ROCHE: For it was a morning's work I done. To the best of my ability, it was a morning's work I done.

SPENS: Give him his bloody wage slip, Hobnails. Did and all. Lunchtime. And what did he do with it? Eh? Screwed it up and throwed it at me.

ROCHE: I said it was more than the wag-at-the-wall antics of a foreman the like of you it would take to get me gone. You re-engaged me!

SPENS: After you did argue. What for you want it now, then?

ROCHE: I changed my mind.

SPENS: Well, I bloody changed mine! Scarpered, didn't you? Didn't have no pay slip, when you bloody scarpered; what for, then, you bloody want one now?

ROCHE: But I changed my mind!

SPENS [*to Roche*]: Shan't listen to you no more. Shakespeare. Nor speak to you. To my way of reckoning, you'm a dead man. Kick me up the crutch with my own bloody mercy....

[*Enter meanwhile* HAWKES *and* GLORIA, *whom* SPENS *now sees.* SPENS *from now on ignores Roche.*]

GLORIA: That man's a dead loss, Daddy. You'll have to write him off.

ROCHE [*clutching at Spens' sleeve*]: Mr Foreman....

[GLORIA *spies pears in his bag.*]

GLORIA: And what are those? Ours? [*Takes out a pear*] Are they? You're paid to pick our pears, not paid to steal them.

ROCHE [*still at Spens' sleeve*]: My halfday's wage. Even the half a dollar of it, only, would be enough.

GLORIA: And listen to me when I speak. Don't you know who I am? [*Tips bag; scatters possessions on ground.* ROCHE *bends to retrieve razor, etc., from rain.*]

ROCHE: Mr Hawkes, sir ... the half a dollar of it, only, would suffice ... Mr Hawkes, sir.... [*Goes to Hawkes, who is inspecting slashed tyres.*] Mr Hawkes, sir! If you please ... I'll be away from you, Mr Hawkes, and not trouble you with worrying about my wage.... But my card ... sir ... my Insurance Card ... I'll be needing that wherever I go. Money I could dispense with. But my Insurance Card, Mr Hawkes, sir; and on it my name.... You'll be giving me my card, Mr Hawkes ... ? A moment only of your time, it will occupy. . . . I can't go out into the world with no address. My wage I'll do without. But my card. . . .

HAWKES: Come along, Gloria.

ROCHE [*horror*]: Mr Hawkes!

[*Exeunt* HAWKES *and* GLORIA *with rubber.* ROCHE *follows to exit.*] Mr Hawkes. . . !

SPENS: See you, then, Hobnails. Up the yard. . . .

[*Exit* SPENS *opposite.* ROCHE *turns, desperate; trails him.*]

ROCHE: Mr Foreman. . . ! [*Pause.* ROCHE *turns to the four at their tyres. They slash grimly; a little blood on their wrists.*] Ah. The Children of Israel was in slavery and bondage, onced upon a time. In the land of Egypt, far away. Did none of youse never hear that tale? Constructing bricks, they were. Labouring away at the bricks, the livelong day. For the great pyramids they did have in Egypt in those times. . . .

[*Suddenly helicopter sounds much nearer, swooping and zooming, though not approaching meanwhile.*]

And they done something. They done . . . something. What it was they done, I don't remember rightly. But they done something, don't you see? Oh, I disremember. I disremember what it was they done. It's a terrible affliction, the defective memory. It's like a sieve. I can mind nothing at all from one minute's end to the next. But they done something! They done some misdemeaniour, don't you see? And the Pharaoh . . . The Pharoah of Egypt . . . A tale of bricks! That's what it was! A tale of bricks. . . !

[*Sudden attention on him from the four at tyres.* ROCHE *caught. Pause.*]

What for are youse . . . What for are youse looking at me with that . . . ?

[*Silent,* JEFF *makes obscene gesture with knife. Enter* JOHNNY *for last crate.*]

Hobnails. Take me . . . to the gate. As you done. . . .

[JOHNNY *shakes his head helplessly.*]

To the road . . . Hobnails. . . .

[JOHNNY, *taking crate off, pauses, turns to look at Roche.* GINGER *is watching Johnny.* JOHNNY *nods to Roche.*]

[*Relief*] Ah . . . I'll not keep you. . . .

[ROCHE *kneels to retrieve possessions.* GINGER *rises, strides across to Johnny, kicking possessions away from Roche's reach.* ROCHE *stands.* GINGER *stabs his knife twice into crate which* JOHNNY *is holding.*]

GINGER: Carter ... Carter. That'm a name they bloody give you. Isn't it? I shall give you a name, shall I? Come into the world without no asking. I s'll give you a name! You s'll go back. For ever. Utter a word, and you s'll go back! No one believes you, no more. And we s'll have you back inside. And you s'll grow old inside, till you'm a old, old man. Not never marry. Not never have no kinder. And you s'll know why, one day. Which am your judgement for coming into the world with out no asking. We s'll have you back in there, Hobnails!

[JOHNNY *seems unthreatened;* TINY *appears, takes crate;* JOHNNY *stretches out hand to Roche.* ALBERT, JIM, *and* JEFF *rise, laying tyres aside, knives in hand but not wielded.* JOHNNY *wavers, drops hand.*]

JOHNNY: Oh, Shakespeare ... [*Torn, helpless, retreats.* JOHNNY *to all*] But Jesus loves me. He loves us all ... [*Turns.*]

[*Exit.* TINY *puts his tongue out at them, exit quickly. Tractor revs up; goes.* GINGER, JIM, ALBERT, *and* JEFF *turn to Roche, their faces blank, transformed and wild.* ROCHE *retreats, but they surround him. Tractor is gone. Helicopter suddenly very near.* ROCHE *gropes with his arms outstretched, trying to break through the circle.*]

ROCHE: Youse will let me go, you. .... Youse will let me go, now.

[*Rises, backs – they converge on him. Thin trails of spray-mist creep on to stage as plane zooms near by.*]

I'll give you my teapot ... Fine aloominum ... My razor, even ... of Sheffield steel. .... If I had more, I'd ... Youse will let me go, now; won't you. .... Youse will let me go. ....

[*They close in; hold him. More mist. Helicopter screams down overhead.*]

Don't bend me ... !

[*Terrible cry from* ROCHE. *Abnormal light.* ROCHE *bent back like a hoop, head front, face slashed.* ROCHE'S *hands, praying, torn from each other by* ALBERT *and* JIM, *thrust against ground, pinned to ground beneath their feet.* JEFF, *suddenly paralysed, hauled forward by* GINGER *who grabs his wrists, thrusts them together, with flick-knife aimed downward. Spray spills over stage in a filmy mist.*

ALBERT *and* JIM *haul Jeff's arms down. Knife plunges.* JEFF *groans.*
GINGER *hauls his wrists down twice more; knife with them each time,
at breast, and heart.* JEFF *is moaning . . . he has slashed on Roche's
chest the form of a cross . . .* ROCHE *falls, is still.*
Spray ceases, plane recedes.
GINGER *thrusts Jeff from them. He lurches away, sobbing; knife falls
to ground. . . .*
GINGER *plunges hayfork into ground about body's neck, hauls on
its handle to crush neck.* ALBERT *and* JIM *watch from hayfork to
neck. Pause. . . .*]

GINGER: Quickly –

[*They gather round head with their knives. They cut it away.* JEFF
*sees, thrusts hands before his eyes; hands are stained; he is going to
cry out. . . .*
Something lies, stretched and scarlet, on ground. JEFF's *voice will not
come. . . .*
GINGER *crawls forward, rolling head; then lies still, his head rested by
Roche's head.* JIM *touches head vaguely with two fingers, strokes it.*
Pause.
Suddenly JEFF's *voice begins to return as he whimpers hoarsely.* JIM
is at him in a flash, hand over mouth. JEFF *struggles.* GINGER *and*
ALBERT *motionless.*]

JEFF: Unwish this . . . I haven't come here . . . I haven't come. . . . It'm
morning. And I'm going to come here. And I won't. . . .

ALBERT: Spens got your name. . . .

JEFF: No!

[*Pause.*]

I give him a false name. . . . Honest, I done. . . .

ALBERT: Tell you, we can, telling a lie. . . . Say so much as a
word, too, Trousers: come for you. . . . Go where Hobnails
gone. . . .

[JEFF *breaks free,* JIM *leaves him.* ALBERT *captures him.*]

There were no Irishman come this day!

[*Pause.*]

Where you live, then, Trousers?

JEFF: I tell you the truth. I live in Headless Cross. Other side of
Redditch. Church with the hollow spire. . . .

[ALBERT *shows him bloodied knife and stained oilcloth, lets him go.* JEFF *hurries off.*]

ALBERT: Where are you, Ginge?

GINGER: I be here, Albert.

[*Pause.*]

ALBERT: Let's get him in his grave.

[*With great respect, they wrap corpse and head in tarpaulin; slowly trail shrouded figure off towards hole off stage. With method and discreet deference, they clear stage of all Roche's possessions.* JIM *takes three knives, cleans on a pear;* JEFF's *knife forgotten; three knives put in* JIM's *belt. Hayfork left prong-fixed centre stage.*]

GINGER: What'm the time, Jim?

JIM: Top of this bloody pear-tree, Jumbo!

[*They laugh softly, remembering.* ALBERT *hands few remaining rubbers and tyres to Ginger.*]

ALBERT: Take up these tyres to Mr Hawkes.

[*Exit* GINGER.]

[*To Jim*] Jim. Dusthouse.

[JIM *gesturing to knives in belt, exit.* ALBERT *takes off ladder. All trace of Roche is gone. Enter, slinking, whispering,* TAFFY *and* JUMBO. *They bear two enormous signboards:* HAWKES OF BROMSGROVE SENDS FRUITS TO ALL PARTS OF THE COUNTRY. *These they carry across stage.*]

JUMBO: None of our business, was it, Taff?

TAFFY: Didn't see nothing, Jumbo.

JUMBO: Painting these signs.

TAFFY: Their affair.

[*Exeunt* JUMBO *and* TAFFY. *Light turns richer, into glow of sunset. Enter* JOHNNY, *shivering, wandering in his mind.*]

JOHNNY: Shakespeare . . . What shall I tell your mom and dad . . . ? On the Day of Judgement. Only, I tried my hardest. . . . Would have saved you, only it'm what they s'll do to us if I cross them, Shakespeare. . . . Send me back inside. . . . For ever. . . . Do that to us if I cross them, Shakespeare. . . . Do you hear me? Do you understand? [*A slight wind blows.*] I tried to save Larry from the witness on it; and I did do. . . . Only I lost him. 'count of I had to lie to him to make him run away. . . . And I liked him, any road.

I liked him more than you.... Only, I lost him.... He don't like me.... Do you understand? Show us, will you, if us'm forgiven...? If you do...?

[*Enter* LARRY, *dressed to go home. Sees Johnny, looks at him.* JOHNNY *becomes aware of his presence, moves away, embarrassed.*]

LARRY: I'm sorry. What I said. I am.

JOHNNY: What did you say? I don't remember.

LARRY: Forget. The best thing I ever had, I'd give it to you; because I know your hands would hold it carefully, you'd respect it, because it had been mine....

JOHNNY: Bungled their murder. Victim escaped....

[LARRY *suspects this is not true.*]

[*Bitter*] I'm just the same as them.

LARRY: I said what I said because you frightened me.

JOHNNY: Why? Why did I frighten you, Larry?

LARRY: When you touched me, you frightened me.

[*They approach each other.*]

I want you to know that –

JOHNNY [*not meaning it*]: I forgotten.... [*Meaning it*] No, really. [*Convincing*] I have. [*Pause.*] Warned you. And you scarpered.

[*Enter* TINY *terrified.*]

TINY: Johnny ... Johnny, gaffer'm roaring down the lane.... 'count of them apples for South Africa! We got to go and weigh them all again.... I'm sorry, Johnny....

JOHNNY: Blimey, Tiny. We s'll never get home!

TINY: In a awful rage. Gaffer. Awful rage. Seen him leaping they ditches, chewing his fingers like they was fish and chips....

[*Voice of* HAWKES, *terrible, off.*]

HAWKES: SPENS!

JOHNNY: Get weaving, then. You heard us, Tiny.

TINY: Don't like to leave you, Johnny, face his mercy. [TINY *still hesitates.*]

JOHNNY: Blimey, Tiny, dead lice am falling off you: get a move on!

TINY: Don't do...

[JOHNNY *dives at him, uttering strange frightening cry.* TINY, *with a tiny bleat of terror, is gone. Pause.*]

LARRY: Johnny. [*Takes fountain pen out of inner breast pocket.*] I'll give
you this. For a present.

JOHNNY: What am it?

LARRY: Fountain pen.

JOHNNY: Is them the kind writes for a long time without no ink?

LARRY: Here. . . .

[JOHNNY *hesitates to touch.*]

No. No. Hold it. . . .

[JOHNNY *takes pen, richly pleased.*]

Pocket?

[JOHNNY *proudly feels pen.*]

JOHNNY: Feel in my bones, in my shoulders, my wrists, like it were
the light of the moon. . . . Oh, it'm wondrous . . . I want to break
it, and then weep me eyes out for not having it no more. . . .

[*Looks at Larry now with some air of proprietorship. Puts pen in
inside pocket.* LARRY *is looking down at his hands.*]

Play the piano, do you?

[*Larry's hands despair him.*]

Know how to make them come up purple? Lupins? Plant copper
nails in, in the autumn. Got gardens there, Black Country, where
you and I come from. . . .

[*Enter, hobbling, mostly hidden behind plasters and bandages,* MRS
TREVIS.]

MRS TREVIS: Spens?

[*Enter, without cape, but with institution jacket on his arm,* HAWKES.]

HAWKES: Carter!

JOHNNY: Sir!

HAWKES: Made a wondrous cock-up, this time; haven't you? I s'd
send you up there, now, and have you weighing them again; all
night. Have you weighing all they boxes till the squeak of dawn.
By rights. But I can't. 'count of your warden'm come for you.

JOHNNY: No. No. . . .

HAWKES: Thought as maybe you s'd be getting lost in the storm. Or
as perhaps you was frightened of thunder. Never know with you
types. Go bonkers, sometimes, your kind, warden was telling me.
Interesting man, warden at the colony. Risk to hire you, he says . . .

JOHNNY: I'm not going back there, Mr Hawkes. . . .

HAWKES: So he'm very kindly come to fetch you home. In his van.

JOHNNY: Tell him I don't need. Tell him, Mr Hawkes, I work for you good . . . [JOHNNY *makes a show of being busy.*] Shouldn't have put us in there to begin with. I had no father. She were ashamed. . . .

HAWKES: If I hears another word from you, Carter. . . .

JOHNNY: All them people. The singing keep me awake. Tell him I run away. . . .

[HAWKES, *struggling, puts on jacket.*]

HAWKES: Warning you. If I hears another word from you, I s'll not ask for you no more. You s'll be in there for ever, Hobnails. You'm lucky. Don't seem to realize. It'm most rare, the way I hire you from the colony, Hobnails. . . .

JOHNNY: No!

HAWKES: Letting you free, twelve hours a day. Working for us. With nice companions. Most rare. Most unique. There. All wrapped up in your swaddling clothes. Reckon, though, as no wise men s'll come to give their gifts to you. . . .

[JOHNNY's *desperation and shame turn to radiance, defiance, pride.*]

JOHNNY: He has done, though.

HAWKES: I don't understand you, Hobnails.

JOHNNY: You might be my father. Any on you. Don't you think so?

HAWKES: Drop dead.

[*Exit* JOHNNY. *Enter* SPENS.]

SPENS: Ah. Mr Hawkes.

HAWKES: What's happened to everybody, Spens? Where's everybody gone?

SPENS: I don't know.

HAWKES: Don't know?

SPENS: Reckon, Mr Hawkes, as things'm gone and got a bit out of hand. . . .

HAWKES: Oh, it's terrible, Spens. You've no idea. And now my Gloria's taken to her bed with a cold. I don't know where to turn. I don't know which dilemma to attend to first. But a cold! Isn't that awful, Spens? But she will insist on helping out with the men. . . .

SPENS: I s'd get they couplings seen to, Mr Hawkes, afore some'at happens as we s'll all be sorry for.

HAWKES [*despair*]: Ohhhh . . . ! Ohhhh . . . ! I'm going home. I'm very worried about my Gloria. I'm very worried about my Gloria indeed. You understand. I must attend to her. Must give her preference. Yes. That's it. Give Gloria preference. . . . [*Exit.*]
[*Pause.*]

MRS TREVIS: Got to have the week off, Spens. Doctor says so. Haven't broke nothing. Got to have the week off, though, all the same. [*Pause.*] Pity about Hobnails.

SPENS: Ah. Homo-bloody-maniac, they calls them blokes, or something.

MRS TREVIS: Still. It all helps keep the birthrate down.

SPENS: Oh, he's a nice bloke, Mrs Trevis.

MRS TREVIS: See you.
[MRS TREVIS *hobbles off. Horn heard off. Light is fading. Enter gradually* JUMBO, TAFFY, GINGER, ALBERT, *and* JIM, *caps on, bags slung. They take off their boots, don shoes meanwhile.*]

JUMBO: Nice, going home in the evenings, Taff.

TAFFY: Yeah. Kind of free.

JUMBO: Calm.

TAFFY: Yeah.
[*Cigarettes are being lit.* SPENS *takes out his book.*]
World's all yours, when the horn goes. Night comes. . . . See you. . . .

JUMBO: See you. . . .
[GINGER, ALBERT, JIM, SPENS, *give murmured replies. Exeunt* JUMBO *and* TAFFY. *Two bicycle bells. Silence.*]

SPENS [*to Larry*]: Got you down, have I?

LARRY: I don't think so.

SPENS: Got one on you down. Remember. Two on you come, this morning. Got the one on you down. Must have forgot the other, somehow. [*Finds entry.*] Ah. Fish. Trousers, that were. Horrible name. Me all over. Only two new workers to look after, and I forgets to enter one of them. Pay packets'd suffer.
[LARRY *frozen.*]
What they call you, then, kid? Leominster, were it?

LARRY: Lewis.

SPENS: Ah. Lewis. Remember, now. Has to know what to call you. Calls you anything, though, when I gets going. That so, Jim?

JIM: Say that again.

SPENS: Any bloody thing. [*Writes.*]

ALBERT: How you come, then, this morning, Jim? You walk it?

JIM: Left bike up the barn.... [*Exit.*]

　　[GINGER *and* ALBERT *begin to go off.*]

GINGER: Proper buggered up that weighing though, old Hobnails.

ALBERT: Ah. It'm that swivel-eyed Tiny let him down.

GINGER: See you, Jim.

ALBERT: Jim....

JIM: Ginger ... Albert ... Spens....

　　[*Exeunt* GINGER, ALBERT. *Exit* JIM. *Silence.* SPENS *closes book, puts away, looks at Larry.*]

SPENS: Ah. You s'll bring rubbers tomorrow, boy. [*Exit* SPENS.]

　　[*Silence. Almost dark now. In distance, rumble of traffic; sound of heavy industry; slight wind again.* LARRY *hoists shoulder-bag; goes slowly; pauses; turns; sees Jeff's knife on ground; takes it up; carefully cleans blade, closes knife; thinking, pockets it deliberately. Exit.*

　　Stage empty, except for hayfork, standing, prong-fixed in ground, in a pale shaft of moonlight that strays upon it. Wind dies. Noises, then moonlight? fade. Darkness, silence, emptiness.]

GILES COOPER

Everything in the Garden

First presented by the Royal Shakespeare Theatre by arrangement with the Arts Theatre Club and Michael Codron at the Arts Theatre, London, WC2, on 13 March 1962, with the following cast:

JENNY ACTON	Geraldine McEwan
BERNARD ACTON, *her husband*	Derek Godfrey
LEONIE PIMOSZ, *a Polish Jewess*	Betty Baskcomb
JACK, *a bachelor*	John Dearth
ROGER, *the Actons' son*	Diarmid Cammell
BILL, *an estate agent*	Dennis Chinnery
BERYL, *his wife*	Carole Boyer
STEPHEN, *in oil*	Brian Badcoe
LAURA, *his wife*	Caroline Blakiston
TOM, *a stockbroker*	Geoffrey Chater
LOUISE, *his wife*	Audine Leith

The play was directed by Donald McWhinnie

On 16 May 1962 the play was presented by Michael Codron at the Duke of York's Theatre, London. The part of Bernard was played by Charles Gray.

The play is set in the Actons' sitting-room
in an outer suburb of London.

ACT ONE

The set is aggressively normal, the well-appointed sitting-room of a house-proud woman, with french windows leading out to a garden which is obviously owned by a keen gardener. Television set, magazines, not many books, no pictures.

Beyond the fence at the bottom of the garden lie playing-fields and, from time to time, shouts of encouragement and the sound of the referee's whistle can be heard.

It is a fine evening in late April though cool enough for a fire to be burning in the grate. A motor-mower can be heard outside going to and fro across the lawn.

> [*For a moment the stage is empty, filled merely by these sounds of work and play, then* JENNY ACTON *comes in. She crosses to the fireplace, and takes a packet of cigarettes from the mantelpiece. It is empty. Carefully she removes the silver paper and crosses to the waste-paper basket. She is about to throw the packet away when she finds another packet in the basket. She picks it up and shakes it. Empty. The mower coughs and stops.* JENNY *opens the cigarette packet and finds some silver paper in it. She takes it out and calls through the french windows, irritated.*]

JENNY: You might remember!

BERNARD [*off*]: What?

JENNY: You might!

> [BERNARD, *in shirt-sleeves and old trousers, comes in from the garden.*]

BERNARD: What?

JENNY: Remember. You always forget, you throw away the silver paper. I want it for my ball.

> [BERNARD *thinks this very funny. He roars with laughter, slaps his thigh, slaps his wife who moves away to smooth the paper on top of the other piece.*]

JENNY: No, it's not funny. It's getting quite big.

BERNARD: What do you do when it's the size of the Albert Hall?

JENNY: Take it to the Cottage Hospital.

BERNARD [*seeing his opportunity*]: I should jolly well think so too. [*He collapses into a chair.*]

JENNY: You are funny. Give me a cigarette.

[BERNARD *takes a packet from his pocket.*]

BERNARD: I must finish.

JENNY: How is it?

BERNARD: Hard.

[*She has taken a cigarette and so has he. He now finds the packet to be empty.*]

Oh, for a four-stroke. Oh, for a Monarch.

JENNY: Monarch?

BERNARD: Grass Monarch. Marvellous. Costs the earth. [*He takes out the silver paper and hands it to her*] Here you are, here's a little bit more. [*As she takes it he sings to himself.*]

> Oh, let's have a little bit more!
> Oh, let's have a little bit more!
> I'm very fond of a bit of fresh meat,
> So let's have a little bit more!

JENNY: Was that the last?

BERNARD [*rising and moving to window*]: Unless you've got some.

JENNY: How could I?

BERNARD: Well, you do.

JENNY: Only on Thursdays.

BERNARD [*looking up at the window*]: You know, it's coming on.

[JENNY *joins him at the window.*]

JENNY: Where shall we put the nemesia this year?

BERNARD: Over there they'd make a show.

JENNY: I thought dahlias by the fence.

BERNARD: They didn't do much last year.

JENNY: No, but....

BERNARD: Yes, perhaps.

JENNY: We're held back all the time with no greenhouse.

BERNARD: We'll have one.

JENNY: When?

BERNARD: Money!

JENNY: You go on saying that.

BERNARD: I go on having to earn it.

JENNY: Jack Foster said he might look in.

BERNARD: When?

JENNY: Sometime.

BERNARD: No, when did you see him?

JENNY: Shopping this morning.

BERNARD: Doesn't he ever do any work?

JENNY: He says he's drawing a strip cartoon.

BERNARD: Odd way to live.

JENNY: He makes money.

BERNARD: Oh yes. But you never quite know where you are.

JENNY: You play golf with him.

BERNARD: Well he's a member, and a neighbour. No, there's nothing against him, I don't say that; just that I'd never be surprised to see his name in the Sundays.

JENNY: That's prejudice.

BERNARD: All right, that's prejudice.

JENNY: When do you want to eat?

BERNARD: When I'm fed.

JENNY: No you won't, you say that but you never do and then it all gets cold while you finish something.

BERNARD: What is it?

JENNY: What would you like?

BERNARD: What is there?

JENNY: Nothing much.

BERNARD: Then I'll have it cold with pickles.

JENNY: There isn't time, if I cooked it now it would take two hours and it wouldn't be cold till midnight.

BERNARD: It was only a joke.

JENNY: I thought you meant the joint.

BERNARD: No, you said nothing much, and I said I'd have it cold with pickles.

JENNY: I'm not there.

BERNARD: Because you said what would I have and I said what was there, and you said. . . .

JENNY [breaking in]: All right, eggs?

BERNARD: Yes, O.K.

JENNY: How?

BERNARD: Bacon.

[JENNY *crosses to the door.*]

JENNY: If there is.

BERNARD: If there isn't I'll . . .

JENNY: Yes?

BERNARD: Have them any way you like.

[JENNY *comes in again.*]

JENNY: No, that's no good. I mean if you want an omelette there's no use my making one now and then you not coming in to eat it. You must make up your mind.

BERNARD: I can't.

JENNY: Think.

[BERNARD *comes into the room deep in thought. There is a long pause.*]

BERNARD: Er . . . well . . . [*a bright idea comes to him.*] We need more cigarettes.

JENNY: So you're going down.

BERNARD: Well, I'd better. I mean tomorrow's Sunday.

JENNY: How long?

BERNARD: No time.

JENNY: Unless you meet somebody.

BERNARD: No, really, just a drink and the cigarettes, that's all.

JENNY: And the lawn?

BERNARD: I'll finish the edge and do the rest tomorrow.

JENNY: Don't be too long.

BERNARD: I could do it later.

JENNY: Dark.

BERNARD: Oh I don't know, the evenings are lighter than they were.

JENNY: Well of course.

[*There is a slight pause as* BERNARD *looks out of the window. From the playing-fields beyond comes the faint sound of two teams cheering each other:* 'Three cheers for Whites, hip, hip, hurrah!' 'Three cheers for Colours, hip, hip, hurrah.' *etc.*]

BERNARD: Three cheers for me. [*He makes a decision.*] If I went down now there'd be plenty of time afterwards. [*He takes his jacket off the chair where it has been lying, and puts it on. He finds a tie in its pocket and starts to put that on too.*]

JENNY: Is there anything in the cupboard? [*She goes to the cupboard in the corner and looks in.*]

BERNARD: Not really.

JENNY [*holding up a bottle*]: Some gin.

BERNARD: Well, yes.

JENNY: There is some.

BERNARD: But if someone came.

JENNY: There's sherry.

BERNARD: Oh yes, quite a bit. Shall I get you a glass?

JENNY: No, they can have sherry if they come.

BERNARD: Who?

JENNY: You said if someone.

BERNARD: Yes, but I like to have some gin to offer.

JENNY: Well, of all the selfish . . .

BERNARD: Some people don't like sherry.

JENNY: And I'm one of them, but can I have gin? Oh no, it's being kept for your friends.

BERNARD: Or yours.

JENNY: What friends have I?

BERNARD: There's Beryl and Muriel, and that Green woman.

JENNY: Green?

BERNARD: With a husband in cement.

JENNY: Hester Brown.

BERNARD: All right then, that Brown woman.

JENNY: They are not friends. I hardly ever see them.

BERNARD: I thought you had coffee together every morning.

JENNY: That's not being friends.

BERNARD: What is?

JENNY [*defiantly pouring herself a drink*]: Knowing people, knowing them well, people you like.

BERNARD: We had a party.

JENNY: Parties don't mean anything.

BERNARD: I wish you'd told me that before you made me have it.

JENNY: Made you! Is there anything to put in this?

BERNARD: Pink. I wouldn't have dreamt of having a party.

JENNY: You suggested it. I hate pink.

BERNARD: I . . . ? Oh no! Oh no no no.

JENNY: Isn't there any tonic?

BERNARD: Orange squash, bottom shelf. But it was your idea, I swear it was.

[JENNY *finds the orange squash and pours some into her glass.*]

JENNY: How can you say that?

BERNARD: You said we ought to return some hospitality.

JENNY [*moving towards the fireplace*]: We couldn't go to other people's parties and do nothing.

BERNARD [*moving towards the cupboard*]: No need to do anything, have them in one or two at a time, for drinks or dinner.

JENNY: It costs more in the long run.

BERNARD: In the long run.

JENNY: You said so.

BERNARD: The party took a cracking great slice in the short run. [*He moves over to the sofa and sits.*] Oh, money, money, money.

JENNY: That's how it has always been. [*She sits in the armchair.*] When we were married.

BERNARD: That's how it is.

JENNY: You earn more than you did then.

BERNARD: Earn, yes.

JENNY: Well, why then?

BERNARD: We've got a house, not a two-roomed flat, garden, school fees for Roger, higher fares, more taxes, everything. You can't have parties and the sort of life you want to lead.

JENNY: Me? *You!*

BERNARD: Oh, now, now really, look now, now. I mean, well! Do you think I need all this? [*He stands and strides around, indicating the luxury of their surroundings.*] Oh no, I could live in one room.

JENNY: If you hadn't got me as a burden.

BERNARD: No, I don't mean that. [*Suddenly reasonable, he goes and sits on the arm of her chair.*] But don't blame me for not earning more, I do my best.

JENNY: Yes, of course.

BERNARD: It's the way it is today.

JENNY: And yet there are rich people. How do they do it?

BERNARD: They get born as Greeks, or Jews, or Yanks, or anything but poor bloody Englishmen.

JENNY: Yes, I suppose . . . [*She looks up at him.*] You know, I hate to feel I'm a drag on you.

BERNARD: Not a drag.

JENNY: No but, oh you know.

BERNARD: I never said you were a drag.

JENNY: I want to be a help.

BERNARD: Oh you are.

JENNY: No I'm not, you're quite right, I'm a drag.

BERNARD: No, look I didn't say that, I never said any such thing. I mean, I married you . . .

JENNY: For better or for worse, yes, why shouldn't you do a little better.

BERNARD: Darling, you do as well as, well, as well as anyone could.

JENNY [*looking into her empty glass*]: No, I could do better, supposing I got a job?

BERNARD: Oh no, oh no, not on your Eleanor.

JENNY: My what?

BERNARD: Nellie.

JENNY: What do you mean?

BERNARD: Oh, never mind. [*He is refilling the glasses.*] But no.

JENNY: Why not? Why on earth not?

BERNARD: Because . . .

JENNY: I don't see why not.

BERNARD: What about school holidays?

JENNY: We could manage. People do. Laura Hicks.

BERNARD: Oh well . . .

JENNY: But she does. Three children and a job speech-training. We ought to have them round some time.

BERNARD: It's different for her, she's qualified.

JENNY: A Friday night would be best.

BERNARD: Or a Saturday.

JENNY: You might give me a drink. But we ought to have someone to meet them.

BERNARD [*crossing and giving her a drink*]: I'm sorry. Someone to meet

149

them makes us six, and it never really works, the table isn't big enough.

JENNY: We've had eight at Christmas, and you've never complained before.

BERNARD: Ah, Christmas. That's different. [*He wanders over to the window.*] My grandfather used to have dinner parties of sixteen before the war, of course, when we had Less-ways.

JENNY: Everyone did in those days.

BERNARD: I know they did, I was just saying.

JENNY: Not that we don't need a larger table.

BERNARD: Need, need, need, oh, yes!

JENNY: That's the sort of thing I mean, if I had a job, we could afford to buy one or two things.

BERNARD: No use having a table and nothing to eat off it because you haven't time to cook.

JENNY: Ah, now I see! I see! All you're thinking of is yourself.

BERNARD: And who are you?

JENNY: I'm thinking of being a useful person, not just a cabbage slaving away in the house.

BERNARD: Cabbages don't.

JENNY: Like that woman in that play.

BERNARD: What play?

JENNY: Oh, I don't know, Strindberg.

BERNARD: Don't go highbrow on me.

JENNY: I thought everyone knew that.

[*There is a pause.* BERNARD *stands looking out of the window; he takes out his pipe and starts to fill it.*]

Do go down if you're going.

BERNARD: All right. Why don't we have them in for a drink?

JENNY: The Hicks?

BERNARD: And one or two others, not a party.

JENNY: We could. When?

BERNARD: Sometime.

JENNY: No, but you must say, if we don't do anything, we won't do anything.

BERNARD: Next month. We're overspent on this one.

JENNY: I only bought some seeds.

BERNARD: That's all right, quite all right. I'm not saying that you shouldn't have, just that we are. [*The telephone rings.* BERNARD *answers it.*]

BERNARD: Hullo, two-seven-double-five. Who? Yes.

JENNY: Me?

[BERNARD *holds out the receiver.*]

BERNARD: Some foreign woman.

[JENNY *takes the receiver.*]

JENNY: Yes, yes it is. Oh yes. [*Doubtfully*] Yes, I suppose so. Where are you? All right. It's called White Walls about half-way down the road on the right. Yes. [*She replaces the receiver.*]

BERNARD: Who on earth is it?

JENNY: Oh, just a woman. Grace put me on to her.

BERNARD: What sort of a woman?

JENNY: A dressmaker. She's coming round now.

BERNARD: I thought you went to them.

JENNY: You do, but she happened to be here. She rang from the box on the corner.

BERNARD: I'll go down then.

JENNY: Yes, she'll be here in a moment.

BERNARD: Not if she knows her left from her right.

JENNY: It's only a step.

BERNARD: But you said on the right, it's on the left coming that way.

JENNY: Why didn't you say?

BERNARD: How was I to know where she was?

JENNY: You knew she was telephoning.

BERNARD: Christ, there are two million telephones in the London area.

JENNY: Counted them?

BERNARD: Don't be childish.

JENNY: It's you that's being childish. You must have known she was somewhere near from the way I spoke.

BERNARD: As a matter of fact, I was doing a job for the G.P.O. the other day. Big contract.

JENNY: So?

BERNARD: So I do know how many telephones there are.

JENNY: You know everything.

BERNARD: No, but I'm not the complete fool you seem to think I am.
    [*Door bell.*]

JENNY: Anyway, she's found it.

BERNARD: That only means she doesn't know her left from her right
    either.

JENNY: Well, are you going?

BERNARD: Yes. I'll let her in and go. [*He goes towards the door.*]

JENNY: Don't be too long.

BERNARD: Only cigarettes. [*He goes out.*]
    [*The front door is heard to open off and* BERNARD *can be heard
    speaking.*]
  Yes, do come in, my wife's in here.
    [*He ushers in the squat, square figure of Leonie.*]

JENNY: Good evening.
    [BERNARD *does a brief pantomime behind Leonie's back, indicating
    what an extraordinary creature she is. He then goes.*]

JENNY: Do sit down ... er ...
    [LEONIE *sits.*]

LEONIE: Pimosz.

JENNY: I'm sorry?

LEONIE: Leonie Pimosz, like primrose but having no *r*'s.

JENNY: Oh yes. Would you like a glass of sherry?

LEONIE: No gin?

JENNY: I'm afraid this is the last of it.

LEONIE: Then sherry, yes, all right.
    [JENNY *crosses to pour a glass of sherry for her.* LEONIE *lights a
    cigarette.*]

LEONIE: You want to work?

JENNY: You saw my advertisement.

LEONIE: Yes.

JENNY [*taking glass to Leonie*]: How did you know where to find me?
  I only put the telephone number.

LEONIE: I find out.
    [JENNY *sits in the chair by the fireplace.*]

LEONIE: You smoke?

JENNY [*taking one*]: Thank you. My husband's just gone out for some.

LEONIE [*indicating door*]: That your husband?

JENNY: Yes.

LEONIE: Why do you want to work?

JENNY: Well, you know how it is. My son's away at school and I have some spare time. Besides, one can always use money, can't one?

LEONIE: One can. [*She is sizing up Jenny, the room, the furniture, everything.*]

JENNY: These days with taxation and school fees, you know what it is.

LEONIE: I know what it is. You are not asking for much, only to keep what you have and each year that is more difficult. What is your husband?

JENNY: In business.

LEONIE [*laughing harshly*]: Ha! So are we all in business.

JENNY: He works for a firm that makes office furniture.

LEONIE: Good money?

JENNY [*taken aback*]: Oh, he doesn't do too badly. What job had you in mind for me?

LEONIE: Job, yes. A job to make money you want, I think?

JENNY: And for something to do, you know how it is. One likes to feel useful.

LEONIE: Yes, useful. [*She dips into her bag and brings out a bundle of notes which she puts on the coffee-table between them.*] Money.

[JENNY *looks at it.*]

For you.

JENNY: No.

LEONIE [*thrusting it at her*]: Here, yes for you, take.

[*She is so forceful that* JENNY *does take it.*]

Fifty pounds, count if you like.

JENNY [*dropping it on the table*]: I don't want it.

[LEONIE *picks it up and throws it into the fire, which flares up.*
JENNY *looks at the fire, half stretches out a hand, draws it back and looks at Leonie. She stands.*]

JENNY: I think you had better go.

LEONIE: Not yet. Let us start again. [*She takes out another bundle of notes and thrusts it at Jenny.*] Here take, or I do the same. [*She withdraws it slightly as if to throw it.*]

[JENNY *takes it.*]

JENNY: Quite mad.

LEONIE: No, very rich.

JENNY [*looking at the notes*]: You must see I can't take money from you like this.

LEONIE: You have, it's yours. There's something you would care to buy?

JENNY: But I can't just be given money. I want to work.

LEONIE: Good then. [*Indicating the money.*] An advance of salary, you work for me.

JENNY: What as?

LEONIE: In the afternoons, from two o'clock, say, to six.

JENNY: But what do I do?

LEONIE: When you are telephoned you come to my flat.

JENNY: Where is that?

LEONIE: In Wimpole Street, you know?

JENNY [*impressed*]: Yes, I know Wimpole Street. Doctors, dentists . . .

LEONIE: Yes.

JENNY: Is it a receptionist's job?

LEONIE: Receptionist?

JENNY: Making appointments, and so on. . . .

LEONIE: I make appointments. For you.

JENNY: For me? Who with?

LEONIE: Clients.

JENNY: What for?

LEONIE: Twenty-five guineas each time.

JENNY: No, I mean . . . Twenty-five guineas?

LEONIE: More if they are generous.

JENNY: But these clients, who are they?

LEONIE: Some businessmen, some visitors. All gentlemen, all rich.

JENNY: I don't think it's quite the sort of thing I was looking for.

LEONIE: No?

JENNY: Some sort of club, I suppose.

LEONIE: No no, nothing like that. Clubs are not good. This is quite private, quite respectable. Here is my card, and here, if you wish, two more days advance. [*She puts card and notes on the table between them.*]

JENNY: Oh no! I mean I haven't really decided to take a job at all.

LEONIE: You advertised.

JENNY: Yes, but I've since found out that my husband's very much against it.

LEONIE: He is here in the afternoons?

JENNY: Only week-ends. But he'd have to know and I'm sure he wouldn't approve of anything like this.

LEONIE: Or like this? [LEONIE *indicates the money.*]

JENNY: Money isn't everything.

LEONIE: All the ladies I offer jobs to say that. But here we sit; money is this house, this garden, these clothes, this drink. What please is not money?

JENNY: It's rather hard to explain.

LEONIE: To an old Jewess, yes.

JENNY: I'm sorry. I didn't mean to be rude, but it's all so vague, isn't it? Couldn't you be more precise?

LEONIE: Yes, I could.

JENNY: I mean, you can't expect anyone to take a job on without knowing exactly what it is.

LEONIE: As I said, then, you wait for me to telephone, then you come to that address. [*She points to the card.*] You have a key to the side door so that you will meet nobody except myself . . . and your client, of course.

JENNY: But what exactly would I *do*?

[LEONIE *laughs slightly. There is a pause. The penny drops.*
JENNY *suddenly picks up the money and the card and thrusts them at* LEONIE.]

Go away, get out of my house.

[LEONIE *does not move and the card and money drop to the floor.*]

I'll call the police.

LEONIE: What for?

JENNY: You know what for.

LEONIE: I have said nothing.

JENNY: You've suggested . . .

LEONIE: That you make money.

JENNY: In the most revolting way one can. Me!

[LEONIE *shrugs this off.*]

JENNY: Did you think I'd think of it?

155

LEONIE: You have a friend who does.

JENNY: Who?

LEONIE: Oh no, we are discreet.

JENNY: That's easy to say.

> [LEONIE *takes out a cigarette-case and offers Jenny a cigarette.* *Without thinking,* JENNY *takes it. She realizes what she has done* *and throws it away.*]

I don't believe you, not a word. People round here wouldn't do that sort of thing. You don't realize, you don't know what we're like. Unless it's one of the tradesmen's wives you're thinking of or someone like that.

LEONIE: I'm thinking of a lady with a nice house, who keeps it nice, who has no more worries about money, who is very happy; so could you be.

JENNY: I'd rather do anything, die!

LEONIE: How very far you are from death to say such a thing. [*She slaps the wall by the window.*] You think all this lasts for ever, and it lasts for you? I tell you something. This house, it don't know you're here, nothing knows about you, nothing cares; what you do is up to you. Once there was a time when I thought the way that you think now, but I am Polish. I was in a camp at your age.

JENNY: I don't care. I'm sorry, but I don't.

LEONIE: Nobody cares, why should they?

JENNY: I'm sure it was all very terrible but you really can't make it an excuse for coming here and offering me money to . . . do that.

LEONIE: You don't have to take the money.

JENNY: You filthy woman. It's disgusting.

LEONIE: Nothing is disgusting, unless you are disgusted.

JENNY: I am.

LEONIE: Not me.

JENNY: You!

LEONIE: Yes, me. Look, I remember when the Nazis said I was disgusting. We were all disgusting, but we were not disgusted. Nothing you are or do yourself offends yourself. Disgust is only hate and hate is for other people.

JENNY: You're evil. Yes you are, evil!

LEONIE: So are we all to others, but what we do is nothing.

JENNY: I shall tell the police.

LEONIE: Then they will perhaps arrest me.

JENNY: I hope they put you in prison.

LEONIE: Oh yes, they will, and I shall admit everything; how you approached me, yes, and we discussed it, yes, but the terms did not suit.

JENNY: That's not true!

LEONIE: They do not seem to suit.

JENNY: You came to me. I shall say.

LEONIE: And that you advertised.

JENNY: Not to you.

LEONIE: To the world.

[*Slight pause.* JENNY'*s tone changes.*]

JENNY: Do please go, please.

[LEONIE *stands.*]

LEONIE: You will think about it and telephone.

JENNY: I shall forget you ever came.

LEONIE: No police then, good.

JENNY: I don't know yet, I shall have to think.

LEONIE: And then telephone, yes.

JENNY: Get out! Get out! Get out!

LEONIE: Do not ring before ten o'clock in the morning, please. [*She goes to the door, looks back at Jenny, and nods, pleased. She goes.*]

[JENNY *stands for a moment, tense, then she picks up the cigarette which she threw away. She lights it and stands for a moment looking out into the garden.*

She shakes her head and moves down. She sees the money and the card lying on the floor. She picks up the card, tears it across savagely, and throws it into the waste-paper basket.

She picks up the money and looks at it. After all, it is money. She goes to her desk and puts it away in a drawer.

Moving over to the fire, she sits, gazing into it. Then with a sudden access of distaste, she throws the cigarette into the fire.

JACK FOSTER *appears outside the french window. He watches her.*]

JACK [*sepulchral*]: Good evening kiddies, this is the mad ghoul calling.

JENNY [*turning, startled*]: Jack! Oh, you horror.
    [*He comes in.*]

JACK: Who was that went out as I came in? Your aunt Becky?

JENNY: A dressmaker. Bernard's at the pub.

JACK: And I am here, my great moment. Alone at last. [*He smacks his lips.*]

JENNY: Ah, but you were seen coming in by the neighbours.

JACK: Oh, no, I crept through the shrubbery like the cat in the crypt. 'id behind the 'olly'ocks.

JENNY: There aren't any hollyhocks.

JACK: No! Jenny don't talk gardening. You know I can't bear it. [*He leafs through a woman's magazine which he has picked up.*]

JENNY: Would you like some beer?

JACK: Is that all there is? No thanks. Too wet. [*He holds the magazine open at a fashion page.*] How d'you like her?

JENNY: I like the hat. Is she yours?

JACK: All mine.

JENNY: Why do you give them such long legs?

JACK: It's the fashion. And I like it.

JENNY: But it's disappointing when you buy things, you never do look like the drawings.

JACK [*looking coolly at her*]: Oh, I wouldn't say that, I think you could manage it.

JENNY: Not that I can afford the sort of clothes you put your models into.

JACK: I don't have models, and even if I did they'd be put into their clothes by some tough number with a mouthful of pins. [*He indicates the door.*] Like her.

JENNY: Who?

JACK: Your dressmaker woman.

JENNY: Oh yes.

JACK: The very type. You can tell 'em from a mile off. Good solid flint from the inside out.

JENNY: Hard?

JACK: You have to be if you're going to make money in that trade, which they do. At the expense of the poor and honest, like me.

JENNY: Are you poor?

JACK: I would be if I were honest.

JENNY: Why?

JACK: Look around.

JENNY: What at?

JACK: Your pictures.

JENNY: There's one in the hall.

JACK [*indicating magazine*]: And dozens in here.

JENNY: One never seems to have any money left for pictures.

JACK: Why don't I give you one, Jenny? An early Foster. Come up to my flat and choose it.

JENNY: I might.

JACK: Monday?

JENNY: I'm having coffee with Beryl, can I bring her along?

JACK: I didn't actually say two for the price of one.

JENNY: She's interested in art.

JACK: Perhaps we could send her to the National Gallery. [*He goes over to her.*] No, but seriously, Jenny . . . Well, fairly seriously.

[*The front door is heard to slam.*]

JENNY: Bernard!

JACK: Curses, foiled again! [*He moves away.*]

[BERNARD *enters.*]

BERNARD: Hullo, Jack. [*To Jenny*] Has the old girl gone?

JENNY: Yes.

BERNARD: Any good?

JENNY: Too expensive.

BERNARD: A member of the chosen race, I should say.

JENNY: Did you get another bottle of gin?

BERNARD [*sitting*]: Lord no, I can't give the Government all that money more than once a week.

JACK [*standing*]: Ah well, I think I'll creep out the way I crep' in. [*To Bernard, indicating Jenny*] Isn't she beautiful?

BERNARD: What? Oh. Yes.

[JACK *blows a kiss at Jenny and goes.*]

What did he want?

JENNY: Gin, or whisky.

BERNARD: Funny chap. He told Tom Palmer the other day that he'd

like to see the whole of Woodfield blown to bits. Didn't say why.
Tight of course. But you want to be careful.

JENNY: Of him? No, I'm not his type. My legs are too stumpy.

[*She stretches them out.* BERNARD *looks at them.*]

BERNARD: Oh, I wouldn't say that.

JENNY: Who was in the pub?

BERNARD: Nobody much. Bill.

JENNY: What did he say?

BERNARD: Nothing.

JENNY: Fun for you both.

BERNARD: If you really want to know, he said 'Good evening'. I said
'Hello'. He said 'What is it, a pint?' and I said, 'Thank you very
much'.

JENNY: But what did you talk about?

BERNARD: The Test selection and asparagus.

JENNY: How dull.

BERNARD: You asked. Anyway I was only down there for a second.
He's getting a second car.

JENNY: Was Beryl with him?

BERNARD: No, she'd been up in Town.

JENNY: Beryl had?

BERNARD: Why not?

JENNY: I wonder what for. She has her hair done at Yvette's in the
High Street, like me.

BERNARD: You can go to Town for other things than hair.

JENNY: Yes, but she said she was fed up with Peggy.

BERNARD: Who's she?

JENNY: Oh you know, Peggy, I told you, the girl who does us both.

BERNARD: Not me.

JENNY: Beryl. She's not bad, at least I don't think so. But she's a bit
casual, of course they all are these days. They get so much money.

BERNARD: Let's become hairdressers, then. 'Maison Acton Coiffeur
des Dames' – and I'll have a white coat and a pair of curling tongs.

JENNY: They don't use those.

BERNARD: Well. A comb sticking out of my pocket. You'd have a
white coat too.

JENNY: And a blue rinse.

BERNARD: You'd look fetching in a white coat. [*He stands.*] **Nice.**
[*He draws her to him and kisses her with some passion.*] **Nicer.**

JENNY: You behave yourself.

BERNARD: I'm supposed to do this, it says so in the Prayer Book.

JENNY: And that I've heard before. Let me go or you won't get
anything to eat.

BERNARD: Don't want anything.

JENNY: Yes, you do.

BERNARD: All right, cut off the joint.

JENNY: Not now.

BERNARD: This very moment. Do you remember Bernard the Blood-
sucking Bat?
[*He tries to bite her neck. She gives a shriek and tries to get away. In
doing so,* BERNARD's *hand knocks off the top of her cigarette*]
Ow!

JENNY: Oh, do be careful.

BERNARD: Oo, burnt my hand.

JENNY: The tip's gone on the floor. [*She throws the cigarette into the
fireplace.*] Where is it? Quick!

BERNARD: It hurt like hell. [*He sucks his hand.*]
[JENNY *is on her hands and knees.*]

JENNY: Look for it, it'll burn the carpet.
[BERNARD *goes down on his hands and knees. They push aside
chairs.*]

BERNARD: Are you sure it came off?

JENNY: Yes, certain. You are a clumsy oaf.

BERNARD: I was cherishing you. Like it says I should.

JENNY: This carpet's bad enough as it is without another great burnt
hole in it.
[BERNARD *is facing her on all fours.*]

BERNARD: Bow wow!

JENNY: Can you smell it?
[BERNARD *sniffs.*]

BERNARD: Let's play bears.

JENNY: Oh, don't be a fool.

BERNARD: All right, let's not play bears. [*He moves away and gives a
sudden cry of pain.*] Ow! Damn!

JENNY: Found it?

[BERNARD *has flicked something off the carpet into the grate and is now standing rubbing the carpet with his foot and nursing the other hand.*]

BERNARD: Put my hand on it.

JENNY: It stinks.

BERNARD: No large damage. But I must say . . .

JENNY [*flops into a chair*]: I'm exhausted.

BERNARD [*also sits, looking at his hand*]: I'm lacerated.

JENNY: There's some stuff in the bathroom.

BERNARD: All for trying to do what I wouldn't be allowed to do with my wife's aunt's niece.

JENNY: Well you see what happens.

BERNARD: You're not my wife's aunt's niece, you're my wife.

[JENNY *gives an enormous yawn.* BERNARD *picks up a magazine. There is a moment's pause and he gives an equally enormous yawn.*]

BERNARD: It's catching.

JENNY: Let's go out.

BERNARD: Where?

JENNY: To eat. I'm bored.

BERNARD: There's nowhere much open now.

JENNY: The Ship Hotel.

BERNARD: That costs a quid before you get through the door.

JENNY: I've got some money.

BERNARD: How much?

JENNY: Enough.

BERNARD: For dinner at the Ship?

JENNY: Yes.

BERNARD: How?

JENNY: M.y.o.b.

BERNARD: Have you been saving?

JENNY: Perhaps.

BERNARD: You said you hadn't a penny on Monday.

JENNY: I don't have to tell you everything.

BERNARD: You haven't done anything silly?

JENNY: I don't think so.

BERNARD: No, I mean that job you talked about. You haven't got one behind my back?

JENNY: Suppose I did.

BERNARD: You could jolly well go and un-get-it.

JENNY: Why? Why? Why?

BERNARD: Have you?

JENNY: No, I haven't. But why shouldn't I?

BERNARD: We've been through this before.

JENNY: No we haven't. We started and then you went on about Laura Hicks and having a party.

BERNARD: Me! That I do like.

[JENNY *rises from her chair and kneels by his. A submissive wife.*]

JENNY: No darling, don't be horrid. I'm quite serious.

BERNARD: But what do you think you're going to do? I mean you don't want to work in a shop do you?

JENNY: No, but there must be something, as a matter of fact I have made a start.

BERNARD: What?

JENNY: I've advertised.

BERNARD: No? In the local paper.

JENNY: In the newsagent.

BERNARD: You haven't? As though you were a lot of old gramophone records or a pram or a tart.

JENNY: What?

BERNARD: That's what they do these days. 'Model aged 25, 34-44-54.' [*Sudden alarm.*] You didn't put our address?

JENNY: Telephone number.

BERNARD: That's bad enough; well, out it comes tomorrow.

JENNY: It does anyway, the week's up.

BERNARD: You haven't had any calls?

JENNY [*slight pause*]: One.

BERNARD: Who?

JENNY: Some woman.

BERNARD: What sort of job?

JENNY: I don't know. I didn't go into it. I didn't like the sound of her much.

BERNARD [*laughs*]: You are incredible, darling, you really are. What a thing to do.

JENNY: It seemed cheap.

BERNARD: And very nasty, darling. But honestly, supposing some-one we knew had seen it, just supposing. If they'd seen the number and known. Bill for instance, or Beryl.

JENNY: Who are they to mind?

BERNARD: Nobody, but we'd never have heard the end of it. He'd probably have rung you up as a joke and offered you something quite appalling.

[JENNY, *a little crushed, stands up.*]

JENNY: Yes, I suppose he might. Oh, what hell people are. [*She is crying.*]

BERNARD [*rising*]: Oh, now look, darling.

JENNY: Yes, they are, they are! I'm not a person at all. I'm just a sort of belonging of yours, and if I try to do anything else you either treat it as a joke or you get angry.

BERNARD: No, darling.

JENNY: Yes you do.

BERNARD: No, look, look here ... [*He takes out his handkerchief.*] Mop up. Then you can take me out to dinner.

JENNY: Can I?

BERNARD: With your miser's hoard. How much is there?

JENNY: About a fiver.

BERNARD: Clever, clever girl.

JENNY: You'd better put things away in the garden.

BERNARD: And wash.

JENNY: Should I change?

BERNARD: You look all right.

JENNY: Would I be better in my grey skirt and red top?

BERNARD: You look fine as you are.

JENNY: But what do you think?

BERNARD [*going to her*]: Good enough to eat.

JENNY: It doesn't make me look skinny?

BERNARD [*holding her from him, looking at her*]: Big Chief Bernard say he like-um skinny squaw.

JENNY: Skinny squaw say 'How!'

BERNARD: Big Chief Bernard show-um how. [*He puts an arm round her and kisses her.*]

JENNY: Big Chief Bernard boasting. Squaw getting skinnier every minute. Let's go and eat.

BERNARD: And then come back to the wigwam. [*He gives her an affectionate pat and moves up to the window.*] We'd better hurry or they'll be shut; put some face on and we'll go. [*He goes out.*]

[*JENNY goes to the desk and takes two five-pound notes from drawer. She crosses to the waste-paper basket and lifts it on to the stool.*]

CURTAIN

ACT TWO

Some weeks later. It is about quarter past nine on a fine Saturday July morning.

[BERNARD *wanders in wearing slacks and pullover. He opens the french windows and stands looking out at the garden.* JENNY *comes in carrying a tray of breakfast things. She is wearing a skirt and blouse which are both very much more expensive than her clothes of the first act.*]

JENNY: Put the cloth on.

BERNARD: Where is it?

JENNY: Where it always is.

BERNARD [*goes to a cupboard by the fireplace and finds the table-cloth which he puts on the table*]: Why does one have a table-cloth for breakfast?

JENNY [*laying the table*]: It's better.

BERNARD: Then why not for other meals?

JENNY: That's different.

BERNARD: Something to do with marmalade I suppose.

JENNY: Do you want an egg?

BERNARD: Are you having one?

JENNY: Do you want one?

BERNARD: If you're having one I will, otherwise no.

JENNY: You are a lazy devil.

BERNARD: No, it's just that I don't want an egg enough to start everything going towards cooking it, but if you were going to do one for yourself, well I'd want it enough for that.

JENNY: I don't think I'll have one.

BERNARD: I'll do you one if you like.

JENNY: You do want one?

BERNARD: No I don't, I'll just do you one. You ought to eat.

JENNY: Toast. [*She sits and takes a piece,* BERNARD *does the same.*]

BERNARD: It's not enough for you.

JENNY: Oh my God! Cornflakes. [*She goes to the bureau and rustles*

166

round until she finds an envelope which she brings back to write on.]

BERNARD: Why cornflakes?

JENNY: Roger's home today, had you forgotten? Matches. [*She writes again.*]

BERNARD: No of course I hadn't, put down envelopes.

JENNY: There are some.

BERNARD: No there aren't, I was writing a letter last night and there's only the belt thing that goes round them.

JENNY [*writing*]: All right, and a dish-mop. Who were you writing to?

BERNARD: We've got a dish-mop.

JENNY: We need a new one. Did you write to Aunt Edith?

BERNARD: No, I paid the coal bill, fourteen pounds nine and three-pence.

JENNY: We've got to have it.

BERNARD: I suppose so. [*He gets up and goes to the door.*]

JENNY: Where are you going?

BERNARD: Papers.

JENNY: Not yet on a Saturday.

BERNARD: Yes they are, I heard them.

[*He goes off.* JENNY *writes down one or two other items and* BERNARD *reappears carrying the* Daily Telegraph *and the* Express.]

JENNY: Shall we go to the cinema on Monday?

BERNARD: Why?

JENNY: Something for Roger.

BERNARD: You two go.

JENNY: Oh come too.

BERNARD: Waste of money.

JENNY: You'll spend twice as much in the pub.

BERNARD: I shan't go to the pub.

JENNY: You will.

BERNARD: Might not.

JENNY: Well, give me a paper.

He folds the Express *and hands it to her.*]

You're reading that one.

BERNARD: No I was only looking at it.

JENNY: Anyone would think I couldn't understand the *Telegraph*.

BERNARD: Have it if you like.

JENNY: No no, this'll do. [*She looks at an advertisement.*] They've got marvellous greenhouses here for thirty pounds.

BERNARD: Oh, for God's sake!

JENNY: Well, they have.

BERNARD: Do you know you've made three suggestions in the last three minutes and they all mean spending money.

JENNY: I haven't.

BERNARD: Dish-mop, cinema, greenhouse.

JENNY: Well!

BERNARD: I know, I know, I know, but there it is and fourteen pounds nine and threepence of coal. [*The letter-box is heard off.*] And there are a whole lot more bills I bet you.

[JENNY *gets up and goes out.* BERNARD *looks at the headlines.*]

BERNARD: Things look bad in Africa.

JENNY [*off*]: What?

BERNARD: Africa.

[JENNY *comes on again holding letters and a small parcel.*]

JENNY: Africa?

BERNARD: Things look bad.

[JENNY *puts a couple of letters and the package down by Bernard and goes back to her side of the table with one letter which she looks at.*]

JENNY: From Mary Verrall. [*She opens the letter, but she is secretly watching Bernard, who looks at his two letters.*]

BERNARD: Gas, plumber. [*He puts them down disgustedly and picks up the package.*] What the hell's this?

JENNY: Mary's having another.

[BERNARD *turns the package this way and that way suspiciously, then wipes his knife clean on a piece of toast, and slits it open. He takes out a bundle of notes.*]

BERNARD: Jenny!

JENNY: What?

BERNARD [*baffled*]: Money!

JENNY: Money?

BERNARD: Notes. Look.

JENNY: How much?

BERNARD: It's incredible. [*He starts to count.*] One, two, three, four, five, six, seven, eight, nine, ten, eleven, twelve, thirteen, fourteen, fifteen, sixteen, seventeen, eighteen, nineteen, twenty, twenty-one, twenty-two, twenty-three, twenty-four, twenty-five, twenty-six, twenty-seven, twenty-eight, twenty-nine, thirty, in fivers making a hundred and fifty and . . . [*he counts the remaining notes out in silence*] forty-eight in ones making a hundred and ninety-eight pounds.

JENNY: Not two hundred?

BERNARD: No, you count. [*He pushes them across to her.*]

JENNY: No no, if you say so, you're better at counting than me.

BERNARD: A hundred and ninety-eight pounds. [*He stands and walks jerkily about the room.*] A hundred and ninety-eight pounds just like that, from nowhere. [*He examines the package.*] No message, nothing, who?

JENNY: Aren't you pleased?

BERNARD: It's so damned odd. I mean, why? Where from? There's no sense in it.

JENNY: But it's money.

BERNARD: I suppose so. [*He holds a note up to the light.*] Of course I can't keep it.

JENNY: What!

BERNARD: Oh no, no, wouldn't do at all. I'll take it to the police.

JENNY: No!

BERNARD: Of course. There's something wrong somewhere.

JENNY: But it's addressed to you, it came through the post, it's not as though you had found it. Someone means you to have it.

BERNARD: Who?

JENNY: Perhaps you did someone a good turn.

BERNARD: Those sort of things don't happen. Not to Joe Soap.

JENNY: This has happened.

BERNARD [*thinking deeply*]: There was an old woman I gave my seat to in the tube the other day, she seemed awfully grateful, but she didn't look rich.

JENNY: Really rich people never do.

BERNARD: But how would she know where I lived? She got out at Green Park.

JENNY: Perhaps she had you followed.

BERNARD: No, no, it couldn't be her. [*He lights a cigarette.*]

JENNY: Can I have one?

BERNARD: Oh, I'm sorry. [*He hands her the packet.*] There's a chap who often sits opposite me in the train, he always seems very interested in me. You know, he asks me questions about how I manage on my salary and that sort of thing, perhaps he's a millionaire.

JENNY: Match.

BERNARD: Oh, yes. [*He is about to hand her the matches but suddenly realizes that it would be more courteous of him to strike one for her, which he does.*]

JENNY: Thank you.

BERNARD: I wonder. At work of course I meet people, you know – clients, directors of big firms, I think that's the answer, it's one of them.

JENNY: Oh, why?

BERNARD: Well, you know, a lot of the people in this business are pretty good oicks and I suppose they find it a change to deal with a ... well, with a ... let's not be ashamed of it ... a gentleman. [*He is gathering up the notes and stacking them neatly together.*] Someone like Sir Henry Vane-Quilter.

JENNY: Do you know him?

BERNARD: Slightly, he gave me a drink in their board room the other day. We talked about gardening, he's interested in roses. I should think it might very probably come from him.

JENNY: Yes it might.

BERNARD [*taking a fiver from the pile and handing it to her*]: Yours.

JENNY: Thank you.

BERNARD: Wait a moment. [BERNARD *takes off three one-pound notes and pushes them across.*] That brings it down to round figures, one hundred and ninety pounds.

JENNY: You're not taking it to the police?

BERNARD: No, I don't think so. As you say it came through the post, someone wants me to have it. It would be silly not to.

JENNY: Would you like more coffee?

BERNARD: Yes I would. My God, we could have a Grass Monarch! Shall we fly over to Paris tonight?

JENNY: There's Roger.

BERNARD: Oh yes, blast!

JENNY: He could come too.

BERNARD: Not if we're having a Monarch as well. But we must celebrate. Shall we have a party?

JENNY: If you like.

[*She takes the coffee off. In her absence* BERNARD *does a little dance of pure joy ending up at the window holding the money.* JENNY *returns with the coffee.*]

BERNARD: I'll get one of those edgers too and a load of hop manure.

JENNY: What about the party?

BERNARD: Yes, let's make it a proper one. Champagne cocktails, caviare, that'd shake them.

JENNY: When?

BERNARD: Tonight.

JENNY: It's Roger's first night home.

BERNARD: He's old enough to enjoy it now, fifteen, he can hand things round.

JENNY: We can't ask people at such short notice.

BERNARD: Yes we can. Let's start with Bill and Beryl. [*He goes to the telephone.*]

JENNY: No, I ought to ask her.

[BERNARD *is dialling.*]

BERNARD: Why?

JENNY: It's done.

BERNARD: Oh, all right. [*Into the telephone*] Hello Beryl, my old woman wants a word with you. [*He hands the receiver to Jenny and goes back to his coffee.*]

JENNY: My dear, how are you? Look, Beryl ... I'm terribly sorry, we didn't decide until now, this very minute, and it's horribly rude to ask you ...

BERNARD: It's a party, nothing to be ashamed of.

JENNY: What? [*To telephone*] Sorry. ...

BERNARD: Nothing.

JENNY: We wondered whether you could possibly come in for a drink this evening ... sort of six-thirty, not really a party, just a kind of celebration. One or two people. ... Yes ... yes, today as a matter of fact ... I'm off to the station now.

BERNARD: Are they coming?

JENNY: ... Oh you know what it is at the start of the holidays ... absolutely filthy ... they always are, they don't seem to teach them to wash at all. ...

BERNARD: Are they?

JENNY: ... I know, something I wanted to say ... Do you know that shop at the corner of ... not the High Street, that other one ... I always forget its name ... near the garage. ...

BERNARD: Willingdon Road.

JENNY: You know ... well they've got some twin-sets in, some sort of reject, but you can't see anything wrong with them and they're reduced to three pounds. They say they won't have them after this week, so I thought I'd tell you. I must go ... so is ours ... absolute hell, everything seems to be coming up at once. Were you able to get that man?

BERNARD: Get that man.

JENNY: He's expensive, but I think he's good, at least the Hicks's say so, they have him on Tuesdays. We really need someone more often ... Must go, good-bye then. [*She hangs up.*] Once you get her on the telephone, you can never get her off.

BERNARD: Are they coming?

JENNY: Yes. Who else?

BERNARD: The Palmers?

JENNY: If you like.

BERNARD: We said we would, some time ago.

JENNY: She talks so much.

BERNARD: Makes the party go.

JENNY: As soon as they can, to get away from her.

BERNARD: Old acid. And the Hicks?

JENNY: If they're there. [*Going to door.*] I'll ring them from upstairs. I must get ready.

BERNARD: Aren't you?

JENNY: My face.

BERNARD: Good enough for British Railways.

JENNY: Roger worries about what I look like.

BERNARD: Nearly two hundred pounds ... nearly two hundred pounds.

JENNY: Lovely.

BERNARD: I wonder why not two hundred.

JENNY: Perhaps he couldn't count.

BERNARD: Or she ... more likely to be she ... I mean if he's rich he can count ... but a rich woman ...

JENNY: Why should a rich woman? Because you're so beautiful?

[She goes. BERNARD riffles through the notes.]

BERNARD: One nine eight ... no, one ninety ... *[He struts about the room, then picks up the telephone. He puts it down again.]* Sorry. *[He calls off.]* Didn't know you were on the line. I was going to order the Monarch. [He goes to the window and looks out. The sound of a cricket bat striking a ball can be heard off. He stands on a stool so that he can look over the fence. Watching the cricket he takes his pipe from his pocket. There is a polite round of applause.] Well held! [He puffs at his pipe but it is blocked. He gets off the stool and comes into the room. He undoes the pipe and blows through the stem. Every now and then he says, 'A hundred and ninety-eight pounds!']*

He wants a pipe-cleaner. None on the mantelpiece. He goes towards his wife's desk and opens a drawer. He takes out a bundle of notes. He looks at them, puzzled. He puts the pipe in his mouth without the stem and counts them. He looks upstairs and puts them back in the drawer. He is puzzled but he still wants a pipe-cleaner. He goes to the mantelpiece again and takes down a vase. He puts his hand in. His expression changes. He pulls out more money. He lets it drop on the floor.

He tries the opposite vase. More money still. He is ankle-deep in the stuff. JENNY returns.]

JENNY: They can come....

BERNARD: Look ... look, what is it?

JENNY: Money, Bernard.

BERNARD: But in the vases, your drawer ... everywhere. ... *[He opens her work-basket. There is more in there.]* Yours?

JENNY: I must go.

BERNARD: Yes?

JENNY: There isn't time to tell you.

BERNARD: You must. Wait ... *[He goes to the table.]* Did you send me that?

JENNY: Actually yes ... well I had to.

BERNARD: Have you been betting?

JENNY: Yes.

BERNARD: Who with?

JENNY: A man.

BERNARD: Called?

JENNY: What does it matter as long as I won?

BERNARD: Called?

JENNY: Edwards.

BERNARD: That's a lie.

JENNY: What a way to talk to your wife.

BERNARD: Well, is it true?

JENNY: Not exactly.

BERNARD [*bending and picking up the money*]: Then it is a lie. How much is there?

[*Telephone.* JENNY *answers it.* BERNARD *stands counting the money.*]

JENNY: Hullo ... [*To Bernard*] Louise Palmer. [*To phone*] My dear, how are you? I was just going to ring you. Yes ... [*She looks nervously at Bernard.*] Look, I know you'll think it awfully rude to ask you at such short notice but could you come round for a drink tonight ... no, not a party, just one or two people ... could you? Oh good ... about seven. Lovely ... [*She listens.*] Yes ... yes ... No, I don't think so. ...

[BERNARD *has counted the money and has moved up beside her.*] Did you know she once played cricket for Gloucestershire? Oh, women's cricket, yes, at least I suppose so.

BERNARD: Hang up.

JENNY: I mean if it had been men's she'd have had to be a man ... [*She laughs.*] Well yes ...

BERNARD: Bloody well hang up.

JENNY: I must go ... All the shopping and Bernard's calling me. See you tonight then, 'bye ... [*She hangs up.*] There's no need to be filthily rude.

BERNARD [*waving the money*]: Where did you get three hundred pounds?

JENNY: Supposing she'd heard?

BERNARD: And that other two hundred. Where did you get it?

JENNY [*moving away from him and beginning to clear the breakfast*]: I didn't steal it.

BERNARD: *Where did you get it?*

JENNY: I earned it.

BERNARD: A job, you've got a job.

JENNY: Sort of.

BERNARD: I said I didn't want you to take a job. Anyway you couldn't have, not this sort of job . . . I mean five hundred pounds, you couldn't have had it long anyway.

JENNY: Six weeks.

BERNARD: No look, darling, look. Tell me. Did someone leave it to you? Did someone die and you haven't told me?

JENNY: Nobody died. I earned it. In the afternoons.

BERNARD: Even if you worked full-time you couldn't have earned this sort of money. Oh no. Come on now, tell me.

JENNY: I make twenty-five guineas five afternoons a week, sometimes more. I spent a little on clothes but there hasn't been time to spend the rest.

BERNARD: Nobody pays that sort of money, and I mean you've no training.

JENNY: You don't need any.

BERNARD: What do you need?

JENNY: Your coffee's still warm, or shall I heat it up?

[*She carries the tray out of the room.* BERNARD *picks up his coffee and tries it. Not nice. He throws it out of the window. There is a burst of applause, off.* JENNY *returns.*]

I could have heated it easily.

BERNARD: Now tell me. [*He goes across to her and takes her by the shoulders.*]

JENNY: There's nothing worth telling.

BERNARD: If you don't, I'll make a bonfire of this money in the middle of the lawn.

JENNY: Don't be absurd, darling. It's money.

BERNARD: I want to know where it comes from.

JENNY: Well do you remember that woman who came here?

BERNARD: The dressmaking woman?

JENNY: Yes, she offered me this job.

BERNARD: By God, you're not at one of these strip clubs, are you?

JENNY: Why should you think that?

BERNARD: I heard of a man who found out his wife was working in one.

JENNY: Do you really think I would?

BERNARD: No, but it must be something.

JENNY: It's a disgusting thing to suggest, taking off your clothes in one of those dreadful places in Soho in front of a lot of provincial businessmen.

BERNARD: Well, I'm sorry, but if you're so secretive, what am I to think?

JENNY: Think what you like.

BERNARD: You'll bloody well tell me what you do!

JENNY: I work as a receptionist.

BERNARD: For that money?

JENNY: It's a very expensive place.

BERNARD: What sort of a place?

JENNY: In Wimpole Street.

BERNARD: A clinic or something?

JENNY: Sort of. For very rich people, and Americans.

BERNARD: And you sit behind a desk arranging their appointments and someone gives you twenty-five guineas an afternoon for it.

JENNY: Yes.

BERNARD: How bloody improbable.

JENNY: Don't you want the money?

BERNARD: The money's got nothing to do with it.

JENNY: Oh yes it has. You don't think I'd do it for pleasure?

BERNARD: Do what? Sit behind a desk?

JENNY: Yes, sit behind a desk.

BERNARD: What's the name of this place?

JENNY: No name, just a number.

BERNARD: Well?

JENNY: It's confidential.

BERNARD: I'm your husband.

JENNY: I'm your wife, do you tell me everything?

BERNARD: I want to know the number of this place.

JENNY: Two forty-two.

BERNARD [*going to telephone*]: All right.

[*He dials quickly.* JENNY *watches rather nervously.*]

Directory inquiries? Can you give me the telephone number of two forty-two, Wimpole Street?

JENNY: Oh all right, there isn't a two forty-two Wimpole Street. It's another number.

[*He replaces the receiver.*]

BERNARD: And you don't like being called a liar. I wonder what you do like being called.

JENNY: I like being trusted.

BERNARD: Well, I like being told the truth by my wife.

JENNY: How much do you talk about your job? To me?

BERNARD: It's a dull job.

JENNY: So's mine.

BERNARD: The money isn't. Hell, it's four times what I get! What can you do that's worth that? [*Contemptuous*] Sitting behind a desk in a clinic . . . sounds more like a high-class whorehouse.

JENNY: I don't like that word.

BERNARD: A knocking-shop then.

[*She does not reply.* BERNARD *looks at her and begins to realize that he has hit on it.*]

No, look, what is it?

JENNY [*looking out of the window*]: Just a place.

BERNARD: A place.

JENNY: Where they pay me.

BERNARD [*seizing her*]: For God's sake, what do they pay me for?

JENNY: It's me they pay. [*Long pause.*] Don't you want the money?

BERNARD [*turning away and collapsing into a chair*]: I don't believe it.

JENNY [*kneeling beside him*]: It's going to make such a tremendous difference.

BERNARD: By God it is!

JENNY: All the things we've been wanting for years.

BERNARD: We!

JENNY: There'll be enough for a new car next month. Two if we did one on H.P.

BERNARD: There's no . . . I don't believe it.

JENNY: No what?

BERNARD: Room in the garage. How could you do such a thing?
Is it really true?

[*She gives a little shrug and moves away from him.*]

No, is it? Can you tell me straight out that you, a woman of your
background, with your parents and education, my wife, is a common prostitute.

JENNY: That's a horrid way to put it.

BERNARD [*rising and going up to her*]: There's no other way.

JENNY: I'm not the only one, you know.

BERNARD: The only one married to me.

JENNY: But it makes no difference to us.

BERNARD: Doesn't it? [*He slaps her face, hard. She gives a cry and drops
into a chair.*] What do you charge for that?

[*She sits, fingering her face, not looking at him. He goes to the window.*]
Pack and go.

[JENNY *does not answer.*]

Or I will.

JENNY: Where?

BERNARD: Anywhere, no by God, I won't. It's my house. I stay here.

JENNY: A lot of the things are mine.

BERNARD [*turning to her*]: Take them, take them, take them! But go.

JENNY: I can't, just like that.

BERNARD: I'll send them after you.

JENNY: No you won't, I know you, you never do anything like that.
I'm the person who has to find a movers and ring them up and
arrange everything.

BERNARD: Oh rubbish.

JENNY: When we had to send Aunt Lily's secretaire back you kept
saying you'd do it and weeks went by and you did nothing.

BERNARD: Hell to Aunt Lily's secretaire. I can tell you this. I don't
want a thing of yours in the house. Nothing!

JENNY: Oh, don't be silly.

BERNARD: I'll send it all to store and you can collect it from there.
So go on, get out!

[*Door bell. They both hesitate, taken aback.*]

JENNY: Well, go on.

BERNARD: Probably the milkman.

JENNY: If you're going to turn me out, you'll have to learn to deal with him.

BERNARD: Very well, very well. Certainly.

[*He marches out of the room. A moment later* JACK *appears at the french windows.*]

JACK: Hello, Jenny, I always find you alone these days.

JENNY: Bernard's answering the door.

JACK: I know. To me. I rang the bell, and then I thought, 'Why stand on ceremony with my old friend Bernard?' [*He goes to door and opens it.*]

Old friend Bernard!

[BERNARD *re-enters.*]

BERNARD: Hello, Jack.

JACK: It was me.

BERNARD: What was?

JACK: Who rang the bell.

BERNARD: Oh, yes, I guessed that when I saw you.

JACK [*to Jenny*]: He's quick this morning.

BERNARD: Quick?

JACK: Yes, quick.

JENNY [*to Jack*]: Cigarette?

JACK [*crossing to her and taking one*]: Thanks. [*Sits on the sofa and sees the pile of money.*] Money.

BERNARD: Yes.

JENNY: I'll get some coffee.

[*She moves to the tray, picks it up and goes,* BERNARD *holding the door for her.*]

Thank you, darling.

JACK: I'd take a cup of sulphuric acid from Jenny, just for the pleasure of watching her go and fetch it.

BERNARD: She's getting coffee now.

JACK: Yes, Bernard.

BERNARD: Have you got a pipe-cleaner?

JACK: No. [*Indicating the money*] Why don't you buy one?

BERNARD: I haven't been out yet.

JACK: On a beautiful morning like this? You frowsty old thing. What about a game this afternoon?

BERNARD: What of?

JACK: Golf, Bernard, golf. You know. The game you're nearly as bad at as I am.

BERNARD [*going to the window*]: No, I've got to get down to it.

JACK: You people and your gardens.

BERNARD: If one has a garden, one's got to keep it up.

JACK: Why?

BERNARD: One can't let it go.

JACK: If I had one I would. I'd let it go wherever it wanted to.

[*JENNY re-enters with coffee, which she hands to Jack.*]

Thank you, darling.

JENNY [*to Bernard*]: Would you like some more, darling?

BERNARD: No thank you ... very much ... indeed.

[*JACK drinks. There is an immense silence.*]

JACK [*to Jenny*]: Have you got a pin?

JENNY: No.

JACK: We might have dropped it and listened.

[*BERNARD has found a pin. He offers it to Jack.*]

BERNARD: I've got a pin.

JACK: No, Bernard, no. What's the matter with you this morning?

[*Pause. BERNARD starts to work at his pipe with the pin.*]

JACK [*putting his coffee-cup down*]: Well, I've got to work. I can't stay here talking to you idle tycoons all morning. I've got to draw a beautiful girl playing tennis in a foundation garment she doesn't need.

JENNY: What for?

JACK [*pointing to money*]: That stuff. You don't think I do it for pleasure.

[*JENNY looks in alarm at Bernard who is blowing noisily and apoplectically into his pipe.*]

JENNY: Darling!

BERNARD: My pin is stuck in my pipe.

JACK: Bernard, do me a favour. Buy some pipe-cleaners. Honestly it's the best way, even if you have to buy them on the H.P. I'll be buying beer at lunchtime, will you be down?

BERNARD [*now having a fit of coughing*]: I might.

JACK: Well take care of that cough. [*He goes.*]

JENNY: What did he come for?

BERNARD [*bitterly*]: He wanted me to play golf this afternoon.

JENNY: You should.

BERNARD: This afternoon?

JENNY: You need the exercise.

BERNARD: Are you trying to tell me what I need? You! You!

JENNY: But you do. You're putting on weight.

BERNARD [*stamping round the room*]: That is it! That is the end! You stand there criticizing me.

JENNY: Not criticizing, I was saying. You told me yourself your blue suit was tight.

BERNARD: Only because the Jew tailor you persuaded me to go to skimped the material. Anyhow it doesn't matter now.

JENNY: Don't be feeble, I never persuaded you. I simply said that Tom Palmer had got a suit for nineteen pounds and why didn't you do the same.

BERNARD: You nagged until I did.

JENNY: You were glad of it.

BERNARD: It doesn't matter! I'm not going to argue!

JENNY: It was a very good suit when you got it.

BERNARD: A businessman's suit, not a gentleman's suit. All right for someone like Tom Palmer.

JENNY: Oh don't be so superior.

BERNARD: Me? You told me yourself only last week that you'd seen him buying a postal order and it must be for his pools.

JENNY: I was joking. Haven't you any sense of humour?

BERNARD: You mean he didn't buy a postal order?

JENNY: Yes, he did buy a postal order.

BERNARD: But?

JENNY: Nothing. Oh for heaven's sake, Bernard.

BERNARD [*quietly*]: For heaven's sake, for heaven's sake. . . . Is he one of your clients?

JENNY: Don't be silly.

BERNARD: Why silly? You tell me what you told me and now you say don't be silly! For all I know you've been to bed with everyone in the district.

JENNY: Of course not! It's not like that at all. I told you, it's the money. You don't think I get any enjoyment out of it?

BERNARD: I don't think of it at all. I can't. I shall go mad. Men kill their wives for this.

JENNY: Oh, darling. . . .

BERNARD [*going towards her*]: Don't you think they do? Read the papers. By God, read tomorrow's . . . [*he is checked by a sound outside. They look towards the door.*]

[ROGER *enters.*]

ROGER: I took a taxi. Have you any money?

JENNY: Roger!

ROGER: He says he wants three times the fare because of the distance.

BERNARD: Oh does he. I'll soon deal with him. [*He goes out.*]

ROGER: Hullo, Ma.

JENNY [*going to him and kissing him*]: Darling! You're desperately early.

ROGER: The train was on time.

JENNY: I was on my way to the station and then something happened, but our clock must be terribly slow or something.

ROGER: About twenty minutes I think. [*He goes to the window.*]

[JENNY *picks up the money from the floor.*]

Are they playing? [*He stands on the stool so that he can see over the fence.*]

JENNY: Good term?

ROGER: Yes, all right.

JENNY: How did you do in the exams?

ROGER: All right. [*He is watching the cricketers.*]

[BERNARD *returns, he beckons to Jenny from the door.*]

BERNARD [*low*]: Money?

JENNY: The clock's twenty minutes slow.

BERNARD: He wants ten pounds.

JENNY: He can't want that much.

[*Hammering on front door, off.*]

BERNARD: I hit him.

JENNY [*fierce whisper*]: Hit him?

BERNARD: Ssh!

JENNY: *Pourquoi?*

BERNARD: What? Oh, *parce qu'il était* . . . bloody-minded.

ROGER [*loudly*]: Jolly good!

JENNY: I'll give him some money. [*She goes out.*]

BERNARD: What sort of term did you have?

ROGER: All right.

BERNARD: Where did you come?

ROGER: Seventh, equal.

BERNARD: Where did you start?

ROGER: Seventh.

BERNARD: Who were you equal with?

ROGER: Blakeney.

BERNARD: Who's he?

ROGER: F. J. Blakeney.

[JENNY *returns.*]

JENNY: *Ça va.*

BERNARD: *Bon.*

JENNY: Do put the clock right.

BERNARD: It is.

JENNY: Not by the train.

[BERNARD *turns to the clock and turns it round.*]

ROGER: Ooh! He's been hit in the crutch.

JENNY: Darling, don't say 'crutch' like that.

ROGER: He's in agony.

[BERNARD *goes across to stand by his son craning to see over the fence.*]

JENNY: Who are they?

BERNARD: No, he's all right, he's going to play on.

[*From the playing-field comes a polite patter of applause;* BERNARD *and* ROGER *also clap once or twice.*]

I don't know who they are. [*He turns back into the room and goes to the telephone. He dials* TIM.]

Ten five.

JENNY: Do set it.

BERNARD: Roger . . .

[ROGER *does not answer;* BERNARD *speaks louder.*]

Roger!

ROGER [*does not move*]: Yes.

BERNARD: Set the clock.

ROGER [*crossing to the clock*]: What do I do?

BERNARD: The top knob clockwise.

ROGER: Do you understand about sidereal time?

BERNARD: No! Clockwise the other way!

ROGER: Oh yes. The sidereal day is four minutes shorter than the solar day, so if you lived by the stars you'd live longer.

BERNARD: Ten eight.

ROGER [*to Jenny*]: Did you know?

JENNY: Fancy, darling. Shopping!

[*She goes.* ROGER *is still turning the clock hands.*]

ROGER: But the sidereal year is quite different and it's longer.

BERNARD [*replacing telephone*]: Too far! Stop! [*He rushes over to Roger.*] No! Don't turn it back. Never do that. Never never! [*He takes the clock.*] Don't they teach you anything at school?

ROGER: Not about clocks, actually.

BERNARD: Only about sidereal time.

ROGER: Not that either really. Only in Scripture.

BERNARD: Why Scripture?

ROGER: The Headmaster's keen on it and we get him talking.

[JENNY *re-enters with a shopping-basket.*]

JENNY: Darling, do take your case up.

ROGER: O.K. [*He makes no move.*]

BERNARD: Now.

ROGER: Oh, all right. [*He slouches out.*]

JENNY: Do be nice to him on his first day back.

BERNARD: Don't you want him to obey you?

JENNY: Oh, yes, but, you know. . . . Money, shall I get some at the bank?

BERNARD: If you must.

JENNY: Oh no I needn't. [*She goes to the pile of notes.*] I can use some of this.

BERNARD: Was it true?

JENNY [*taking some money*]: We can't go into all that now if I'm going to get the shopping done. Did you really mean caviare? How do you buy it?

BERNARD: By the pot.

JENNY: I'd better get several.

BERNARD: One big pot would be cheaper.

JENNY: And you'll do the drink?

BERNARD: Do the drink.

JENNY: You will, won't you? It would be awful if they turned up and there was nothing.

BERNARD: Awful, yes.

JENNY: Why did you hit the taxi-driver?

BERNARD [*tensely*]: Because I had to hit somebody and I can't hit you.

JENNY: It was an awful thing to do, suppose you'd hurt him.

BERNARD: I meant to hurt him, I wanted to hit his stupid face and if he hadn't moved I would have. I hit him on the shoulder.

JENNY: It's lucky we had the money.

BERNARD: If we hadn't had the money there wouldn't have been any reason for me to hit him.

JENNY: No, well we'll talk about that later. If I don't go now there won't be a decent banana left. [*She goes.*]

[BERNARD *lights a cigarette, he stands smoking it for a moment then he does a left hook into the air. That was how he should have hit the fellow. . . . And follow up with the right. He puts his cigarette down and adopts a boxer's stance. He swings wild lefts and rights at the air. Now he has his man down he looks at him on the ground by the sofa, aims two vicious kicks at the sofa itself, picks up his cigarette, and goes over to the telephone. He dials.*]

BERNARD: Farrow and Leeming! Acton here. I want a case of champagne and two bottles of brandy. Can you deliver them this afternoon?

CURTAIN

ACT THREE

It is early evening, still daylight.

[ROGER *stands on the stool watching the cricketers.* JENNY *enters, dressed for the party.*]

JENNY: Oh do hurry!

ROGER: He scored a six just now.

JENNY: But you don't like cricket.

ROGER [*remembering that he doesn't and stepping off the stool to go to the fireplace*]: No, I don't. It's fiddling, don't you think, while Rome . . . you know what.

JENNY: Fetch the table.

ROGER: I don't think Nero really did fiddle.

JENNY: The table.

ROGER: It's a popular fallacy.

JENNY: The table!

ROGER: From the dining-room?

JENNY: No, the hall. Do listen.

ROGER: Listen?

JENNY: To what I say.

ROGER: O.K.

[*He starts to go off as* BERNARD *comes on with the table.*]

BERNARD: You might give a hand, Roger.

ROGER: I was going to get the table, but . . .

BERNARD: Get something else. There's plenty.

ROGER [*going off*]: Glasses.

JENNY: No.

BERNARD: Why not? He's fifteen.

JENNY: Sure to break something.

BERNARD: A glass, they're only hired. Half a crown.

JENNY: Half a crown's half a crown.

BERNARD: I know half a crown's half a crown.

JENNY: We're not made of money.

BERNARD: No, but . . .

JENNY: But what?

BERNARD: Here are the glasses.

[*As* ROGER *enters with the tray.*]

ROGER: Where shall I put it?

JENNY: Table.

ROGER: One fell over.

BERNARD: You broke it?

ROGER: Sort of.

JENNY: Never mind.

BERNARD: Either you broke it or you didn't. There's no 'sort of'.

ROGER: Yes, there is.

JENNY: Don't contradict your father, darling.

ROGER: I didn't.

BERNARD: Or your mother. Half a crown those glasses cost.

ROGER [*producing one*]: Here you are, then.

BERNARD: Give it to your mother.

JENNY: Oh don't be silly, darling, I don't want it. Do hurry or they'll be here. I'll get a cloth. [*She goes.*]

BERNARD: You know, you mustn't be rude to your mother.

ROGER: No.

BERNARD: After all, she is . . . your mother.

ROGER: Yes. [*Pause.*] Shall I put the Monarch away?

BERNARD: No, that's all right. I'll do it.

[*He goes out.* ROGER *watches him. After a moment there is the sound of the engine starting . . .* JENNY *re-enters with the table-cloth.*]

JENNY: Oh no!

ROGER: First pull.

JENNY: Please.

[BERNARD *pushes the mower into view. He switches it off.*]

Not now, darling.

ROGER: Can I have a go?

JENNY: No you cannot, they'll be here in a moment. Go and wash and put on a clean shirt.

ROGER: Oh, all right.

[*He goes out.* JENNY *puts the cloth on the table.*]

JENNY: Table-cloth.

[BERNARD *stands outside looking at his machine.*]

BERNARD: It's a pity the paint doesn't last.

JENNY: Darling, there's no time. Do get ready. You can't leave it there.

BERNARD: They'll want to see it.

JENNY [*who is distributing ashtrays*]: You're not to disappear into the garden with all the men.

BERNARD: No need to if it's here.

JENNY: It looks like showing off.

BERNARD: I don't mind. [*He comes in and looks round vaguely*] Table-cloth . . . table-cloth.

JENNY [*indicating the table upon which it lies, folded*]: There. You always say Tom Palmer's showing off when he leaves his car outside his garage.

BERNARD: I say, you say. [*He begins to spread the cloth.*]

JENNY: You did, last time.

BERNARD [*shaking his head*]: No.

JENNY: As we got out of the car.

BERNARD: You said 'He's left his Mercedes outside for us to admire'. All I said was that I didn't blame him.

JENNY: You said you weren't surprised.

BERNARD: Whore.

JENNY [*going towards the door*]: What do you want besides champagne and brandy for the cocktails?

BERNARD: Angostura and lump sugar.

JENNY: I'll get the sugar.

[*She goes out.* BERNARD *wanders out to the mower. He pushes it so that it is just out of sight, looks at it and pulls it a little closer to him; there is a cry of* 'How's that?' *from the cricket-field and a burst of clapping.*]

BERNARD [*looking up and calling to an upstairs window*]: What was it?

ROGER [*off*]: Lbw.

BERNARD: Don't take all night about changing.

[*He comes in and takes a cigarette from some that Jenny has placed in a glass. She enters with a bowl of sugar.*]

JENNY: No, not from there.

BERNARD: I've sucked it now.

JENNY: Well don't put ash on the carpet.

BERNARD [*indicating around*]: Ashtrays.

JENNY: Oh no, let's have them clean for the start.

BERNARD: Fireplace, then.

JENNY: I wonder about the windows.

BERNARD: Open.

JENNY: You don't want people to be cold.

BERNARD: It's warm, warm.

JENNY: But when the sun's down.

BERNARD: We can shut them. Let them have a look at the garden.

JENNY [*at window*]: Pity. The tobaccos are really gone.

BERNARD: The roses are all right. And the lawn.

JENNY: You only think of the lawn.

BERNARD [*loudly*]: Do I? Do I really?

JENNY: What's the matter?

BERNARD: As if you didn't know.

JENNY: Darling, with Roger here and people coming . . .

BERNARD: Well?

> [JENNY *makes a kind of helpless gesture which enfolds the whole situation.*]

Exactly. You've no need to worry.

> [ROGER *enters.*]

ROGER: 'A bumping pitch and a blinding light,
  An hour to play and the last man in.'

JENNY: Do try and be useful, won't you? Hand things round and talk sensibly when people talk to you.

BERNARD: They won't play for another hour.

ROGER [*to Bernard*]: Quotation. Like The Raven. 'Nevermore.' [*To Jenny*] They'll only ask me whether I had a good term.

BERNARD: Oh I know. 'The Colonel's dead and the Gatling's jammed.'

ROGER: 'And the voice of a schoolboy rallies the ranks,
  Play up, play up, and play the game.'

> [BERNARD *is arranging the drinks table to his satisfaction.*]

JENNY: Do you want ice?

BERNARD: No, the bottles are in the fridge.

ROGER: What do I drink? Champers?

JENNY: Where did you learn to say champers?

ROGER: Some of the chaps at school.

JENNY: They drink it?

ROGER: No, say it.

BERNARD: No brandy in yours. And not too much.

ROGER: I don't like it, actually.

[*Sound of a car.*]

JENNY: Here's someone.

BERNARD: Early.

JENNY: Bill and Beryl.

BERNARD: Another bottle, Roger.

ROGER: One?

BERNARD: Yes, yes. Hurry up.

[ROGER *goes.*]

BERNARD [*looking at Jenny*]: What the hell are we doing?

JENNY: Having a party.

[*Door bell. She goes out.* BERNARD *starts to open a bottle.*]

BERNARD: Having a party, a jolly, bloody party.

[BILL *and* BERYL *are heard in the hall.*]

BERYL: No, it's been lovely, but oh for a drop of rain. Everything's going brown.

BILL: There won't be a splash of rain till we start on our holidays.

[*They enter,* BERYL, JENNY, BILL.]

BERYL: Last year, my God, last year.

JENNY: And us too.

BILL: Hullo Bernard. This is a very pleasant occasion.

BERNARD: Hi, Bill, Beryl . . . [*He shakes hands with her.*]

BERYL: Are we too early? I told Bill we'd be first.

BILL: And I said 'what of it?' [*He sees the drinks table.*] I say, genuine high-class sarsaparilla.

[ROGER *enters with another bottle.*]

BERYL: Hullo Roger, bigger every time I see you.

[*She shakes hands with him.* BERNARD *is mixing the drinks.*]

BILL: Back from school? Had a good term? Two silly questions one after another. Got any silly answers?

BERNARD: He keeps those for the exams.

[*General laughter as drinks are handed out.*]

BILL: All the best.

BERYL: Cheers.

JENNY: Cheers.

ROGER: Why do people say cheers?

BILL: Why not?

[*Door bell.*]

JENNY: Someone. Roger, you go.

[*He goes. She speaks to the others*]

Probably the Palmers.

BERYL: Oh good, I can kill two birds with one stone and you're one of them, Jenny.

BILL: Jenny a bird?

JENNY: I can't give blood. I've had jaundice.

BERYL: No, Civil Defence. We all ought to do it.

BERNARD: What happens?

BERYL: Lectures and first aid. You know what to do if they start dropping the things.

BILL: Harp lessons, that's all we'll need.

[JENNY *has taken a quick look out of the door.*]

JENNY: It's not the Palmers. Stephen and Laura Hicks.

BERYL: Oh.

BERNARD [*to Bill*]: Not too much angostura?

BILL: Perfect. Do you know Le Touquet?

BERNARD: Not well, why? Hullo!

[STEPHEN *and* LAURA *have entered.*]

STEPHEN [*to Jenny*]: Splendid surprise being rung up and asked to a party.

BERNARD: Not really a party.

LAURA [*kissing Jenny*]: Your Roger's terribly good-looking.

JENNY: Oh, but untidy. You all know each other?

[ROGER *has re-entered and is handing round a tray of canapés.* BERNARD *gives drinks to the newcomers.*]

BILL: Of course. How are the oil-tycoons?

STEPHEN: Bearing up. Are people still buying houses?

BILL: Yes, but I can always dispose of a nice deep cave.

JENNY: Beryl, you ought to rope Laura into your Civil Defence.

BERYL: Oh no, I'm sure she's much too busy with her job.

LAURA: It does take up time.

BILL [*to Stephen*]: I call them Beryl's harp lessons. That's what we'll need; we will.

BERYL: Harp, my dearest, is what you do.

ROGER [*to Beryl*]: Did you go on the March?

BERYL: March?

ROGER: We had fifteen Old Boys who went all the way from Aldermaston.

JENNY: Darling, Civil Defence isn't the same as whatever it's called.

LAURA: Anti-Nuclear something.

BILL: Bomb.

[*General laughter. Door bell.*]

JENNY: Roger ... [*He goes out.*]

STEPHEN: I shall dine out on that.

BERNARD: Bill, you've an empty glass. [*He takes Bill's glass.*]

BILL: Careful! Beryl's driving.

BERYL: Sometimes I think Bill has a book full of old jokes and learns a page a day.

BILL: Well, at least it's a different page.

JENNY [*to Beryl*]: I'm ashamed of the garden. Everything's withering up.

BERYL: Your roses are marvellous. And the nemesia.

[*They move up towards the window.* BERNARD *is at the table with* BILL, *giving him another drink. For a moment* LAURA *and* STEPHEN *are together.*]

LAURA: Bitch.

STEPHEN: Who?

LAURA: Beryl Wilson.

STEPHEN: Why?

LAURA: She said I was busy.

STEPHEN: Oh well, local yokels.

[TOM *and* LOUISE PALMER *enter.*]

JENNY [*turning to them*]: Hullo!

BILL: Tom! How are you? How's the Stock Exchange?

TOM: All right. How are you?

BILL: All right.

[JENNY *has embraced Louise.*]

JENNY: You do know Stephen and Laura, don't you? Yes, of course you do.

LOUISE: Of course. [*To Laura*] How's your elocution going?

LAURA: Speech therapy actually.

BERNARD: Roger! [*To Tom*] Let me arm you with a drink.

BILL: And a very good drink too.

BERYL [*to Louise*]: You are the very person I want to see.

[BERNARD *has given them drinks. He goes to the door.*]

BERNARD: Roger!

ROGER [*appears*]: Yes?

LOUISE: Hullo, Roger, how are you?

ROGER: Hullo, Mrs Palmer. Fine.

BERNARD: Another bottle. Where were you?

ROGER: Nowhere. [*He goes.*]

TOM: Growing up.

[*He turns to Stephen down stage. The conversation is simultaneous.*]
How are you?

STEPHEN: Fine. You?	LOUISE: It seems only yesterday
TOM: Splendid. Been on your holiday yet?	since he was on his tricycle.
	JENNY: This is a terrible age.
STEPHEN: We took a fortnight in June, we're taking another in September.	BERYL: They all are, my dear. Wait till he starts falling for girls.
TOM: Of course you don't have to worry about school holidays.	LAURA: Surely it's worse with girls.

STEPHEN: No, but Laura's work ties us down a bit.

[BERNARD *has refilled Bill's glass.* BILL *calls across to Beryl.*]

BILL: This puts up the local standard all right, all right. No trotting out the old South African the next time the Actons come round.

STEPHEN: There won't be much more of that to trot.

JENNY: What?

STEPHEN: South African. The way things are going.

TOM: No, my God.

LAURA: All over Africa.

[*They have now all turned towards each other.*]

BERYL: We nearly went to Kenya.

BILL: After the war.

[ROGER *enters with two bottles which he stands holding.*]

LOUISE: How thankful you must be.

BERYL: That we didn't? Thankful.

BILL: All right then, though; bags of booze, bags of servants, plenty of sun.

STEPHEN: And no taxes.

LAURA: Ah, but now . . .

BERYL: Finished.

BILL: *Kaputt.*

TOM: Mind you, I blame us.

BERNARD: Handing over to them, you mean?

LOUISE: Of course one's not supposed to say it, but . . .

BERYL: Grinning apes, I call them.

LAURA: They make good nurses.

STEPHEN: Oh well, yes, but, that's hardly everything, is it darling?

BILL: I don't say anything against them, nothing at all, but there are some things you just can't deny.

LOUISE: Daddy always said it was a pity the Germans ever lost their colonies.

STEPHEN: Yes, they knew.

BERYL: Firm handling.

BILL: Twelve with a rawhide whip.

JENNY: Or a sjambok.

LOUISE: Which they understood.

TOM: Mind you, they'll still need capital.

[*This last comes out pontifically and is followed by a momentary pause at the happy thought.* ROGER *is standing watching them. He starts swinging a bottle like an Indian club as he speaks.*]

ROGER: Actually there won't be any solution to the colour problem until we're all coffee-coloured.

BERYL: Roger!

JENNY: Darling!

STEPHEN: Where did you pick up that theory?

ROGER: A book.

BILL: Theories that come out of books are best kept in books.

BERNARD: And stop waving that bottle about.

[*He takes it from Roger and gives him a glass already poured out.*]
Here take this and start handing things around.

[*He hands him two dishes of canapés and turns to Bill.*]

That's the sort of education one gets for four hundred a year.

[STEPHEN *and* TOM *are slightly apart from the others.*]

BILL: My God how right you are.

TOM: How are you?

LOUISE: We've got to have Martin coached if he's to get his A-level.

STEPHEN: Fine, you?

TOM: Oh, yes, fine. How's oil?

STEPHEN: Not bad.

BILL: If we could only take it off income tax.

TOM: Your shares are steady?

STEPHEN: I wish I had some.

LAURA: No government would dare.

LOUISE: I don't see why not, after all, we save them pounds.

[ROGER *comes up to them with the dishes.*]

STEPHEN: Thanks. I say, caviare!

BERYL: Caviare!

[*They are now one group again.*]

You must have had a legacy.

BERNARD: I'm a Russian spy. This is how they pay me.

LOUISE: Sort of immoral earnings.

BERNARD: Sort of, yes. Ha, ha.

JENNY: Darling, shut the window. It's getting cold.

BERNARD: I'll just put the Monarch away.

ROGER: I'll do it.

BERNARD: Oh no you won't.

BILL: A Monarch? Who's got a Monarch? Bernard?

STEPHEN: Have you? Let's have a look.

LOUISE: I've been wanting Tom to get one for ages. Come and look at it.

BERYL: Give us a demonstration.

[*They are going out of the french windows.*]

JENNY: You've asked for it now.

[*Door bell.*]

JENNY: Who's that? We didn't ask anyone else.

BERYL: Probably Jack Foster, he can smell a party a mile away.

JENNY: Roger, go and see.

[ROGER *goes out of the door. The others are now in the garden, except* JENNY *who empties an ashtray into the waste-paper basket. The mower starts up outside.* ROGER *returns.*]

ROGER: It's a woman to see you.

[LEONIE *enters.* JENNY *stares at her, aghast.*]

LEONIE: Good evening, dear.

JENNY: What do you want?

[ROGER *has slipped out into the garden.*]

LEONIE: I want to talk. [*She sits.*] Oh my feet. I do hate to walk.

JENNY: You can't come here, you mustn't.

LEONIE: It is very indiscreet, yes. But important.

JENNY: I've a party on. Guests.

LEONIE: So I am one of them.

JENNY: No, I'm sorry, but no.

LEONIE: Why not?

JENNY: These are friends, local people, they all know each other. They'd think it odd.

LEONIE: Me odd?

JENNY: Yes, if you want to know, they would. And my husband . . .

LEONIE: Does he know?

JENNY: Today. It would be the worst possible thing if he met you now.

LEONIE: It cannot be helped.

JENNY: But how can I explain you?

LEONIE: Some little lie. That you met me on holiday last year.

JENNY: We went to Cornwall.

LEONIE: And the weather was terrible, good, I can do it.

[STEPHEN *and* LAURA *enter.*]

LAURA [*as she enters*]: It's chilly now.

JENNY [*stepping forward*]: Laura, this is Miss Pimosz, we met down at Mevagissey last year and she happened to be passing, so she dropped in, what a surprise.

[*The mower has stopped.* LAURA *and* STEPHEN *glance at Leonie, who smiles.*]

LEONIE: Hullo, Laura dear.

JENNY [*looking at Laura*]: You!

LAURA: And you?

[*The others enter.* BERYL, LOUISE, TOM, BILL, *and* BERNARD.]

BERYL: Oh it's a wonderful machine, Bill, you'll have to keep up with the Actons even if . . . [*She sees Leonie and stops dead.*]

LOUISE: Oh!

[*They stand in a small group by the window looking at her.*]

LEONIE [*to Tom*]: You I have not seen before. Dear Louise's husband, yes?

TOM: Yes.

[*There is silence. The men look at Tom, they look at each other.*]

BILL: Look here . . . does this mean . . . ?

STEPHEN: It does.

BERYL [*at Laura*]: Speech therapy!

LAURA: In the mornings.

LEONIE: You see how discreet I am.

BERNARD: I don't call this discreet.

BILL: No, by God.

[ROGER *enters through the french windows.*]

ROGER: Funny, you know, it's still quite light but you can see Venus as clear as anything. At least I think it's Venus. [*To Bill*] Do you know?

BILL: Venus I think, yes, Venus.

STEPHEN: I say Bernard, I wonder if I could ask Roger to do something for me? I'm right out of tobacco. If he could slip down to the Royal Oak and get me some.

BERNARD: Yes, do that, Roger.

ROGER: What sort?

STEPHEN: The curly-cut. Say it's for me, they'll know. [*He takes out a note.*] Have a drink.

ROGER: It's not allowed.

BERNARD: Lemonade.

STEPHEN: Tomato juice.

JENNY: Coca-cola.

BILL: Ginger beer.

STEPHEN: Anything like that, yes. Don't hurry.

[*He more or less hustles Roger to the door.* ROGER *goes.*]

LEONIE: And please a drink for me.

[BERNARD *picks up a bottle of champagne.*]

Brandy I prefer, or I gurk.

[BERNARD *pours a glass of brandy and gives it to her.*]

Thank you. Good health.

[*She raises her glass to the girls, then to the men.* STEPHEN *bows slightly.*]

Where were you on Thursday, Beryl dear?

BERYL: At a first-aid lecture.

LEONIE: Ten guineas, that will cost. Someone was disappointed.

BILL: Now look . . .

LEONIE: Yes?

BILL: Is it true? That all of us . . . all of them . . .

LEONIE: Yes.

TOM [*to Louise*]: And this is . . . ?

LOUISE: Yes.

TOM: My God. [*To Leonie*] It's not on, you know.

LEONIE: What not on?

TOM: Well you know, I hope I'm broad-minded, but . . .

STEPHEN: It's a bit of a flanker.

LEONIE: But you knew. [*She points to Laura.*] She tell me that she tell you, to explain the money.

STEPHEN: I didn't know there was anyone else involved.

LEONIE [*with a coarse laugh*]: Ha, you should read a book about the bees or something.

TOM: That sort of talk's not going to help. Are there many others?

LEONIE: Two girls at Orpington and one at Muswell Hill, but she is moving.

JENNY: Nobody else here?

LEONIE: No.

BILL: Odd we should all be together like this.

STEPHEN: Coincidence.

TOM: Just as well we all see eye to eye on most things.

BERNARD: I don't believe it.

BILL: What?

BERNARD: That you've known all the time.

BERYL: One had to explain the money.

BERNARD [*to the three men*]: But when we played golf you knew, when we met on the train, you knew, in the pub you knew.

TOM: I don't see what's so odd about it.

BERNARD: You never gave a sign.

STEPHEN: Neither did you.

BERNARD: I only found out today.

LEONIE: Jenny has not been long with us.

TOM: All the same, you know, Mrs um . . . it's not on. Coming here, I mean . . . well, it doesn't do.

STEPHEN: Hardly discreet.

LEONIE: It was not my wish to come, but there has been trouble.

BERYL: What sort of trouble?

LEONIE: So that I dare not use the telephone.

BILL: Police?

LEONIE: Yes.

JENNY: At Wimpole Street?

LEONIE: A Superintendent McRoberts.

BILL: Asking questions?

LEONIE: Telling me to clear out or else.

LOUISE: He didn't ask for names?

LEONIE: He knew he wouldn't get them.

LAURA [*with a sigh of relief*]: Well . . .

BERYL: Yes.

BERNARD: That's that.

LEONIE [*sips*]: Good cognac.

BILL: I suppose you're selling up.

LEONIE: To a psychiatrist, yes.

STEPHEN: What about . . . er . . . them . . . ?

LEONIE: I do not have addresses.

TOM: Bit of a surprise for some of them when they find a psychiatrist there.

[LEONIE *shrugs.*]

STEPHEN [*catching Laura's eye*]: Well, er . . .

LAURA: Yes, we must go.

JENNY: Oh no, not yet. Hardly arrived.

LAURA: Really we must.

BERYL: So must we.

LAURA: Lovely party.

BERNARD: For Christ's sake!

BILL: No point in a fuss, old man.

TOM: What can't be helped, can't be helped.

JENNY: No, don't go, don't! Give them all another drink.

    [BERNARD *grabs a bottle.*]

LOUISE: No really . . .

STEPHEN: Better save it Bernard.

TOM: Money's going to be tighter from now on.

BILL: That's a true word.

LEONIE: Why?

BILL: Obvious enough.

LEONIE: This has happened to me before.

STEPHEN: So one imagined.

LEONIE: It is never the end.

STEPHEN: Rather different for you. You're used to it.

LEONIE: Everybody can become used to anything.

BILL: Not jug.

LEONIE: I am the only one that is in danger. [*Indicating the girls*] They
    commit no crime. And you know nothing.

TOM: They'll have their eye on you now.

LEONIE: In the West End, yes.

STEPHEN: I don't see that you could operate anywhere else.

LEONIE: Why not out here?

BERNARD⎫
TOM   ⎬ : Out here?

LEONIE: Frequent trains to City and West End. At your station it
    says so.

BILL: Yes, there's a jolly good service, but . . .

    [BERNARD *fills his glass.*]

  Oh, thanks.

LEONIE: If one could find some suitable property. . . .

LOUISE: I don't think one could, well, you know . . . here.

STEPHEN: Absolutely not on, not on at all.

TOM: Wouldn't do.

LEONIE [*about to go*]: Then I must see what I can find in Orpington.

STEPHEN: Er . . .

LAURA: No, much too far.

LOUISE: Cross country.

BERYL: Of course if there was somewhere round here it would be . . .

LEONIE: Yes?

BERYL [*lamely*]: Handy on my Civil Defence days.

LAURA: And for my mornings at the school.

JENNY: And the shops.

BERNARD: There's such a thing as messing your own doorstep.

TOM: That's a pretty rotten thing to say.

BERNARD: True.

LEONIE: I think perhaps we keep this a business discussion, yes?

BILL: Yes.

STEPHEN: Not much to discuss.

BILL: Oh, I don't know.

LEONIE: Jenny dear, take the girls out for a little.

JENNY: All right. Come and see the roses.

[*All the women go off demurely.*]

BERNARD [*to Leonie*]: I find that rather high-handed.

TOM: Easier without them.

BERNARD: This happens to be my house.

BILL: Come off it, Bernard, we're all in this together.

STEPHEN: Lucky not to be in court together.

LEONIE: No, no, it will not come to that.

BILL [*to Stephen*]: How much do you stand to lose?

STEPHEN: About four thousand a year.

BILL: Yes. Tax free.

BERNARD: Is it?

BILL: Well, of course. You can't declare it.

STEPHEN [*indicating Leonie*]: And she makes no return of payments.

LEONIE: Only for the maid.

BERNARD: Tax free.

TOM: Worth about seven thousand taxed.

STEPHEN: On top of your normal income. If you retired it would be worth more.

BILL: Ah, but you don't want to retire. Beryl and I talked this over.

BERNARD: You did?

BILL: Naturally. Oh, I know how you feel. I felt just like that at first.

TOM: Wanted to break the place up.

STEPHEN: I did break the place up. Gave us an excuse to redecorate.
[LEONIE *nods every now and then with approval.*]

TOM: Funny really, how quickly you get used to the idea.

STEPHEN: You feel it's no worse than giving someone a blood transfusion or something.

BILL: That's the way I look at it.

TOM: And there's the money.

STEPHEN: I must admit I don't know how we're going to manage.

TOM: We can't take Martin away from school at this stage.

STEPHEN: Same here with Jeremy. And Jennifer's pony. I'm paying through the nose for its keep at the stables but I can't sell it, she's entered for the Gymkhana.

BILL: I've got a new greenhouse half up. Can't tell them to take it down.

TOM [*to Bernard*]: That's the trouble, we're all involved in things. We can't just stop.

BILL: And between these four walls I don't mind admitting that Beryl and I get on much better these days.

TOM: So do we. Most of our rows were money.

STEPHEN: Hell to go back. [*He picks up a bottle.*] May I?

BERNARD: Yes, do.
[*The others hold out their glasses mechanically.* STEPHEN *fills them.* LEONIE *holds out her glass.*]

LEONIE: Please.
[BERNARD *fills it.*]
You understand better?

BERNARD: Yes. I hadn't thought of it being tax free.

TOM: Makes a difference, yes.

STEPHEN: And we do spend the money on worth-while things, education, the garden, and so on.

BILL: That's forced on us in a way. You can't make too much of a splash in case the tax people notice.

STEPHEN: No yachts.

TOM: That's why you want to keep your job.

BILL: I do a good bit of betting. Helps to explain things. Funny, you know, I win. I never used to.

TOM: Your luck's quite different when you're rich.

BERNARD: Rich . . .

[*In the momentary pause the women can be heard chattering, off.*]

BILL: They're away. Like a hen-house.

LEONIE: Should we perhaps start talking business?

BILL: Only too ready. [*To the others*] Yes?

TOM: But look we ought to do it properly, I mean treat it as business, keep off side issues.

BILL: We need a chairman.

STEPHEN: Bernard.

BILL: Yes.

BERNARD: Oh no.

TOM: They're your chairs.

BILL: Do you propose him?

TOM: I do.

STEPHEN: Seconded.

BILL: Carried *nem. con.* [*He indicates a chair*] The Chair.

[*They sit.*]

BERNARD: Do we keep minutes?

LEONIE: Nothing in writing.

BILL: Sound principle.

BERNARD: Well . . . er . . . any ideas?

BILL: Yes, Mr Chairman, I have. I happen to know of a little property that's just coming on the market which I think would suit this lady.

STEPHEN: Where is it?

BILL: That's the joy of it. East Woodfield.

TOM [*to Leonie*]: One station up the line.

STEPHEN: Not on our doorstep.

LEONIE: How much money?

BILL: Four and half thousand.

BERNARD: Very cheap.

BILL: There's work to be done. It's a draughty old place.

STEPHEN: Oil-fired central heating. I can help you there.

BERNARD: Of course, you're in the trade.

LEONIE: How many rooms?

BILL: Twelve with a kitchen and two baths, all mod. con., half an acre of garden and two minutes' walk from the station.

BERNARD: One of those big houses backing on the railway?

BILL: That's it. The rates are less than they might be because of the trains. It's a snip.

LEONIE: When can I move in?

BERNARD: Any idea, Bill?

BILL: September the first.

TOM: That's good. We don't want too much of a gap.

LEONIE: Tomorrow I will come and see.

BILL: Splendid.

BERNARD: What about your ... well ... customers?

LEONIE: Clients.

BERNARD: How'll they know?

STEPHEN: That's a good point.

LEONIE: I shall inform them.

BERNARD: You said you hadn't their addresses.

LEONIE: But their names I have, and a copy of *Who is Who*.

STEPHEN: Get them through their clubs.

TOM: They're a pretty distinguished crowd.

BERNARD: Are they? Are they?

BILL: Miss Pimosz had better put down a deposit in the morning.

LEONIE: Ten per cent.

BILL: Non-returnable.

TOM: Perhaps we could ...

STEPHEN: No we couldn't. We must stay right out of this, don't you agree, Mr Chairman?

BERNARD: Oh, absolutely.

TOM: Are we agreed then?

BERNARD: All those in favour ... ?

[*All half-raise their hands.*]

Carried.

BILL: Unanimously.

BERNARD: Any other business?

LEONIE: The telephone.

BILL: Vital.

TOM [*to Leonie*]: Apply at once.

BERNARD: As a matter of fact I've been doing a contract for the G.P.O. I know the area manager.

BILL: Nothing like the Old Boy net.

BERNARD: Well if that's everything I declare the meeting closed.

STEPHEN: There's one thing ... not business ... just a thing we must agree on.

BILL: Yes?

STEPHEN: It's pretty important that we carry on normally.

BILL: Press on regardless ...

TOM: As it were.

STEPHEN: I mean we shouldn't talk about it among ourselves.

BILL: Forget it.

BERNARD: I don't quite see how one can forget it.

LEONIE [*jumping up*]: Oh yes, if a thing is not convenient to live with, you can forget. Easy to forget. You must forget if you want to live at all. Or else you are like young boys who think all the time of death. But soon they put it from them, not because death has gone, but because they want to live. We all must live in the way we want to live, and forget what does not help us so to do. This you know. You are men of family and education.

STEPHEN: A certain amount of background, yes.

BERNARD: So we don't refer to this again.

BILL: Not unless we have to.

TOM: Even when we're alone together we don't want to talk about it, really.

BILL: After all, what would we say?

BERNARD: It's a purely personal matter, between ourselves and our wives.

LEONIE: I will go and tell them.

[*She goes out.* BERNARD *has filled their glasses.*]

BILL [*raising his glass*]: Well, here's to us.

STEPHEN: Good luck.

ALL: Cheers.

TOM: Half an acre of garden?

BILL: It's been let go.

BERNARD: Should we grass it?

STEPHEN: That means a lot of work.

TOM: A gardener?

STEPHEN: Tricky.

[*The women return, led by* JENNY.]

BERYL: I find it quite hopeless trying to grow azaleas here, I don't know why.

JENNY: Lime in the soil, they hate that. Can we all have a drink?

LEONIE: Not me, I go.

JENNY: Must you?

LEONIE: Yes dear, but I will give you a ring.

BILL: And me. At the office tomorrow.

TOM: You know, we ought to get cracking on this garden.

LOUISE: Which garden?

TOM: Oh the one . . . you know, with the house.

BILL: It runs right down to the railway line.

STEPHEN: The best thing might be to get a firm to do it.

LAURA: Much the most practical.

BERYL: But soulless, don't you think?

[ROGER *enters with* JACK FOSTER.]

JACK: Hullo, hullo. Enter a gate-crasher!

[*They turn and look at him. For a moment there is complete silence.*]

BERNARD: Oh, hullo Jack.

JACK: I met young Roger boozing at the pub and he told me the stuff was flowing round here.

ROGER [*to Stephen*]: Here's your tobacco and some change. I didn't have to have a drink because Mr Foster bought me some beer.

BERNARD: Beer?

JACK: Only a pint of bitter.

BERNARD: He's only fifteen.

ROGER: It was jolly good. Do you know Van Gogh cut off his ear?

JENNY: I think you know everyone.

JACK: Er . . . [*He looks at Leonie.*]

LEONIE [*to Jenny*]: And very nice to have met you again, Mrs Acton, and all your friends. Now I must go, perhaps we meet again and talk of Cornwall, yes?

JACK: That's funny. You were a dressmaker last time.

LEONIE: I am a dressmaker this time. What are you?

JACK: Me? I call myself an artist.

LEONIE: Successful?

JACK: Well – er – yes.

LEONIE: Good. Then perhaps we also shall meet again. Good-bye, good-bye, good-bye. [*She goes.*]

JENNY: I'll see her out.

JACK: Cornwall, but what's she got to do with Cornwall?

JACK [*to Bill*]: How's crime?

BILL: Taxed as usual.

STEPHEN: Still you can't complain being your own employer.

BILL: Don't you believe it.

TOM: Schedule A and a whacking great claim.

BILL: Oh never. P.A.Y.E. for me. I'm paid as a director.

STEPHEN: Who's the other?

BILL: Beryl.

STEPHEN: That's cunning.

TOM: Very cunning.

STEPHEN: Car on the firm?

BILL: And drink.

TOM: Cunning.

STEPHEN: Very cunning.

JACK: What about Beryl?

BILL: I did have her down as secretary but they wouldn't wear it.

LOUISE: Did you hear Monica Jessel's gone to hospital?

BERYL: No, when?

LOUISE: Yesterday.

LAURA: I heard she was going.

BERYL: Everything out?

LOUISE: The lot.

LAURA: Sensible.

BERYL: But all the same . . .

JENNY: She'll be much, much better.

LOUISE: Yes, but all the same . . .

LAURA: Should have had it done years ago.

JENNY: Where is she?

LOUISE: St Michael's.

LAURA: That's a dump.

BERYL: I'll send some flowers, is she in a ward?

[*Laughter from the men.* ROGER *who started with the women has now drifted across to them.*]

JACK: Because she was your wife or because she was a director.

BILL: All three. [*He hears Laura and turns to her*] Who has the money?

BERYL: The Jessels.

LOUISE: Not Monica, Monica in a ward? Oh, no. Private room.

LAURA: Of course they've got the money.

[*The two groups now turn towards each other.*]

BILL: Oh well.

STEPHEN: Naturally.

LOUISE: They don't look it.

TOM: They don't have to.

BERYL: Funny how you can always tell.

BERNARD: Always, always, always.

ROGER: Tell what?

BILL: When someone's a member of the chosen race.

LAURA: Not that there aren't some decent ones.

STEPHEN: Quite, but you can tell.

ROGER: Some people say we're all Jews.

JENNY: What?

ROGER: The lost ten tribes.

BILL: Some people will say anything.

ROGER [looking eagerly round the party]: And quite a lot of us are circumcised.

    [JACK roars with laughter. BERNARD turns with effort.]

BERNARD: Leave the room.

ROGER: Why?

BERNARD: Leave the room at once.

JENNY: He didn't mean to say anything.

ROGER: What did I say?

BERNARD: Will you do as you're told and leave the room!

ROGER: I want to know what I said wrong.

BERNARD: Don't stand there defying me!

ROGER: But it's not fair. You say much worse things.

BERNARD: I am your father, do you hear? Your father and I tell you to leave the room. You're not fit to associate with decent people.

JACK: Oh, I say Bernard . . .

BERNARD: This is my house and my son. I tell him what to do. Go on.

ROGER: But it comes up all the time in the Bible.

BERNARD: So do the Ten Commandments. Do you know the Ten Commandments?

ROGER: Yes.

BERNARD: Say them.

ROGER: Now?

JENNY: Darling . . .

BERNARD: Now!

ROGER: Thou shalt not . . . [He pauses.]

BERNARD: There . . . and a liar as well. Go upstairs and wait for me.

ROGER: But . . .

BERNARD: Go upstairs, sit on your bed, read your Bible, and wait for me!

[ROGER *goes*.]

JENNY: Don't be too hard on him, darling; after all, it is a party.

JACK: And he really said nothing.

BERNARD: I think I'm the best judge of that. [*He goes*.]

STEPHEN: I'm with him every time.

BERYL: Yes, they do need discipline.

BILL: A good caning from his father never did any boy harm.

TOM: Mine used a belt on me.

STEPHEN: And you never resented it, did you?

TOM: Of course not.

LOUISE: It's the only way if you want respect.

JACK: I resented it all right, my God I did. I made it as hard as I could for them too [*clutching his behind*].

LOUISE: Jeremy tried that on.

STEPHEN: A tap on the fingers soon changed his mind.

JACK: How savage you are tonight. Have you been eating meat?

[*A moment's awkward pause*.]

JENNY [*jumping in*]: Look, do have another drink everybody. Stephen, fill us all up.

[STEPHEN *crosses to the table*.]

JACK: Do you think old Bernard's got a drop of Scotch hidden away?

JENNY: I expect you'll find some in the cupboard.

[JACK *moves towards it*.]

LAURA: Really Jack, you can't drink Bernard's private supply.

JACK [*finding the bottle*]: Can't I just?

BERYL: You'd soon hear about it if it was my house.

JACK: Six of the best? [*He raises his glass*.] Cheers. After all, I haven't been drinking champagne. I didn't know this party was on. Why not? Because I wasn't invited. [*He moves to Jenny*.] But you don't mind, do you, Jenny? Please say you don't [*kneeling*].

JENNY: No, of course not.

JACK: There, forgiven. [*He rises*.] Kiss and make up.

[*He kisses her as* BERNARD *enters*.]

BERNARD: What do you think you're doing?

JACK: Kissing your beautiful wife.

BERNARD: Then stop it.

JACK: I have stopped.

BERNARD: I don't care for that sort of behaviour.

JACK: Come on – don't take the whole thing so seriously.

BERNARD: I regard it as a serious matter.

JACK: My dear fellow, it might have been anyone.

BILL: Oh might it?

JACK: What is the matter with you all this evening?

TOM: Nothing's the matter with *us*.

JACK: Yes it is, you've all joined some stuffy Victorian club that I'm not a member of. I believe it's something to do with that old madam. If you're going to burst into song, I'll give you the note.

LAURA [*to Jack*]: You're not being particularly funny.

JACK: One can't win a coconut every time. But she is like a madam, you know. I went to a place in Rome once, and it might have been her sister in charge.

BERYL: We really don't want to hear about it.

JACK: Beryl, you have heard about it, and laughed, now don't pretend you haven't. I see it all! I am standing in the centre of the white-slave market of Woodfield Green.

[*Pause.* BERYL *gives an artificial laugh.*]

No, Beryl, it's not as funny as that.

STEPHEN: It's not funny at all.

JENNY [*to Jack*]: Let me give you another drink. [*She takes his glass from him.*]

JACK: And now I'm plied with liquor. Splendid. You hope I'll become too fuddled to unmask your guilty secret.

BERNARD: What guilty secret?

JACK: Some skeleton in the cupboard.

JENNY [*handing him back his glass*]: No, no, a body in the garden.

LOUISE: What?

BERNARD: That's right. In the rose-bed.

[*Hearty laughter from all.*]

JACK: Anyone I know?

JENNY: No, just an old friend.

JACK: For his money?

JENNY: Of course.

JACK: I knew you'd been up to something this afternoon.

BERNARD: Why?

JACK: There was so much money on the table that you could hardly see over it. [*To the others*] Hundreds of pounds. Cash. Well, I mean to say, you can't come by that honestly, not in Woodfield Green, not without selling something of value. Like your car or your wife.

    [LAURA *gives a gasp.* JACK *notices.*]

JENNY: No, Jack. I told you. Murder.

JACK: I prefer white slavery. It goes with the old madam, and with the money and everything.

BERNARD: Everything?

JACK: You behaving like Mr Barrett.

BERNARD: Mr Barrett?

JACK: Of Wimpole Street.

    [BERYL *and* LOUISE *gasp.*]

    Another coconut?

TOM: All right, joke over.

JACK: Joke hardly begun as far as I'm concerned. [*He drinks up.*] Well, I must leave you. Thanks for the spiffing party. [*He moves towards the french windows.*]

JENNY [*urgently*]: Don't let him go!

JACK: Darling, it's nice to be wanted, but I must.

BERNARD [*taking him by the arm*]: No, wait . . . Where are you going?

JACK: To prop up the golf-club bar.

JENNY: Oh no!

JACK: Why not? I'm famous for it.

    [BERNARD *lets him go.*]

    What do you think I'm going to do?

JENNY: Talk.

JACK: Probably.

    [*He moves towards the window.* TOM *checks him.*]

TOM: No.

JACK: Let me go!

    [*He pushes him aside.* BILL *grabs at him. He struggles.*]

    Let me bloody-well go!

[STEPHEN *steps in to help restrain him. Two of the girls shut the window.*]

Bernard! For God's sake! What's the matter? Have you all gone mad?

BILL: Get him down.

[STEPHEN *does so.* JACK *is struggling underneath them.*]

JACK [*shouting*]: Stop! Stop!

BERYL: Roger will hear.

JENNY: Keep him quiet.

BILL: Knock him out.

[STEPHEN *punches at him.* JACK *kicks and shouts.*]

LAURA: Someone will come.

TOM: I'll shut his mouth for him.

[*He takes a bottle from the table and strikes Jack with it. If possible, the bottle breaks.* JACK *goes limp.*]

STEPHEN: He's out.

[*They draw back.* BERNARD *kneels by him.*]

BERNARD [*to Tom*]: You've hurt him.

BILL: Had to do something.

LAURA: He asked for it.

[BERYL *bustles forward and kneels beside him.*]

BERYL: Probably shamming. [*She examines his head for a moment and her manner changes. She looks up at them all, then rises and moves towards the other girls. She speaks uncertainly.*] There's a test you can do . . .

[BERNARD *moves Jack's head to and fro.*]

BERNARD: No need. I've seen them like this before.

TOM: So have I.

STEPHEN: In the War.

BILL: By the dozen.

LOUISE: Take him away, put him somewhere. He looks awful.

BERNARD: We should call a doctor.

TOM: That's no damned use.

JENNY: I do think you might move him instead of standing round talking. Put him out there.

BERNARD: In the open?

[BILL *goes to the windows and opens them.*]

BERYL: You're lucky not to be overlooked.

JENNY: That's why we chose the house.

LAURA: All the same, I think you ought to put something over him.

[JENNY *goes across to find the table-cloth.*]

JENNY: In case someone looked over the wall.

LOUISE: Or a helicopter.

TOM: For God's sake stop nattering!

[*He and* BILL *pick up Jack and move towards the window with him.*]

LOUISE: There's no need to talk to me like that.

TOM: Here Bill . . .

[JENNY *hands the table-cloth to* BERNARD *who is watching stupidly.*]

JENNY: Here . . .

BERNARD: It's our table-cloth.

JENNY: Yes, darling.

[BERNARD *slowly unfolds it. He follows the others out.* STEPHEN *is the only man left in the room.* JENNY *turns to him.*]

I think some brandy, Stephen. [*To the others*] Or champagne?

BERYL: Brandy for me.

LOUISE: Not really the moment for champagne.

[STEPHEN *is trying to pour, but is unable to.*]

STEPHEN: I . . . I'm sorry. My hands are shaking.

LAURA [*crossing*]: I'll do it, darling. You sit down.

[STEPHEN *sits in the nearest chair.* LAURA *competently pours drinks. The other men return having put Jack out of sight. They enter, aghast at what they have done.*]

TOM: Now what?

BERNARD: The police, I suppose.

JENNY [*unbelievingly*]: Police?

BILL: Only make things worse if we delay.

STEPHEN: It was an accident.

BERYL: Oh, but of course!

LAURA: If he hadn't struggled like that there'd have been no need to . . . [*She gestures vaguely with the bottle.*] Anybody else like a drink?

[*The men decline.* BERNARD *moves towards the telephone.*]

BERNARD: I'll ring them.

JENNY [*sharply*]: Bernard!

BERNARD: I must.

JENNY: Don't be absurd. [*She goes up to the telephone and puts her hand on it.*] It's the last thing we want to do.

TOM: Jenny, we've got to.

LAURA: Why?

STEPHEN: Besides they'll find out sooner or later.

BERNARD: Besides ... well ...

BILL: Yes, it's only right.

TOM: It'll look far worse if we try to conceal it.

JENNY: Worse than what will happen if everything comes out? I never heard such rubbish in my life. [*To the other women*] What a feeble lot they are, aren't they?

LOUISE: Feeble.

BERNARD [*desperate*]: But what can we do?

JENNY: Take the others out into the garden and we'll have a little talk about it.

[BERNARD *moves towards the window.* STEPHEN *and* BILL *go out.* TOM *still sits.*]

LOUISE: Oh Tom, do go!

[TOM *goes.*]

BERNARD: What are we supposed to do out there?

JENNY: You could dig a hole.

BERNARD: Yes.

[*He goes out. All the men go off.*]

JENNY [*with a half-humorous sigh*]: Men ... !

LAURA: My dear, I know. Hopeless.

LOUISE: They just give in.

[*In the course of the scene all the girls kick off their shoes.*]

BERYL: Do you think a hole is the best idea?

JENNY: My dear, I don't know, but it gives them something to do.

LAURA: They are so helpless.

LOUISE: Hopeless.

BERYL: They don't seem to see that this is the best possible thing that could have happened. I mean if he'd gone up to the golf club he'd have talked, and you know what they are up there.

JENNY: People like Hester Brown.

BERYL: Or Muriel. Those shoes are new. [*She picks one up.*]

LOUISE: I noticed them too.

LAURA: Most awfully nice.

JENNY: There's a place in Wigmore Street.

LAURA: You must give me the name. I could go there next . . . oh no. Damn.

BERYL: We must decide.

LOUISE: A hole is the simplest.

LAURA: Of course it was an accident. Perhaps we could make it look like one.

JENNY: How?

LAURA: Put him in the road as though a car had run over him. Tip and run.

BERYL: Hit and run, dear.

LAURA: You know what I mean.

BERYL: But it wouldn't work. They can tell from the type of injury what caused it.

LAURA: Only in thrillers, surely.

BERYL: No, really, really. A police surgeon came and talked to us the other day. [*To Jenny*] You must come along, it's fascinating. You see in this case there'd probably be microscopic fragments of glass in the wound and they'd analyse it and find out where it came from.

LOUISE: Could they do that?

BERYL: They're terribly clever these days. No, if we were to do anything like that it would be better to put him in the river.

LAURA: Oh, no, no, no, quite hopeless. Surely you know there has to be water in the lungs to prove that he drowned.

BERYL: Of course I know that, my dear, everyone knows that, but he could have been set upon by thugs and thrown in after he'd been hit.

LOUISE: Not with a champagne bottle really.

LAURA: I don't think that could be proved.

BERYL: You can't be certain, dear.

JENNY: It does sound rather complicated. [*She goes to the window.*] Oh no! My brussels sprouts were going in there.

BERYL: Very late.

JENNY: The ground had been turned.

LAURA: I expect that's why they chose it.

LOUISE: Lazy.

BERYL: But sensible. I mean it'll be much quicker, and we don't want things to – well, hang about.

JENNY: That's true, I suppose. They're well down now. [*She turns back into the room.*]

LAURA: What will happen when they find he's disappeared?

LOUISE: I shouldn't think anything. I mean he's done it before, don't you remember? Off he went for six weeks without a word to anyone.

JENNY: Oh yes; they won't bother for ages this time.

    [*Door slams off.*]

    Roger!

    [ROGER *enters.*]

BERYL: Oh, hello Roger.

ROGER: I thought I heard a noise.

JENNY: Of course you did, darling, we're having a party.

ROGER: I'm hungry.

LAURA [*handing him a plate of caviare*]: Here!

ROGER: I don't like fish.

JENNY: Caviare isn't fish.

ROGER: Yes it is. It's the eggs of a female sturgeon, and a sturgeon is a fish. Not like a porpoise, that's a mammal you know. It suckles.

LOUISE: It *what*?

ROGER: Nothing.

JENNY: You'd better go up now before Daddy comes in. [*Hands him nuts.*] Here, and I'll bring you something proper later. [*She hustles him out of the room.*]

LAURA: I expect one or two people knew Jack was coming here.

JENNY: With Roger, you mean?

LAURA: Yes, from the pub.

JENNY: We can say he left. After all, nobody saw him not leaving.

LOUISE: What time?

LAURA: Oh, we wouldn't remember that.

JENNY: After all, it was a party.

BERYL: I must say, I think it was disgusting nerve to give Roger beer like that.

LAURA: Typical.

LOUISE: And to gate-crash.

BERYL: But then so many of that sort are like that.

LOUISE: Just because they do something that other people don't, they think they own the world.

JENNY: Not that he was particularly good.

LAURA: Jennifer once asked him to draw a horse and he made a fearful hash of it.

[*The men appear at the window, soiled and sweaty. The girls slip on their shoes.*]

JENNY: Done already?

BERNARD: It's easy digging and the top was off.

LAURA [*to Stephen*]: Darling, you're filthy.

JENNY: If you'd like a wash . . .

STEPHEN: No, it's all right. [*He sits.*]

TOM: Have we decided?

JENNY: Yes. To go ahead.

BILL: Mind you, it's not quite as straightforward as that.

BERYL: We've been into it all, darling, and it's perfectly simple.

LAURA [*to Stephen*]: We'll explain it to you later.

BERNARD: Well, in that case . . .

STEPHEN: Yes.

[*He rises wearily.* BILL *checks him kindly.*]

BILL: No, it's all right, Stephen. Bernard and I can manage. [*To Tom*] You'd better take a rest too.

TOM [*sitting*]: I must say, I've just about had it.

[BILL *and* BERNARD *go out.*]

LOUISE: Darling, I thought you were fit. You play golf.

TOM: Digging uses different muscles.

STEPHEN: Yes, you know, even after that little bit we'll feel it to-morrow.

LAURA: It's like riding.

BERYL: Or swimming.

LOUISE: Or anything if you haven't done it for a long time.

JENNY [*to the men*]: Would you like a drink?

TOM: No thanks, Jenny, I think I'll wait a bit.

STEPHEN: What I really feel like is a pint of bitter.

TOM: Same here. Digging and beer seem to go together.

STEPHEN: I wish I'd had a pint for all the slit trenches I dug in the Army.

[*The girls turn to each other leaving* TOM *and* STEPHEN *to talk.*]

LAURA: They're away.

BERYL: Bill's the same. Get him started on the War and you can't stop him.

LOUISE: It all seems such a long time ago now.

JENNY: Ages. One forgets. Roger wasn't born till quite a time afterwards. Oh dear, that terrible place.

BERYL: Hospital?

JENNY: Nursing home. Nuns. They believed in letting one suffer.

LAURA: That's almost better than being told one ought to be enjoying it.

LOUISE: And expecting your husband to come and watch.

BERYL: They'll suggest confinement parties next.

[BERNARD *and* BILL *enter.*]

TOM: My God, how one longed for one's beer.

STEPHEN: Standing around waiting for something to happen.

TOM: Or on a twenty-mile march.

STEPHEN: Train journeys were the worst.

TOM: Bombay, Calcutta.

STEPHEN: Alex to Matrah.

TOM: Or one of those long road convoys.

STEPHEN: Naples to Rimini.

TOM: Dimapur Imphal.

STEPHEN: A drink and a smoke was all one ever wanted in those days.

TOM: And sleep. I could always do with a zizz.

STEPHEN: Quick work.

JENNY: Does it look all right?

BILL: For the moment.

TOM: I should grass it.

JENNY: You could take some turf from the other side of the path

[BERNARD *wipes his hands on his clothes.*]

Darling, not on that suit.

BERNARD: Sorry, sorry.

BILL [*heartily*]: Well, there we are.

TOM: Quite a business.

BILL: Never imagined I could do it, you know.

JENNY: I think you're marvellous.

BILL: Funny thing. The more you get used to things the better you get.

BERYL: What at, darling?

BILL: Getting used to things.

[BERNARD *looks round them all, desperately.*]

BERNARD: I think he moved as we laid him down.

JENNY: Oh Bernard . . .

BERNARD: I don't believe he was dead.

[*There is a pause. They are embarrassed rather than horrified.*]

STEPHEN: Well, he is now.

LAURA: And we really must be going.

BERYL: So must we.

JENNY: Oh no, you've only just come.

STEPHEN: Lovely party, Jenny. Jolly good show, Bernard.

LAURA: Thank you so much, my dear.

BERNARD: No! Look, we can't do this. We won't be able to live with it.

[*They look at him for a moment, coldly, with menace.*]

TOM: We have done it, old boy.

BILL: And we're living. [*To the others*] Aren't we?

[*General assent.*]

LAURA: Come along, Stephen . . . [*They go.*]

BILL [*clapping Bernard on the shoulder*]: Be seeing you, old son.

JENNY: Coffee on Monday, Beryl?

BERYL: Of course.

BILL: As if we weren't all going to be at the Royal Oak sharp on twelve tomorrow.

[*General laughter as he and* BERYL *go out.*]

LOUISE: You must come to us next time.

JENNY: No, you mustn't go too. Not all at once.

TOM: We're taking Martin out tomorrow.

LOUISE: Besides, we're last.

JENNY: Someone has to be.

TOM: It's generally Bill and Beryl.

LOUISE: They love a party.

TOM: Work hard and play hard, that's their motto. Mine too.

LOUISE: Nonsense darling, you never do a thing in the City except eat enormous lunches till three o'clock when the Stock Exchange closes.

TOM: The busiest part of the day starts then.

LOUISE: I know.

TOM [*giving her a sharp look*]: Well, it has been fun, great fun. Thanks a lot, Jenny, and well done, Bernard.

BERNARD: I'll see you out.

[JENNY *starts tidying up. At the spot on the floor where Jack fell, she stops and rubs at something with her foot. Cars are heard starting off. She goes to the fireplace and takes off her shoes.*

BERNARD *returns.*]

JENNY: Oh ... feet. Is Roger in bed?

BERNARD: No.

JENNY: Did you beat him?

BERNARD: Yes.

JENNY [*standing*]: I'll take him up something nice for supper.

[BERNARD *crosses to her and takes her by the shoulders.*]

BERNARD: Do you know what I am and what you are?

JENNY [*taking him by the wrists and looking at his hands*]: I know what you are, darling. Filthy. Better go and wash and I'll get something to eat. What would you like?

BERNARD: What is there?

JENNY: Nothing much.

BERNARD: Then I'll ... [*He changes his mind, sighs and goes to the window. He shuts the doors.*]

JENNY: The garden didn't look too bad.

[BERNARD *is silent. He takes his pipe out of his pocket without knowing he has done so.*]

But we do need rain.

[BERNARD *has put his pipe in his mouth. He takes it out and turns.*]

I've been thinking ...

BERNARD: Where are my pipe-cleaners?

JENNY: About the house ...

BERNARD: Where are my goddam bloody pipe-cleaners? [*He turns away and starts looking through the desk drawers.*]

JENNY: The garden of the house that we're taking. It must be kept up. If it backs on the railway line we can't afford to let it go. You notice them from the train, the gardens that people have let go. You know at once there's something wrong in the house. Ours must look like all the others, don't you think?

[BERNARD *has found a pipe-cleaner and starts to use it.*]

CURTAIN

Other Penguin Plays by Arnold Wesker

ROOTS · PL19

I'M TALKING ABOUT JERUSALEM · PL25

ANGER AND AFTER
A Guide to the New British Drama

John Russell Taylor

A641

The first explosive performance of John Osborne's bombshell, *Look Back in Anger*, in May 1956, shook the audience, delighted the critics, and let a lot of badly needed fresh air into the post-war British theatre. In this well-informed survey John Russell Taylor takes a calm look at what has been going on on the stage and television screen since that shattering first night.

Avoiding both woolly theorizing about the 'new wave' and neat categorizing of writers and plays, he distinguishes four streams of new drama: Osborne's various successors at the Royal Court; Joan Littlewood's achievement in Theatre Workshop; provincial playwrights such as Arnold Wesker, whose work first appeared at the Belgrade Theatre, Coventry; and the amazing success of television drama, notably A.B.C.'s 'Armchair Theatre'. Detailed analyses of the plays of more than a dozen writers and critical conclusions on them make this a knowledgeable, comprehensive book on an exciting subject.

'Writes clearly and persuasively, furnishing a most intelligent and well-balanced guide to the post-Osborne drama in Britain today' – *Guardian*

'An excellent book, indispensable to anyone genuinely interested in contemporary drama' – *Listener*

For a complete list of books available please write to Penguin Books whose address can be found on the back of the title page